History and Politics

THE CAISSONS ROLL
A Study of European Rearmament, 1938
by Hanson W. Baldwin

WHEN CHINA UNITES
An Interpretive History of the Chinese Revolution
by Harry Gannes

VOLUNTEER IN SPAIN
by John Sommerfield

BURGOS JUSTICE
by Ruiz Vilaplana

THE SIEGE OF ALCAZAR
A History of the Siege of the Toledo Alcazar, 1936
by Major Geoffrey McNeill-Moss

THE TRAGIC FALLACY
A Study of American War Policies
by Mauritz A. Hallgren

AN ATLAS OF CURRENT AFFAIRS
AN ATLAS OF EUROPEAN HISTORY
AN ATLAS OF EMPIRE
by J. F. Horrabin

These are Borzoi Books, published by
ALFRED A. KNOPF

MY AUSTRIA

Translated from the German by

JOHN SEGRUE

CHANCELLOR SCHUSCHNIGG ADDRESSING THE
FEDERAL DIET, FEBRUARY 24, 1938

MY
AUSTRIA

by

Kurt Schuschnigg

WITH AN INTRODUCTION BY
Dorothy Thompson

NEW YORK · ALFRED · A · KNOPF

1938

Published May 23, 1938
First and Second Printings before Publication

Originally published as DREIMAL ÖSTERREICH *by*
Thomas-Verlag Jakob Hegner, Vienna

INTRODUCTION

by Dorothy Thompson

THE last chancellor of Austria here tells the moving, tragic
story of his country since the war, and though he keeps
himself modestly in the background, the story of his country becomes his own.

The book came out in Vienna in November 1937, and
it covers events until early summer of that year. It was begun in 1936, when, as the head of the state, the chancellor
was most heavily pressed by public affairs, and found time
to write only two or three hours a day, usually in the dead
of night. It is as though a prescience of what was to come
drove the chancellor thus to write the apologia for that
Austria which he and his predecessor, Engelbert Dollfuss,
founded, and thus to bear fervent witness to the very idea
of Austria. His book is therefore a declaration of faith and
a memorial.

Its author is, today, in April 1938 under guard, imprisoned in the beautiful Belvedere palace on the Prinz Eugen-
strasse, which was once the residence of the heir to the
Habsburg throne—whose assassination in Sarajevo started
the World War. His eyes, if they look out through the wide
windows, travel across the stepped terraces, adorned by
dimpled baroque cherubs, so characteristically Austrian,

v

through the lovely gardens, their elegance undiminished by twenty years of political turmoil, and their very physical aspect is an echo of the cry repeated often in this book: Austria! Austria! Always Austria! A confirmation of his passionate belief that Austria, a German country, has a mission in another dimension than that of Hitler's Reich, a mission as the amalgamator and mediator of cultures, as a bridge between German, and Slav, and Latin. It is the point where the Latin mind, full of clarity and grace, meets and tames the German. The very architecture of his prison—indeed, the very name—testifies mutely to the truth of its occupant's conception. For a German, born in Genoa, built in—Johann Lukas von Hildebrandt— deriving his inspiration, not from the north but from the south, and translating the genius of two races into something specifically and recognizably Austrian.

Inside the palace is imprisoned a man who loved Austria so much that he was willing to die for her. And perhaps will.

Outside the palace a man rules who, though born in Austria, hated her from his boyhood, and determined to destroy her—as an empire, as a tradition, as a dynasty, as an idea, and as a culture. And has.

In a world which is full of heroics but lacking in heroes, Kurt von Schuschnigg is without the one and embodies the other. I met him only once. A dry man, rather stiff; formal and intellectual, with the precise and subtle mind of one trained by the Jesuits. He had been a soldier in his youth; a lawyer; a politician without the politician's facile urbanity. Ungifted, one would say, for public life. Now, as one reads his book, one realizes how much poetry was behind that rather bureaucratic exterior. He is steeped in the poetry of Goethe, and of the Austrians—Grillparzer, and Wildgans and Hugo von Hofmannsthal! Von Hofmannsthal! Happy that he is dead these few years and has not lived to learn that his Jewish blood makes him—in the eyes of racists—neither Austrian nor German! He who wrote the librettos of Richard Strauss's operas and some of the noblest poetry of our times.

In the poets of his language and culture, Kurt Schuschnigg found comfort in the years of his stewardship, as chancellor of Austria. He listened to them, amid the turmoil of the streets, and he kept his faith in Austria. The last words which he spoke to his country were over the microphone, while Nazi guards stood ready to take him into custody: "God Save Austria!"

What he did not do, to save Austria, was to call up the army of which he was the chief, and ask his country to die fighting. He risked his own life, and forfeited his own freedom. No human being can personally do more for love. I have the feeling, nevertheless, that his predecessor would have risked other lives as well, and forfeited them, too, as the final testimony of Austria's will to existence. Nor can anybody tell what turn history might have taken had the final consequence been drawn, and a last stand made—a stand in arms. As it was—and we must try to construct the last, unwritten chapters of this book—Kurt von Schuschnigg was given an ultimatum: a fantastic ultimatum, with exactly one hour, just sixty minutes, to decide the fate of his nation. That was on March 11th.

In the chancellery, in Vienna, Schuschnigg heard the jangle of a telephone bell. He answered. Berlin was calling,

Adolf Hitler, alone in his own chancellery, was on the telephone.

Hitler spoke. He said: "You are planning to hold a plebiscite. It must be called off. You must resign. A man of my choosing must be put in your place. If this is not done, the German army will march into Austria. You have just sixty minutes to decide."

Did any man ever have a harder choice? Sixty-five million Germans, the most powerful army in Europe, against a nation torn with dissension and undermined by revolutionary cells, its whole people one tenth that of its neighbor, its army negligible against the titan next door?

Schuschnigg went to the council room, where the Austrian cabinet was sitting. He tendered his resignation. The President refused it. There were forty minutes left.

Silently, the Chancellor left the council room. He went to the telephone. He called London. He asked his minister there to ask the help of the British Foreign Office. Then he put down the phone and waited. It rang. London would do nothing. Schuschnigg called Rome. Mussolini could not be found. Italy would do nothing. Schuschnigg called Paris. But the French government was in a serious crisis. Paris would do nothing.

The independence of Austria was guaranteed by all these powers. The last vestige of international law in Europe was being challenged. And Europe was paralyzed.

The sixty minutes were nearly up—only ten were left— when Schuschnigg went to the microphone and spoke his last words to his country. Addressing himself to the Austrian people, he made clear that Chancellor Hitler had asked him to cancel the plebiscite and to resign; that if he didn't yield within the hour German troops would invade Austria; that he was yielding to force, and had tendered his resignation only to avoid bloodshed. With extreme vigor he testified to the world that the accusation that Austrian workers had caused disorders were "false from A to Z," and he ended with the poignant cry: "God save Austria."

Airplanes with the Swastika painted on their wings were booming over the chancellery before his words were spoken. German bombers were dropping pamphlets. They read: "Nazi Germany welcomes Nazi Austria."

Schuschnigg, walking out of the room where he had spoken, was seized by Nazi officials and put under arrest.

And the German troops marched. Austria was invaded and annexed. "Without a drop of blood being spilled."

It is necessary for the record to take note of an extraordinary procedure, a procedure quite unique in the history of the last twenty-four years, years which saw ultimatums given, a world war fought, peace treaties dictated, accepted, and broken, and many an injustice done. Yet, it is unique that a friendly power offers an ultimatum to another friendly and sovereign power threatening armed invasion; that the ultimatum should be accepted; that invasion should follow the acceptance of the ultimatum; and that the man who entirely correctly served and represented his country should then be arrested, and threatened with the charge of High Treason by the invader. Kurt von Schuschnigg delivered his country to Germany, rather than see his countrymen mowed down by German guns. For this, and because he previously sought, by every non-violent and political means, to preserve his country's independence, which he was solemnly sworn to protect, he is imprisoned; treated by his victors as a traitor; greeted by a trained chorus of vituperation; pilloried before the public with every sort of contempt—that the world shall learn what, today, constitutes chivalry and "reconciliation."

One recalls the "Hang the Kaiser" campaign, which began after a world war that cost ten million lives. But even
in those ghastly times, the campaign turned against its
makers. There was still some ounce of chivalry left in the
human breast. It was enough to defeat the enemy—not
utterly to destroy him.

The democratic and socialist revolution that followed
the 1918 collapse on the war front dethroned and exiled
the Habsburgs, and confiscated their estates. But it did not
accuse them of High Treason. It is left for Germany to
issue a warrant for the arrest of the Habsburg pretender
on this charge!

When Kurt von Schuschnigg resigned on March 11th, he
expected the Nazification of Austria. It is doubtful whether
even then, he dreamed that the annexation of Austria was
to follow in forty-eight hours! It is doubtful whether, even
then, he dreamed that there would be no more Austria at
all. Certainly, he expected that a Nazi Austria would be
run by Austrian Nazis. But that also did not happen. Josef
Buerckel from the German Saar came to conduct the Hitler plebiscite, substituted for Dr. von Schuschnigg's. German soldiers and German S.S. guards were put over
Austrian soldiers and Austrian Nazi storm troopers. What
happened was a systematic occupation of the country.

And it is even highly doubtful whether Hitler himself
planned in that moment to annex Austria, or occupy the
country. Perhaps he thought he would step across the border and see whether anyone, whether any foreign office in
the world, protested. Nobody did. His entry became tri-
umphal, as the masses shouted their approval. This would
not surprise Chancellor Schuschnigg. In the course of trou-

bled years he had formed his own opinion of the fickleness
of the mob, and Austria was near enough to Germany to
know what Nazi revolutionary terror can be. Climb on the
bandwagon, and the sooner the better! In this book
Schuschnigg quotes the poet Goethe:

Heroes have often vanished
But who will protect the masses
Against the masses? The mass has become the masses' oppressor.

To bring this book up to date, we need a continuation
of the history of Austria's relations with Germany, from
the time of the agreement reached between Hitler and
Schuschnigg on July 11, 1936, until the recent events
which precipitated the annexation.

Dr. Schuschnigg makes perfectly clear, in Chapter XVI,
what that agreement was. Both partners, Germany and
Austria, agreed to undertake certain observances and certain duties. The government of the German Reich "recognized the full sovereignty of the Austrian union, and promised to regard the Austrian form of government and its
domestic policy, *including the question of Austrian Na-*
*tional Socialism,** as a purely Austrian affair, upon which
it promised to exert *no influence either direct or indirect.*" *
Austria, on the other hand, agreed that it would "in general and in particular in its relations with the German
Reich hold to those fundamental principles which correspond to the fact that Austria is a German state."

"The treaty," said Dr. Schuschnigg, "did not contain a
word which could not, on some similar occasion, have been
subscribed to . . . by Dollfuss."

In an aide-mémoire accompanying the agreement, it was
laid down that the "chancellor is prepared to the end of

* Italics are mine. D.T.

achieving genuine peace, at a *proper time,** which is envisaged as being in the near future, to admit the collaboration and political responsibility of representatives of the
former so-called national opposition, in which case it would
be a choice of personalities; and the chancellor would reserve the right of choice. The agreement consists herein
that these persons, *in the confidence of the chancellor,**
shall be entrusted with the task of providing for the inner
appeasement of the national opposition."

The meaning of the treaty is not ambiguous. The complete sovereignty of Austria as an independent state is
recognized. Germany agrees not to meddle in any way, directly or indirectly, in her internal affairs. Germany recognizes that Austria, furthermore, is not a many party state,
but is ruled by the constitution and the Fatherland Front,
into which everyone who wishes to participate in Austrian
affairs is admitted. The Nazis—the *former* * so called national opposition—must enter on the same terms as former
socialists.

Chancellor Schuschnigg expected great things of this
treaty. "If the general sense of the contract could be made
operative throughout the world, the universal recognition
of the fundamental principle that no influence, direct or
indirect, must be exerted upon the chosen form of government of another state, it might be an effective means of
keeping the peace in the small and the great. But so long
as only a part of the world demands that the other part shall
not mix in, but at the same time finds ways and means to
penetrate with its ideas and its own arms deliveries, so long
the danger will be present."

And, decisively, the Chancellor writes: "Those to whom
* Italics are mine. D.T.

Austro-German amity was dear, and not the triumph of
National Socialistic Totalitarianism in Austria, had no
ground to force the state to intervene. . . . We bound ourselves . . . to respect the political constitution of the
Reich. *We have not and could not have bound ourselves to
give immunity to those who transgress against the laws of
the state, and thus give them a privileged position above all
other citizens of Austria."* *

This treaty followed two years of extremely strained relations due to the revolutionary activities of the Nazis in
Austria. These had reached their climax in 1934, with the
brutal assassination of Chancellor Dollfuss as an incident
in the Nazi attempt to seize the state. Before that the Nazis,
using tactics already made familiar by the extreme left, had
carried the fight to the streets, and supported it by violence,
by murders, by bombings. Schuschnigg says unequivocally
that this party "economically, and as regards its leaders relied on forces not domiciled in Austria, for in the course of
time a decisive influence was gained by an ever-growing
number of political emigrants, most of whom consisted of
people who had lost their Austrian nationality."

And he had been advised to deal with the Nazis harshly
—advised, it ironically happened, by an officer who later
became a Nazi himself. He had said to Schuschnigg,
"Against the Nazis there is only one weapon to be used—
brutal force. There is no good in merely licking them up.
Justice and mildness are of no use in dealing with them!
There is only one thing to be done—"

Schuschnigg does not name that one thing, but he adds,
"I have not forgotten what he told me to do, but we did
not do it. . . ." And, writing at a time when he still hoped

* Italics are mine. D.T.

that the treaty of July 11th would mean peace, he added, "There is no purpose in recalling it now."

The fact is that although the Nazi party was declared illegal, and its uniforms and insignia forbidden, the same sort of drastic steps that were taken against the Socialists in February 1934 were never taken against the Nazis. The reasons may have been manifold. There were many Nazi sympathizers amongst the police. But the chief reason, of course, was always the fear of Germany. Austria had agreed not to persecute National Socialists, as such, but only to suppress revolutionary activities, and to insist on the "national opposition" operating inside the Austrian front, and as Austrians. Germany had agreed to give neither direct nor indirect aid to the Austrian Nazis.

The Austrian part of the agreement was undoubtedly kept. From July 1936 to the end of the year, 18,648 persons were amnestied who had come into conflict with the law on account of illegal National Socialist activity.

But the German part of the agreement was not kept. National Socialist cells existed from one end of the country to the other, organized under exactly the pattern established first by communists, and contact with Germany was never stopped. Peasants in the most remote nests were advised in letters bearing the signature "Adolf Hitler"— whether used with the Fuehrer's knowledge or not—that the day was coming when their pigs would bring twice as high a price, under Greater Germany. In the half-world of partial legality, the Nazis carried on a latent, smouldering civil war, and "the campaign of hatred set at variance . . . even families, invaded the realms of art and sport, and . . . sought to engage the very children in the broil." "That phenomenon," comments Schuschnigg, "was very new, and has as little in common with the Austrian character as it has with the cultivation of the healthy national spirit."

It is unfortunate that we do not yet know, provably, and on the basis of incontrovertible documentary evidence, exactly what inspired Chancellor Schuschnigg to visit the German Fuehrer on February 12th, 1938. Nor do we know positively what transpired at the interview.

Incontrovertible documentary evidence is almost impossible to get under all the circumstances. But Austrians close to Chancellor Schuschnigg and foreign correspondents and diplomats who enjoyed the confidence of Schuschnigg and the Austrian Foreign Office agree that the following is what happened:

After the July 1936 agreement, a committee of seven was set up in Austria whose task was to liquidate the illegal Nazi activities and bring the so-called national opposition into harmony with this agreement. It was headed by Captain Josef Leopold, an Austrian Nazi, and Dr. Leopold Tavs, a Sudeten German—from the German part of Czechoslovakia —who lived in Vienna. Far from appeasing the Nazis and bringing them into harmony with the agreement, these men continued their illegal activities building up Nazi cells all over Austria and copying in this way the strategy first designed by the Communists.

Hitler was convinced that this internal activity would eventually deliver Austria into his hands without any movement from Germany at all.

But by the end of last year and the beginning of this one, he had begun to doubt this very seriously. In the first place, the Nazi movement in Austria was losing much of its financial support. Previously a number of Austrian industrialists had been helping it with money, but now they found,

that the trade agreement which had resulted from the July
11th agreement was not working to their advantage. They
were selling goods to Germany for which they got no money
and they began to realize that Austria's sound currency and
free exchange were a great advantage. Austria's economic
condition was improving and a certain unity was asserting
itself in the country.

Furthermore in the last days of January 1938, representatives of Italy, Austria and Hungary met in Budapest and
the Italian representatives again promised Dr. Schuschnigg
that they would support Austrian independence and improve their trade relations with Austria. And Dr. Schuschnigg came back from Budapest so convinced that he had
friends that he arrested Captain Leopold.

Now, he arrested Captain Leopold because he was involved in a very dark revolutionary plot. That plot was to
create an incident in Austria, which would give an excuse
for German interference. A crowd would have looted the
German Embassy and shot at the German Military Attaché,
General Muff. The intention was to wound him, not kill
him. The plot had been discussed with Heinrich Himmler,
the Chief of the German Secret Police. The blame, of
course, was to be put either on Austrian monarchists or on
Austrian communists. Himmler wanted the plot amended.
He suggested that instead of shooting to wound General
Muff, they shoot to kill the German Ambassador Franz von
Papen, whom he cordially hated, thus accomplishing two
ends—getting rid of von Papen, who has been a great in-
triguer in and out of all camps—and furnishing the necessary incident.

This information came to Schuschnigg through his own
secret police and it also came to Herr von Papen, the pro-

spective victim, and made him very fidgety.

Now let's skip a moment back to Germany. Before Hitler could take steps in Austria, he had to come to terms with his own army which was headed by General von Fritsch, and with his own war minister, General Blomberg. These men and a number of old line Prussian officers put their faces rigidly against an Austrian invasion. They were against it for the following reasons:

First, they thought it below the honor of the German Army to shoot at sparrows with cannons. They asked Hitler why he wanted to extend his frontier by 500 miles which might some day have to be defended, and they pointed out to him that Italy might be their enemy some day instead of their friend. And furthermore, they reminded him that for over a year an agreement had existed between the Chief of Staff of the German Army and General Jansa, the Chief of Staff of the Austrian Army, according to which if Germany became embroiled in a war in Czechoslovakia, the Austrian Army would permit it to march through Austrian territory. In return for this the German Army had guaranteed General Jansa not to exploit the use of Austria as a corridor into an excuse for occupying her, and thereby the German Army had agreed to respect Austrian sovereignty. General Fritsch was therefore asked by Hitler to break his word of honor, which he refused to do. And therefore Fritsch and at least seventeen other generals were purged out of the German army. That occurred on February 4th. Hitler now had an army amenable to his wishes. He also had a good moment in which to move.

Now let's go back to Austria. Keep the dates in mind. On February 4th, the German army was purged. On February 6th, German Ambassador von Papen, fearing for his own life, went to Berchtesgaden and proposed that Hitler issue an invitation to Schuschnigg to visit him and settle everything. He returned on February 8th to Vienna and saw Schuschnigg on February 9th and issued the invitation. Schuschnigg promised to give an answer on the 10th, and consulted an important official of his own Foreign Office. This official immediately got in touch with the Italian ambassador in Vienna, and by noon of the 10th Mussolini knew of the invitation. Since he had not been consulted by Germany, he knew that there was something phony going on, and immediately on the evening of the 10th wired his ambassador in London: "Inform Chamberlain [British Prime Minister] that now or never is the time for negotiations between Italy and Britain."

Mussolini still thought he had time to play Britain against Germany.

On the 12th, Schuschnigg went to Berchtesgaden. He took with him his secretary, Baron von Froehlichsthal, his aide Major Bartl, the chief of the official news bureau, Hofrat Weber, and the foreign minister, Guido Schmidt. He was also accompanied by his personal bodyguard and six detectives. He went to Berchtesgaden via Salzburg, but at Freilassing, the German border, the German authorities refused to permit the entrance of anyone except Schuschnigg, his aide, and the Foreign Minister—an unheard-of treatment of one sovereign state by another. The others returned to Salzburg. But Hitler sent as a "guard of honor" for Schuschnigg an S.S. captain, Spitze, whom Schuschnigg's aide recognized as an Austrian legionaire, who had left Austria to join the Nazis—an egregious insult.

In Berchtesgaden the critical interview took place, I understand, with only Hitler, Schuschnigg, Colonel Bartl, and

Herr von Papen present. In this interview Hitler gave his ultimatum: either put the five most important cabinet positions—including Defense, Interior, Justice and Education—into the hands of pro-Nazis or be invaded. Schuschnigg demurred that he had no power to make such a promise, inasmuch as the Austrian Cabinet was constituted by the President and not by himself. Hitler was adamant. The conference was followed by a luncheon at which General von Keitel, the Chief of Staff of the German Army, and other important officers were present. This stunned Schuschnigg for it indicated that Hitler's threat of invasion had the backing of the armed forces. Schuschnigg was in Berchtesgaden for ten or eleven hours. During the conference, luncheon, and as long as he was in Hitler's presence, he was not permitted to smoke, a nerve-racking experience for the Chancellor for he is a heavy smoker, and like all smokers depends on tobacco when he is nervous. He was also served exactly one meal, in eleven hours.

Schuschnigg went back to Austria and carried out the exact letter of the demands, but he tried to pick Nazis for the Cabinet who still believed in an independent Austria, even if she be a Nazi Austria, resolving to use every peaceful and political means to save his country's sovereignty.

Therefore, on March 9th, in a radio address in Innsbruck, Schuschnigg called for a plebiscite, to be held on March 13th, in which the people could vote whether they wanted an independent Austria. Hitler knew that Schuschnigg would win that plebiscite, and now he had to do something, for if Schuschnigg had won, Hitler not only would lose Austria, but would get the worst slap in the face he had ever got, and the effect in Germany would be very serious.

So, on March 11th, Hitler called Schuschnigg on the telephone and told him that if he did not resign in sixty minutes and call off the plebiscite, Austria would be invaded. To save his country from this fate, Schuschnigg resigned after telephone calls to London, Paris, and Rome indicated that nobody was prepared to send him help. He announced his resignation on the radio to the people of Austria, ending with the words "God Save Austria." As he walked out of the room, he was arrested and has been imprisoned in his own residence, the Belvedere Palace, ever since.

Despite the fact that he accepted the ultimatum, Austria was invaded the next day and has been occupied by German troops ever since.

The only men who knew the whole inside story are either dead or in prison. General Jansa, Chief of Staff of the Austrian Army, who made the agreement with General Fritsch, committed suicide. The private secretary of Chancellor Schuschnigg, Baron von Froehlichsthal, was murdered. The private secretary of ambassador von Papen, Baron von Ketteler, was reported murdered. A subsequent report stated that he had escaped to Sweden. Most of the members of the last Austrian Foreign office are in Concentration Camp at Dachau, in Bavaria.

Visitors to Austria who talked with Chancellor Schuschnigg and other members of the Austrian cabinet in the weeks immediately preceding the visit to Berchtesgaden, found them more optimistic than they had been in a long time over the "Nazi menace." This opinion was supported by Chancellor Schuschnigg himself in an interview which he gave the London *Morning Telegraph* on *January 5th*. In that interview he said:

"There is no question of ever accepting Nazi representatives in the Austrian cabinet. An absolute abyss separates Austria from Nazism. We do not like arbitrary power, we want law to rule our freedom. We reject uniformity and centralization. . . .

Christendom is anchored in our very soil, and we know but one God; and that is not the State, or the Nation, or that elusive thing Race. Our children are God's children, not to be abused by the State. We abhor terror; Austria has always been a humanitarian State. As a people we are tolerant by predisposition. Any change, now, in our status quo, could only be for the worse."

The Nazi revolution in Austria thus follows a pattern amazingly repetitive of Germany. In this book, Schuschnigg describes an interview which he had with General von Schleicher, then Chancellor of Germany, in January 1933, just a fortnight before Hitler became his successor. At that moment, General von Schleicher believed the Nazi movement to be "finished." Actually, Hitler came into power in Germany when his popular following had passed its zenith, as the elections of November had definitely shown. And in Austria the story was the same.

Disinterested observers, including almost the entire foreign press, were convinced that Schuschnigg would win the Austrian plebiscite, even with the votes of many Austrian Nazis, who wished an independent Austria, though a Nazi one. Mrs. Anne O'Hare McCormick, the extremely able reporter of the New York *Times*, told me that a few days before the plebiscite was to take place Nazi leaders, with whom she spoke, openly admitted that they could not get more than 20 percent of the votes in the city of Vienna.

And that the outcome of the plebiscite would be unfavorable for him, was indicated by Hitler's own move. For to prevent it, he risked a European war, and he engaged in a procedure so preposterous that it will live as a black blot on German history forever—if anyone, except the Germans, writes any future European history. Beside what he did the rape of Belgium was a justified invasion! And the precedent which he set lives as a menace to every small country in the world. He did it, I think, not only to get Austria, but because a vote against him in Austria might have meant his downfall in Germany. For Austria is a German country, dominated for centuries by an ideology very different from that of Hitler, and the repudiation of Hitlerism by so old and so civilized a part of the German world, would have had tremendous repercussions in Germany itself. Therefore his telephonic demand that the plebiscite be called off, that the Chancellor resign, that Austria capitulate her sovereignty.

The results of what happened in Austria in March 1938 will not be apparent for some time to come. I am firmly convinced, however, that it was the most cataclysmic event of modern history, and that as a result of it, one of two things will happen: Germany will dominate the continent of Europe, or millions of lives will be spent in another war. Austria lay at the center of the most important cross-roads in Europe, where East meets West; it impinges on, and divides northern and southern Slavs, Germans and Italians and Magyars in a basin inhabited by the most various peoples. There were historical reasons why the old Austro-Hungary was never a national state, but instead existed as an integrating force based upon a dynasty, a culture, and the universalism of the Catholic religion. Chancellor Schuschnigg speaks very movingly of the Austrian mission: "To bring together various nationalities, their civilizations and languages, for the purpose of achieving political and economic welfare—that was her historic European mission. . . . From the standpoint of German culture she should unite the various contending national forces for the benefit of each and all, and for the sake of a common pacific development, founded and led by German traditions."

And again: "Not force, not the instruments of war, but rather the spirit and work of culture discharge the task of the mediator. Such a service for Europe can be performed only by a power which does not fall under the suspicion of discharging imperialistic aims."

And one might add that such a task, a task imperative if peace is to be preserved permanently in this area, can never, never be discharged by a Power, living under a system of ideas so exclusive, so atomizing and explosive, as German racialism. In Germany proper, racialism may prove to be, temporarily at least, a centripetal force. In Central Europe and the Danubian basin inhabited by 80,000,000 non-Germans it *must* prove to be a centrifugal force. The tradition of Austrian imperialism, which Schuschnigg dreamed that small and neutral Austria would exercise in the realm of culture and the spirit, was Christian and Roman. "In my father's house are many mansions." The dream of a Realm, a Reich, wherein men of many races and of many-faceted genius might find a mediator, a roof, and a culture tolerant and universal enough for all.

Against that spirit the young German-nationalist Adolf Hitler set his face. It was his first great hate, preceding even his hatred of the Jews. Now is the time to read again the early chapters of "My Struggle" and see how anaesthetic he was to this spirit, how deeply hostile.

A death blow delivered at this spirit is a death blow at Europe, and a death blow at the western mind. Schuschnigg knew it. And Europe will one day know it, too.

Under all her vicissitudes—recounted vividly in this book—Austria kept that spirit, and that is why from one end of the world to the other, men of culture feel the passing of Austria as a pain in their hearts. For there, of all countries in the world, any human being with the spirit of western civilization in his heart and in his mind, could find a home. What names are not written in her architecture, in her literature, signed to her pictures, signed to her music! Who has not, at some time, felt more at home there than in his own land? Beethoven from the Rhineland, and the austere north German, Johannes Brahms. Great and brilliant Jews: Mahler, Freud, Schnitzler, Werfel, Wassermann, Zweig, von Hofmannsthal. Names Slavic and Latin and Magyar. Vienna was never the Cosmopolis. It was less cosmopolitan than New York. Its spirit did not collect. It fused, to create something unique and universal. It is typical of Austria that the first great and painstaking Life of Beethoven should have been written by an American consul and translated into German and then, years later, when the English manuscript was lost, translated back into English. It is typical of Austria that her greatest geniuses should have been men who came there from other soils. And it is typical of Austria that she was the homeland of all those who spoke the world's most universal language: Music, and that Music vibrated in her very air.

And it is an omen of what has happened that today, Sunday, April 24th, I read in the New York *Times* that Austria's conquerors have begun a raid on the great Austrian National Library, one of the finest in the world, tearing from the books, collected over centuries, those works hostile to Nazi ideas. Ominous. For libraries belong to no country, no nation, but are the common property of all civilized men, the heritage of man's common cultural past, the sum of man's painfully accumulated hopes, and thoughts, and visions. There was a roof for all books in Vienna, yesterday.

This then is a memorial, with even the introduction written by one who would have died for Austria—not for Austria, the state, but for Austria, the idea; supra-national, integrating, all-inclusive, Christian, and humane.

Only a chapter of history has been written. It is too soon to write the name of the final victor. The Austrian idea is the western idea—from Rome, through the Middle Ages universalized by the Christian Church, through the Renaissance universalized by a common source of art and inspiration, to the very dream of the United States of America: the idea of mankind of many origins finding a common language and a common home: a Realm of the Spirit.

If that spirit wins through, Europe lives. If it perishes Europe dies . . . and we, too, children of Europe, men and women of the western world.

FOREWORD

I⊤ ɪs a question whether it is expedient to embark on the narration of events while they are still in progress, when we are still in the thick of the struggle, with our work not yet crowned with success and with the sound of battle still in our ears. There is much against such an undertaking. And a man who, like the writer of this book, was present when the events came to pass can scarcely avoid a strongly subjective coloration. But that, in the present case, can hardly be a defect. For it is impossible to keep the narration of events separate from the avowal of one's own position: to keep one's own will, one's own point of view, one's conception of the fundamental and the decisive, out of a record of historical processes, of resolutions taken at crucial moments and their justification, of the courses chosen out of a number of possible ones. Anyhow, it seems a very short time since certain events, especially since the personal factors in them were decisive and the important actors are still alive. This is true particularly of the last and decisive stage of Austrian events. Thus certain precautions and omissions are unavoidable, and therefore much may seem incomplete or even unclear. That cannot be helped. But it seemed to me that the weightier reasons were on the side of publication. For the fact that the events are so near and immediate is in itself a great advantage, particularly in a period when one year of crowded happenings followed another, each bringing a host of precipitate developments in its train; so that it is in itself a difficult task to remember and describe their sequence.

But the aim of this attempt to remember and describe is to bear witness for Austria: for the inevitability of its present state and the profound significance of the shape it has taken. That would not be possible without an account of the course events took. For if one only sees things as they are today, not knowing or having forgotten why she took such shape, or why—according to my profoundest conviction—things could not have resulted otherwise, then one can never see Austria aright, never understand her, and thus never be able to judge her, even though guided by the best intentions. A right understanding of the new Austria, particularly as seen from abroad, is most requisite to her acceptation and her position in the world. Thus to promote and effect this understanding is to perform a service to the Fatherland.

What I purpose is by no means to write my memoirs. Today is not the time for that, nor do I feel any call to do it. If nevertheless my personal feelings and experiences here and there find expression in what I write, that is because they have appeared to me in the light of a contribution to a clear perception of the Austrian scene today and to an understanding of the attitude of those who represent the Fatherland.

Austria! Austria! And again Austria! In a twofold sense of the words.

Whoever would understand the mind and thoughts of the present-day Austrian, whoever would go beyond that to inquire into the mission and significance of modern Austria, must learn to know the Passion of this hard-tried land, so unique, so rich in irreplaceable cultural values. He must know what Austria was immediately before the catastrophic downfall of 1918; he must remember the events of the fifteen years after the war, the ideas and views which governed the State and the people—both of them theory-ridden up to the very edge of the abyss—until by superhuman efforts and grievous sacrifice it emerged in new life out of the ruins and the wilderness.

May this modest contribution to a political history of the new Austria be at once a stone in the foundation of its ideology and also a wreath which I would lay at the feet of Engelbert Dollfuss's historical monument, his life-work, the new State; erected in the sight of all the world, and, as I profoundly believe, imperishable.

May these words of mine, to utter which I have long been urged by those who have stood closest to me and my work, be dedicated to his memory. Austria! Austria! And again Austria! And this in a figurative sense as well. On the third anniversary of the constitution it came to me with redoubled clearness. In view of the road which already lies behind us, and the road which we must still traverse, in view of the obstacles which malice or short-sightedness still heap up in the path; and under the direct impression of the imposing march of the Vienna Fatherland Front on the day of the Constitution. Great love, loyalty, courage, and glad confidence were vocal in that march of the hundred thousand. It has been borne in upon me of late that in the cities the workers, and the now and then too much despairing administration; in the country the peasants, in the whole State the army—these are the strongest and most certain supports of the activist Fatherland idea, reinforced by considerable sections of the lower and middle classes in their various corporative groupings. Further, I have learned anew the surpassing importance and significance to be ascribed to the problem of the youth of Austria. Everything depends on our gaining hold on wider and wider sections of the younger generation and winning them to an understanding of Austria. Who would deny that in this field there is still much valuable work to be done? Particularly the secondary schools still show a regrettable hesitation to take up a unified position towards the Austrian idea. Is youth to blame for that? In small part, perhaps; and even so, as may be shown later, in many ways with some excuse.

But particularly in these days, which should serve for a searching of the conscience and be in a peculiar degree devoted to thoughts of constructive work in State and society, all shadow of doubt or fear should vanish in face of the lofty faith of the great mass of genuine Austrians. All disappointment, weariness, reluctance must vanish before the compelling knowledge of the State's command that all must set their powers fully to work. Certainly it is not easy to bear responsibility at this hour and in this land. But the conviction that we are treading the right and inevitable path, the passionate love for the Austrian idea, the faith in its ultimate and undying triumph, proved and confirmed again and again throughout the centuries, must always be stronger than any ifs and buts. Again and again, ever more clearly, more positively, more inevitably there stands, at the end of all questioning, the clear, proud, German utterance, defying all storms and reverses, all cheap detraction: Once for all and for all time: Austria! Austria! Again, and forever, Austria!

Let my book, then, be nothing else than the profession of an Austrian, urged from his inmost soul, to the end of demanding justice, summoning understanding, and serving truth.

When, on May 1, 1937, I took up my pen, it was at first not at all clear to me what period might elapse before I could put the last full stop to the last chapter. I tarried long over the beginning and the first fifty pages, and for managing to get along at all I am indebted to a fortunate spell of leisure, more particularly in the following August. Political controversy, after a violent phase in July, subsided into the wished-for summer truce during which those who dabble in politics throughout the year had to fall back on the variations of an old and seemingly always attractive theme: namely, that of the "impending reconstruction of the government," with all the accompanying storiettes. I, for my part, was in a position to enjoy the exquisite peace of St. Gilgen on the Wolfgangsee, where in rain and sunshine alike there was enough opportunity for me to write down what for a long time had been occupying my thoughts.

I take this occasion to express my sincere and cordial thanks to my faithful collaborators Councillor Edmund Weber and Administrative Counsel Dr. Josef Seidl for their valuable and willing aid in collecting and sifting the material to be presented. I am equally obliged to the veteran former chief redacteur and head of the Press Bureau, Ambassador Eduard Ludwig; and to the Federal Commissioner for the Home Service, Colonel Walter Adam, retired.

Meanwhile over half a year is passed and Christmas is at

hand. In the first days after publication the book won many friends, probably because it called to mind and gave voice to much that many people witnessed, much that they felt was part of their own fate, and probably, too, because with us Austrians—often even when we believe we have long since overcome old feelings—the heart is always stirred when the talk turns to our home and our country.

It is the love of Austria that always binds us afresh, that love of Fatherland as supreme rule of thought in all questions concerning the State, the love to which Fichte refers when he says in his *Addresses to the German Nation:*

"For this very reason love of the Fatherland itself must rule the State as the supreme, last, and independent authority."

Vienna, December 1937

CONTENTS

xxxiii

inet of Dr. Buresch.—Minority Cabinet of Dr.
Buresch. My Entry into the Government.—
Dollfuss Forms a Government.—The Lausanne
Loan.

ILLUSTRATIONS

MY AUSTRIA

CHAPTER ONE

Austria's Historical Mission

PRE-WAR Austria was often reproached with being the second Sick Man of Europe; her critics saw only her difficulties, they overlooked what she stood for, and forgot how she had come into being. That attitude afterwards became the Dual Monarchy's destiny and doom.

With an area of 240,456 square miles, reaching from Bregenz on the Lake of Constance to Czernowitz in the Carpathians, from Lemberg in Poland to Ragusa on the Adriatic, with between 50,000,000 and 60,000,000 inhabitants, in extent this Empire occupied the second place in Europe, in population the third. It was colonized by twelve different nations, who were by no means everywhere to be found in compact settlements. Such, then, was the Dual Monarchy of Austria-Hungary, among the other great powers of Europe.

But in respect of constitution this great power was divided

into two parts—the Kingdom of Hungary, and the "King-doms and Provinces represented in the Reichsrat" (Parliament of Austria proper), without any common legal appellation.

Thus the old Austria was a term, an idea, a reality, an administrative organization; but her politicians, for the most part, were not willing to accept as the common denominator the designation "Austria." Moreover, those who were ready to do so were not strong enough to enforce the practice.

And yet this Austria was by no means a mere legal fiction. As a rule, the peoples of all the tongues of the Monarchy were quite aware they had much to lose that was of value, hardly anything more to gain. About the inner disposition of the house, styled Austria-Hungary, they squabbled noisily, as was the habit in Austrian parliaments—so noisily, indeed, that outsiders as a rule, judging by those shrill wrangles only, had come to the conclusion that the wish for a house in common was not at hand and that the centrifugal forces prevailed. But, for all that, down to the war such a belief was on the whole erroneous.

The great majority of Austrians wanted to occupy their house in common, but in respect of its name and inner structure there could be no unity. Even Thomas G. Masaryk admits this general feeling when he writes: ". . . I was at pains to make up my mind definitely to have to oppose Austria and the Austrian idea by acts."

Under such conditions every Austrian government was perforce required to follow laboriously a policy of pacification and postponement, of bartering and haggling, a policy which used up and destroyed men and nerves, time and money; and on whatever strength it had been left with, a heavy strain was imposed by the continuous efforts to arrive at a compromise with Hungary, a country which stood up for her own constitutional rights with energy and persistence.

Side by side with the two governments, and representing the Monarchy in its foreign dealings, there was a sort of joint government of the Empire, consisting of the Ministries for War, Finance, Foreign Affairs, and the Imperial Household. For a long time some of these ministers were allowed to call themselves "Ministers of the Empire," but afterwards, when dusk was falling over Austria, even this nomenclature was eliminated on account of constitutional considerations. There then remained only the highly complicated distinction, comprehensible to the initiated only, between "K.u.K.," [1] "K.K.," and "K.U."

Apart from the common army, there existed an Austrian "Landwehr" (Second Reserve) and the Hungarian "Honved" (Reserve with special privileges). Landwehr and Honved, the armed forces of the two divisions of the Monarchy, were each controlled by its own ministry, the Austrian Landwehr with German as its official language, the Honved with Hungarian, supplemented by some formations where the use of Croat was authorized.

Above all those bodies there was the Crown, personified, until just before the downfall of the Empire, in the Emperor and King Francis Joseph, whom many called the last representative of the old-style Monarchy, the Last of the Knights.

Become, through grief and personal destiny, a legendary

[1] "K.u.K." (Imperial and Royal) was used for the joint ministries and their subordinates, while "K.K." (Imperial Royal) designated Austrian, and "K.U." (Royal Hungarian) Hungarian state institutions. Thus everything pertaining to the joint army was "K.u.K.," the Austrian railroads were "K.K.," and the Hungarian ones "K.U."—TRANSLATOR.

figure, the monarch, so to say, towered in lonely greatness into the dusk of historical Austria. As a young archduke he had been given his first lessons in constitutional law by the famous Chancellor Prince Metternich, and after Metternich his personal experiences had extended down past Felix Schwarzenberg, Alfred Windischgrätz, Ludwig Kossuth, Cavour, Napoleon III, the Emperors William and Alexander, Bismarck, Moltke, and Andrássy, through the epoch of Liberalism and the Christian revival, until long after the days of Lueger.[1]

Between the period of the post-chaise and the arrival of the airplane, there stretched his reign of nearly seventy years. Seventy years of technical progress, revolution in thought, advancement of nations, radical transformation in the conceptions of constructive statecraft. When Francis Joseph ascended the throne, there had been much talk about the renewed German Empire to come. Friedrich List, the protagonist of the German Customs Union idea, had just died, and whoever spoke of the Reich and called himself a "Great-German" moved in historic tracks, where Austria had a particular and leading part to play.

At the time of Francis Joseph's death, the Reich in the old sense (and even outside Austria) had been interred, not only theoretically but in fact, although there was an outside appearance of it existent and although in the jewel room of the Hofburg in Vienna still rested the old German Imperial crown.

When Francis I, in 1806, discarded the title of a German Emperor, this had been nothing other than the formal recognition of a historical fact accomplished long before. In Goethe's *Faust* already the students sitting together in

[1] Dr. Karl Lueger, 1897–1910 Mayor of Vienna, principal leader of the Catholic movement in pre-war Austria.—TRANSLATOR.

Auerbach's wine-cellar wonder how long the Holy Roman
Empire will still survive:

The dear old holy Roman realm,
How does it hold together?
A nasty song! Fie! a political song—
A most offensive song! Thank God, each morning, there-
fore,
That you have not the Roman realm to care for! [1]

The nationalistic tendencies of the nineteenth century
led up from the Risorgimento to the Wilhelmine epoch in
Germany. Austria was now evidently isolated from the
general movement. The old feeble Reich had to yield before new vigorous states. Austria struggled against the
stream till the year 1866 [when the Prussians defeated Austria at Sadowa]. Then a new task offered itself to her—in
fact, it was imposed upon her by the stern fate of historical
development, though not the less great and significant on
that account:

To bring together the various nationalities, their civilizations and languages, for the purpose of achieving political
and economic power and welfare—that was her historical
European mission in the new form. From the standpoint
of German culture she should unite the various contending
national forces for the benefit of each and all and for the
sake of a common pacific development founded upon and
led by German traditions.

For this purpose it was important to preserve historical
continuity, and, indeed, the old Imperial idea has worked
from the distant past—from Wallenstein's camp during the
Thirty Years' War, down past the bivouac of Radetzky in

[1] Translation by Bavard Taylor.

Italy, down to the mobilization under Conrad von Hötzen-dorf in 1914.

The Austro-German Dual Alliance of 1879 was merely the logical extension of an old and inevitable historical path, and whoever on this side or that might think that an alternative course could have been possible would sin in imagination against the spirit of History. This is by no means to assert that the policy of the Dual Alliance proceeded always along the right lines. Indeed, many a blunder involved Vienna and Berlin in a common fate of tragedy.

This line of reasoning leads to the conclusion as follows: The first Reich, the Holy Roman Empire, had become in the course of the centuries a hollow, empty form, a mere fiction. After it came, still induced by a just perception of geo-political and national appropriateness, several cautious experiments—the German League, for instance, an inadequate constitutional construction—and then a makeshift: an alliance between two separate states, a matter of international law.

The triumph of nationalism in the course of the nineteenth century presented Austria with a new political task. In a territory inhabited by different nationalities she should, through her long experience and her talent, build the bridge towards a new realization of the Reich idea in the modern age.

Upon this task Austria broke. It is idle to debate whether the attempt would have miscarried also without war, or had the war ended differently. If conditions had remained as they were until 1914, then, I believe, collapse would have been a question of the next decades only—and why? Because Austria had not succeeded in finding a way from the old to the new Reich. Federalism alone has not the power to call into being an empire, for that is not merely a question of constructive administration. More than anything else was the dualism created by the compromise with Hungary an obstacle in the way towards the establishment of a genuine new empire. And thus it came about, as it was bound to come: the magnetic force of neighbouring states, each impelled by the ideal of national unity, together with national sentiment, proved stronger than judgment and insight. For we know today that the year 1937, as a reality, looks very different from what many a nationalist dreamer anticipated in his visions in 1914.

In fact there is no Reich today, in the old sense of the word, and a glance at the British Empire as well as at the new Italian colonial Empire only confirms this, although on the continent of Europe there are many states, big and strong ones, small and weak ones, and among the strongest and most concentrated the National-Socialistic Germany.

That the idea of the Reich should be kept alive—though transferred to the sphere of Spirit and Civilization—continues to be Austria's hereditary duty, historically confirmed.

It is true that the conception of the Holy Empire has ever been borne on a world of romantic ideas, bordering even on the transcendental; but the realm created by Charlemagne was also a material reality and power of the first order. This Emperor intended to establish a world Empire, consciously continuing the task of ancient Rome, the heritage of which had fallen to a new age. To unite the West in the Christian spirit, to place the symbol of a common Imperial crown above the various kings and princes of the individual nations—that was the aim and purpose of this Holy Roman Empire. Certainly, such a conception could, at that time, only be realized by imperialist methods, but in the last analysis this Reich was based upon and justified by a great civilizing design.

The more vigorously the states and peoples strove after unrestricted freedom and took up an attitude of defence against any kind of union and restraint, the looser the bands of the Empire became, the fainter its idea. With the passage of the centuries and with technical and cultural advancement the range of its influence grew ever narrower, until of the World Imperium, of the Continental Reich, there was left over only a loosely organized central Europe, still called Holy Roman Empire of German Nations. Yet ever, within this compass, considerable cultural values and uniting spiritual forces were streaming forth from the conception of this Empire. But what had once been a fact now gradually became an appearance, and a sharp conflict arose between the Imperial and the national idea. Thus even Austria, the historic upholder of the Empire, could now preserve the Imperial crown only through the territorial possessions of the House of Habsburg, which had grown to the size of a great state.

When, in 1804, the last Roman-German Emperor, Francis II, proclaimed himself Emperor of Austria, he thereby created a new political entity, but not an Empire in the traditional sense of the word. Thus when the Holy Reich was wound up formally, and the attempts in the first half of the nineteenth century to revive it proved abortive, the task of Austria was to foster a new Imperial conception, upon a new plane, though on a smaller scale; and for this task she was more qualified by her history than any other state. It is an open question whether it was still possible at all to unite in one family and lead in the spirit of Teutonic culture the non-German peoples which had become of age, were ambitious, and dreamed of their individual nationalisms. Anyhow, the inexorable realities of the age proved stronger than the attractive romanticism of what was in itself doubtless a true and reasonable idea.

What remains over today from old Austria—32,400 square miles, expressed in terms of surface measure—certainly offers no scope for a renewal of the Imperial idea and another Imperial crown. Austria is become a small state. Yet there are even smaller states in Europe, smaller in population or in extent, which nevertheless play a notable part in Continental politics, and that precisely because theirs is a historical task. This refers to Switzerland, Belgium, Holland, or the Scandinavian countries, for example.

Our new state would not be Austria, would not be worth while persisting, if its inherited mission, in new and modern form, was not able to break through. Yet not force nor the instruments of war but rather the spirit and the work of culture can discharge the task of the mediator in an arena resounding with many tongues and organized into separate states, but which still needs some kind of spiritual and economic unity in order to survive. Such a service for Europe can be performed only by a power which does not fall under the suspicion of following incidental imperialistic aims.

Thus "Empire" and "State" are today still totally different conceptions, not to be looked upon as synonyms. The possible scope of such an "Empire" has been revolutionized. It persists only in the spiritual sphere and has apparently been thrust back into the dematerialized, well-nigh transcendental state, where, in a different age and under different conditions, the first Holy Empire had found the sources of its strength. Certainly these new trends have nothing in common with what the word "Empire" stands for in colloquial usage.

Historical Austria still makes her influence work in a new form and in new, fundamentally altered conditions, across the past into the new age. Faithful to her tradition, she has left us not only a task of extra-national importance to perform, but also a conspicuously German task, a task which we Austrians alone can discharge to the advantage and avail of the German people to which we are bound through our civilization—the people from whose midst Faust came, whom Goethe made to say: "In the beginning was the spirit of things."

CHAPTER TWO

My Country as I Saw It
on the Eve of War

IN THE following pages I shall record some personal impressions from my youth, and certainly these should not be looked upon indiscriminately as if they represented the feelings of my entire generation.

In most respects life was simpler thirty years ago than it is today, but even then young people of fifteen to twenty displayed a lively interest in politics and grappled earnestly with their problems—of which Austria had more than her share. One anxiety at any rate we were spared: anyone who wanted to work and was able to work, anyone who had a sane ambition for achievement, possessed average gifts and health to match, had no need to worry over his earning a living, according to his free choice and within the frontiers of his country. How much that meant, only the young Austrian of the present day can appreciate properly.

Problems of a category entirely different from today's

13

faced the pre-war generation. In the first place the social question aroused intellectual discussion and heated debate, although few people ever contemplated a real reform of the existing order of things. The leading part in this controversy had fallen to the Socialists. Previous to the war the number of their followers was steadily increasing, but still they had more or less reached the limits of their field of activities. And since Socialists have always aspired to capture the masses, they had begun to deviate from objective reasoning; for even in those bygone days one could not appeal simultaneously to Reason and to the Mass Mind. On the other side the Christian Social Reformers were gradually increasing and this movement was taking deep root, though it never secured a compact and politically important following.

As a rule, the prevailing classes within the smaller municipalities, the educated people of the provinces, and the bulk of the well-to-do middle class had no economic anxieties at all and for the most part took no real interest in social problems. But still everyone realized in some way that Capitalism had produced certain abuses, and people who had suffered under these abuses or who merely went about with their eyes open displayed at a quite early date a tendency to put forward radical solutions for the abolishment of the social evil. In the cities particularly, young people who were alert mentally and had the realistic outlook were concerned with the question how best to check the growing proletarianism and improve the position, then deplorable, of the manual worker—problems aggravated just then by the rapid spread of industry.

Model programs of social reform had at that time a certain vogue among the young. They debated them, wrote and read about them; but as a rule this interest was confined to the study or to evening gatherings, for, as a fact, those young men were almost never in intimate touch with the realities of life. In this respect the post-war period has brought about an undeniable progress, of which the artisan-student movement [1] may be mentioned as an example.

But what most interested the young Austrian, in the period of which I treat, especially if he lived in one or another of the mixed-linguistic frontier zones, was the national question. He was bound, sooner or later, to find himself involved in the maze of problems connected with the different nationalities of which the Monarchy consisted. The part he took in this matter generally shaped his entire attitude towards his State and Fatherland.

The conflict of nationalities lasted right up to the eve of the war, all the time taking forms more and more violent. Everywhere in Europe nationalism had developed since the middle of the nineteenth century, although its progress varied from country to country. Within the framework of the old Dual Monarchy the movement had one special feature: it did not really spring from the spirit of the population, nor was it originally fought out on a wide field. Among all the nationalities it was rather diminutive groups of intellectuals who first stirred up the fire.

These groups magnified national discontents even where, judged by post-war conditions, there was no legitimate ground for them, and they provoked quarrels in order to keep aglow, particularly in exposed areas such as the mixed-linguistic districts, the sparks they would need to fan, at

[1] In Austria, as well as in Germany and other European countries, many poor students earn their living today by doing some kind of manual or intellectual work besides their studies. This artisan-student movement is largely encouraged by the universities and the State.—TRANSLATOR.

the appropriate occasion, into the flame of political passion.

And all this was done in the face of a lenient executive which repeatedly changed its course, hushed up or smoothed over disputes, and, in the noisy parliaments of universal suffrage—in force in Austria since 1907—offered to loyalists a picture that was the reverse of encouraging and attractive.

Above the waves of passion there was the Crown alone.

"If Francis Joseph vaults into the saddle, his peoples will follow him." Bismarck had once said this to those who doubted Austria's military value as an ally, and 1914 proved him right. There were people afterwards who did not want to recognize this, and when it was not possible for them, in view of the historical facts, to sustain the charge of Austria's inadequate loyalty, they attempted to allege her worthless-less as an ally altogether. To bolster up this theory, Imperial Austria was classified as a "living corpse." [1] But, indeed, only by using very dark tinted glasses could one see things in such a light.

Undoubtedly the really logical anti-Austrians, in their struggle against the old state, had also put the obliteration of the dynasty upon their program, yet up to the beginning of the war only a few Irredentist fanatics went as far as that. They represented but a miserable minority which generally shunned the daylight. At any rate there was no majority among the Austrians of German language behind the Hohenzollern furore artificially worked up in different parts of the country. "Long live the Hohenzollerns!" had been the slogan of some rabid Austro-German nationalists

---

[1] In certain controversial writings of the post-war period, as for instance *My Struggle* by Adolf Hitler, the alliance with Austria-Hungary has been represented as having been in opposition to the interests of the German Empire.—TRANSLATOR.

before the war, and afterwards this was transformed into the cry "Home to Germany!" [1]

Hungary had to deal with her own problems in this regard, the solution of which was mostly a constitutional matter; but as regards Austrian domestic politics, the quarrel with the Czechs was of the most urgent and recurrent importance.

Particularly the so-called "Badeni disorders" aroused heated discussion among young people before the war. Like many another Austrian statesman before and since, Prime Minister Count Badeni, a Pole, had endeavoured to cut the Gordian knot of the paralysing national dissensions. That he was not fortunate in his attempt must be admitted, and his efforts gave offence in quarters where loyalty to Austria was beyond all question. But, for all that, I believe that an unbiased judgment formed today leads to a milder opinion of his intentions. For the sake of Austria's prestige abroad and her domestic prosperity every true patriot must at that time have striven for the union of all constructive forces within the country that were ready for active co-operation. This, precisely, had been Count Badeni's aim, and in order to obtain the goodwill of the Czechs he was ready to accept in principle a bilingual system among the public bodies of Bohemia and Moravia. Every subject should have the right to employ his mother tongue in the courts and in all his dealings with the authorities. At that time the Austrians of German nationality looked upon this plan as a frivolous challenge to their predominant position in the Monarchy. But if we look back at Badeni's program today and compare it with the solution of the Czech problem brought about in

[1] The slogan of Austrian National-Socialists since 1933.—TRANSLATOR.

1918, we find that the German population had not so much
reason to complain as they had believed thirty years earlier.

Those were the days when the plan of establishing Slovene
classes at the classical grammar-school at Cilli in South
Styria (nowadays called Celje and belonging to Jugoslavia)
led to a cabinet crisis in Vienna, when the motion to in-
augurate a law-course in Italian at the University of Innsbruck provoked the resignation of the Governor of the
Tyrol. On the other hand it was taken as a matter of course
that officials of the various tongues should make use of
German in intercourse among themselves and not feel their
national susceptibilities hurt thereby. This was done, not
on account of regulations, but simply for obvious practical
reasons, and no one came off badly. Undoubtedly the various nations of the Monarchy would have continued to live
together in peace, had they not been persuaded into the belief that by quarrelling they could better serve their individual interests.

This state of things was not altogether disadvantageous
to the cultural predominance of the German element.
Everyone could see that, if he wished to see it—provided
one did not identify the nation with imperialistic and
monopolistic aims.

But even after the revolution and the collapse of the Dual
Monarchy many Austrians of German language were still
unable to recognize what Austria had stood for, what the
idea of Empire she embodied had meant. Although in the
meantime the German element had itself become a minority
in some of the new states and experienced the hardships
and inequalities characteristic of the post-war minorities
policy, those people still saw in the breakdown of the Monarchy a national advantage. The rabid nationalists of yes-

terday developed into the scorners of new Austria as well, notwithstanding that this much derided Monarchy had brought them national freedom and even predominance, while the new State is still carrying on a persistent fight for the maintenance of German culture.

An attitude such as this certainly belóngs to the singularities of political evolution and is only to be explained in part by the fact that in many fields of life, and particularly in the plane of politics, hatred makes her victims blind and shoves aside all sound judgment.

Old Austria could have achieved her mission only had a vigorous and general acceptance of her true idea led to the suppression of extreme nationalism. The German-speaking Austrian was just the one who should, in view of the distribution of the German settlements throughout central and south-eastern Europe, have recognized that the existence of the old Monarchy was a great advantage to him, provided he felt himself Austrian first and German in the second place. And if he could not rally to that view himself, then clearly he had no right to expect that Poles, Czechs, and Slovenes should put Austria above their individual nationalisms.

It was certainly not by mere chance that the unbridled phase of national conflicts should have coincided with the general belief in parliamentary democracy as the most perfect form of government. With us the parliamentary system was not built upon old tradition as it is in England. It had rather abruptly sprung from the ideals of the nineteenth century. One may estimate its values as one wishes, but this much can be asserted: parliamentary democracy was not in a position to produce an adequate solution for problems so thorny as those of the nationalities in Austria. For such a

task everything was lacking—institutions as well as personalities sufficiently strong to bring opponents together, to
weld divergent aspirations into a peaceful co-operation towards the common end.

Judged by human standards, the old Empire could have
been aroused to new life only by a wise authoritative leadership which, at the appropriate time and in the light of the
country's organic evolution, had established some kind of
national federalism and thus remodelled the Monarchy into
a real "Reich" consisting of autonomous territories. Trans-
forming, at any rate for the interim, the system of parliamentary representation, a government with far-reaching
powers could have carried the whole operation through
during a period of peaceful prosperity.

This hope, however, was shattered on June 28, 1914!

It is strange how this fateful day remains fixed in the
mind. On Sunday evening, during supper at Feldkirch College, one of the servants gave us the frightful news. The end
of the term was at hand and we boys were in a holiday mood.
It may have been half past seven.

The tragic event made an overwhelming impression upon
myself and my companions, all boys who were completing
the Septima.[1] We would not at first believe it, and when it
was confirmed, the vague presentiment of impending hor-
rors caused in myself, then a sixteen-year-old boy, a shock
such as I have seldom experienced in later life.

Our way of education accounted for that.

We Austrian boys had been accustomed to look on the
Archduke Francis Ferdinand as the living embodiment of

[1] Seventh class of the Austrian eight-class system for classical grammar-
schools which start at the age of about ten with the "Prima" and end with
the "Octava."—TRANSLATOR.

KURT SCHUSCHNIGG

our patriotic hopes. Therefore no one could now picture what would come afterwards. National reorganization and consolidation, the conception of a stronger Austria—this hope was associated with his name in our minds, a name, moreover, that had long been a rallying cry for the more active forces of the country.

And I might remark in passing that malicious reports of the Archduke's alleged anti-German outlook and pro-Czech tendencies, assiduously put about by circles hostile to the dynasty, particularly by the Pan-Germans, had come to the ears of us boys, together with the first hints of an un-savoury story, then taking shape, regarding the Archduke Charles Francis Joseph, heir to the throne, afterwards Emperor Charles I [who lost the throne in 1918]. It was plain that efforts were already afoot to sap the authority of the dynasty, and the most mendacious and noxious methods were employed in the campaign. The person of the Emperor alone was still treated with respect even by those scandalmongers, and that because of his overwhelming popularity among the masses. The beer-cellar politicians and self-elected reformers of the age opposed to the dynasty preferred to slink into the background when there was even a question of the Monarch's position.

Like thousands of my contemporaries from the different Austro-Hungarian nationalities, I had grown up in a rigid monarchical and loyal atmosphere where particular stress was put upon our cultural relationship with the German nation.

And now a word or two about our upbringing.

Families whose heads served the State as soldiers or civil administrators were a class typically Austrian, a strong prop whose branches spread into every province of the old Monarchy. Numerically the German-speaking element among these families was a strong one, and since German was the language used in the army and civil administration, all those officers and officials became interpreters of German civilization as manifested in the Austrian spirit. These forces, upon which the State rested, thus had an obvious national importance, a consideration which is in itself a refutation of the shallow conception of Austria as an organism deleterious or even dangerous for German culture.

That, nevertheless, many Germans who lived in the mixed-linguistic frontier territories should have lapsed into such a superstition and awaited with impatience the collapse of the Monarchy is one of the strangest paradoxes, rich in irony, of the story of Austrian domestic politics. It was not at all difficult to foresee what must be the result of this attitude. If it were not so tragic, one would be tempted to recall the words: *"Volenti non fit iniuria"* ["He who wishes a thing must not complain if he gets it"—a principle of Roman law].

Born at Riva, on Lake Garda, then the garrison town of my father, I was sent to an elementary school in a Vienna suburb. I had never seen extravagance at home. The Austrian who lived on a fixed income drawn from the State always led a Spartan, frugal existence, with no pretension to luxury. This applied to officers and officials more than to anyone else. But I owe a debt of gratitude to my parents for my sunny, peaceful, and untroubled childhood, for the spectacle I was offered of self-control and simplicity, for the joy of our happy family life.

My mother came of a family long settled in Innsbruck, in the Tyrol. One of her uncles founded the well-known

Tyrol glass-painting industry, another was a much loved doctor, and the third a master craftsman. Dr. Theodor Kathrein, for many years chief of the provincial government of the Tyrol, a leader of the conservative party, and once, in stormy days, President of the Chamber of Deputies, also belonged to the family, as an uncle by marriage. Kathrein started life as a poor student and he died an acting Privy Councillor to His Majesty and a hereditary baron. A career such as his was by no means out of the ordinary in the Austria of those days, when the son of a non-commissioned officer or a gendarme would often become an excellency. In the diplomatic service and the political administration alone things were somewhat different.

On my father's side the family came from the district of Klagenfurt [capital of the province of Carinthia]. My great-grandfather's career as a Klagenfurt property-owner was an honourable one, and my grandfather became a soldier and served under Radetzky [1] in Venice as a cadet, in subsequent grades spending most of his active career in the Tyrol, where he retired with the rank of provincial inspector of gendarmerie, after fifty years' service. His wife came of a middle-class family long settled at Rosenheim in Bavaria, and so when the title of nobility was conferred afterwards, the Austrian and Bavarian colours (black and yellow, and blue and white respectively) were united in the family coat of arms.

My father was born at Kufstein, passed through the Wiener Neustadt military academy, was gazetted to the "Kaiserjäger" [the celebrated Tyrolean regiment of Imperial Sharpshooters], and served afterwards in the Tyrolean second reserve.

[1] Famous Austrian general in the first half of the nineteenth century, who mostly fought in Italy.—TRANSLATOR.

Of all this I was reminded later, when in the heat of political controversy, which unfortunately often tends towards personal slander, I was reproached with Croatian, Slovene, or Italian origin. Of course, even had this been true, I should have had no reason whatever to be ashamed of it, but since it was alleged in the course of highly objectionable polemics, its untruth had to be established.

Like many another army family in Imperial Austria, we, too, had to reckon with having to live in garrison towns where school facilities would be inadequate—Galicia [in Poland] and Dalmatia were among such spots, little loved, to which the wearer of the Emperor's uniform might find himself banished for a great part of his life. That was why it was the practice in army circles for the children—who for the most part would inherit nothing except a good education—to be sent at an early age to a boarding-school.

For this purpose in Austria there existed several military institutes, from grammar-schools up to the cadet colleges and, finally, the military academies, as well as the famous Theresianum [1] in Vienna, intended first of all for the sons of the aristocracy and the well-off, and a large number of boarding-schools, middle-class in character, administered mostly by the Catholic teaching orders.

Thus before I was ten years old my way had taken me to Feldkirch, in the Vorarlberg, where the Jesuits had a school known as Stella Matutina, a noted institution then able to look back on some thirty or forty years of useful activity.

Having been a pupil of the Jesuits, I had in later years to listen to reproaches concerning this kind of education, re-

[1] A college founded by the Empress Maria Theresa for the benefit of young noblemen, but later accessible also to other boys. The Theresianum was and is still regarded as one of the most distinguished colleges in Austria, in some ways comparable to Eton.—TRANSLATOR.

proaches coming from friendly and unfriendly critics alike. I have always been grateful to my teachers—a point that would be hardly worth referring to, were it not that this school exercised a decisive influence on my career and outlook, especially as regards those very questions round which conflicts have arisen in the new Austria. This fact I cannot deny, and the older I get, the more conscious I am of it.

The influence of the school was all the more marked because it worked on the boys throughout the entire school year. The college in my day was run on severe and Spartan lines. Sport at Stella Matutina was looked upon as a matter of duty long before it became fashionable elsewhere.

On the other hand the boys were required to stay on at the school for the Christmas and Easter holidays, during the eight years of the curriculum. Only at the end of the last term there was a six days' vacation previous to the final examinations.

Originally barracks, the school buildings at Feldkirch were a gift, in his day, of the Emperor Francis Joseph to the German province of the Society of Jesus when its members were driven from Germany by order of Bismarck. That was why the masters and "prefects" were, with few exceptions, of German or Swiss origin—though it would be wrong to imagine that their expulsion had stamped the German Jesuits with the mark of the refugee. Such was not at all the case, and when on national holidays the black, white, and red flag of the German Empire floated side by side with the Austrian colours from the school buildings, that was not only due to the fact that the college had a purely German department run on the lines of schools in the Reich, and consisting of eight classes, in addition to the Austrian section. This flag also bore witness to the ardent German spirit of our teachers and to their feeling of unity with the German people. Anyhow, they knew how to combine this feeling with perfect loyalty towards the Austrian State.

In common with hundreds of other young Austrians, peasant boys as well as sons of aristocrats, I received my first lessons in Austrian national harmony in the truest meaning of the word.

This fraternal atmosphere was not always quite easily maintained, the more so as our defects were pointed out discreetly to us Austrians, and German energy and German progress were often held up to us as a pattern. For all that, we grew up into good Austrians, recognizing the worth of our own country, yet with no disposition to belittle the qualities of our comrades from the Reich. The rivalry encouraged, consciously or unconsciously, between us and them was a commendable one and from it the spirit of real comradeship grew.

And here I might remark incidentally that I never supposed myself to be a model schoolboy and was never looked on as such, though the school course presented few difficulties to me. Nor can I assert that, as a youth, I found school work particularly inspiring. As in the case of my contemporaries, the urge towards liberty was very strong within me.

It was in after life only that I recognized the great and permanent benefits for which we had to thank the school. On that account and in an age when there is so much confused thinking and so many false ideas are purposely encouraged I feel the more impelled to do a service to the cause of truth by asserting that never in all my life have I met men more nationally conscious than those German Jesuits. Indeed, so much stress did they put on their nationality that I, as an Austrian, occasionally felt they were overdoing it.

No word of religious intolerance, no criticism of events and conditions in Germany ever fell from the lips of our educators. We were taught that Catholicism requires the extra-national outlook, indeed, but not the "international," as opposed to the patriotic. It was urged upon us that real Catholic sentiment is nowhere in conflict with a national manner of thought and, further, we Austrians were brought to understand that loyalty to the State and loyalty to the nationality ought to supplement each other.

More ridiculous still than the reproach, constantly brought against the Jesuits, of "internationalism" and a wholly anti-national system of education is the attempt to interpret so-called Jesuit methods by the saying: "The end justifies the means." Quite the reverse was constantly hammered into our minds. We learned that the attainment of a presumed or really praiseworthy end in no circumstances justified a prevarication, and that one ought to forgo an end, even though worth attaining in itself, if it was only to be attained by untruth, injustice, or the violation of conscience. Judged by the standpoint of the agitator or political organizer, such doctrines might appear of questionable value, but it is not to be disputed that they are sound ethically. I was taught them, I understood them to be right, and to the best of my knowledge and conscience I have always striven to model my practice upon them.

There is, in short, nothing particularly bizarre about the pupil of the Jesuits, though I am ready to admit that many who were of our set have followed a different path in life. But the Jesuits are not to be blamed for that, since they taught otherwise. The Fathers themselves would have attained many a success had they deviated from their rules of ethics. But this they would not do, and in the long run the results of such an attitude are bound to be of higher value than one or another advantage gained through inconsistency.

Five hundred boys were living together at Feldkirch in the conditions I have described, when war broke out. The school, besides being well known in Germany and Austria, enjoyed international repute. We had boys from all parts of the world and I can remember French, Spaniards, Americans, and many Polish schoolmates. Moreover, in my own class there were Germans from the Volgaland. Far from hampering our patriotic education, as babblers and know-alls would be ready to assert, this national mixture worked in the reverse sense. All the pupils were imperceptibly influenced in the spirit of Austro-German culture, and that remained the case right up to the outbreak of the war, when, to be sure, only Austrians, Germans from the Reich, and Swiss remained at the school.

As was to be expected, during the first year of the war we lived in a state of intense and uninterruped excitement. Rivalries between Austrians and Germans which found expression from time to time in a too tumultuous patriotism were, with much patience and persistence, directed into quieter channels. Not a few of the members of the Society were called up for war service and my recollection is that they served, without exception, in the German forces.

One incident continues in my memory. Towards Christmas 1914 I summoned up courage and asked for permission to spend the holidays at home, mentioning my father's service at the front as the reason. But I was told (exceptions never being made at the school) to stay on quietly at Feld-kirch, "as the war will be over next year and you will then be able to spend your Christmas vacation with your family."

Instead, I joined as a volunteer on July 1, 1915, and four Christmases at the front followed the eight I had spent at school, away from home. To join up was an outstanding event in our lives and each of us took up arms with enthu-siasm and from a deep sense of duty, though by this time the miseries and hardships of war had already lasted a year. Of course no youth straight from school could be expected to know what war really was.

As I have mentioned, I was about to move up to the top class when war broke out and so I lived through the open-ing months of hostilities as a schoolboy on holiday at Mar-burg, the chief town of South Styria [now called Maribor and belonging to Jugoslavia], where my father was in gar-rison.

These few months left a deep impression on me and were calculated to give me an insight into one of Austria's grav-est difficulties. South Styria, an incomparably delightful country of sunshine, rich in fruit and colour, was one of the mixed-linguistic districts. The towns were for the most part German-speaking islets set in Slovenian peasant land. There in the summer months, particularly on Sundays when the traditional festivals were celebrated, singularly striking con-trasts came to the surface. The very exterior of the towns bore witness to German industry and well-being and helped the intelligent inquirer to get an impression of many a na-tional problem.

There were to be found Bismarck Squares or Bismarck Streets everywhere, while only here and there a monument to Emperor Joseph II reminded one of Austrian history.

Emperor Joseph [son of Empress Maria Theresa, Emperor from 1780 till 1790] was still universally held in great esteem as the monarch of the age of enlightenment. Besides his monument one would be reminded of the House of Habsburg by one or another statue of Archduke John, who lived on in popular esteem as Regent of the German League [which preceded the Empire of 1870] and as a cordial friend of the peasants and mountaineers.

There would be a German club-house everywhere, serving as the headquarters of different national organizations, and generally a Slovenian club-house would stand opposite. Moreover, there would be in each of the large German frontier parishes a Protestant church, which as likely as not had not been standing there for more than a generation.

The black, red, and gold flag would dominate the scene whenever the fire department or choral society held their annual feast, the Austrian colours on these occasions generally being in the background. *The Watch on the Rhine* enjoyed great popularity as the anthem of defiant Teutons, the more so as its singing was supposed to create difficulties with the Austrian police authorities, though that was no longer the case in my time.

Before, and particularly during, the war the local newspapers just published about Austria what the authorities insisted on and nothing more. All this clearly indicated that down there, in the mixed-linguistic zone, the conflict of the nationalities was carried on at the cost of the Austrian Imperial idea. To the black, red, and gold of the Germans the Slavs opposed their blue, white, and red, and both parties compromised on the legal black and yellow [of the Habsburg Monarchy] only when it was the Emperor's birthday or the district governor was expected.

The symbolic meaning of flags in Austria had always been a matter queer and complicated. As the black, red, and gold had once been the colours of a German Reich in which Austria played the leading part, precisely this fact gave a deeper meaning to their display in our country. But most people were not aware of that and they waved the tri-colour—black, red, and gold—merely to prove their anti-Austrian, Pan-German zeal. This was done at a time when the Reich of the Hohenzollerns had for a long time adopted black, white, and red as the Imperial colours.

A similarly odd situation arose after the war. The German Republic, set up at Weimar, chose black, red, and gold as the national flag, and consequently Austrian Pan-Germans displayed these colours wherever they could, although what they really wanted was not the democratic Republic of Weimar at all, but a system entirely different. Even nowadays black, red, and gold are frequently used, in Austria, as a disguise for Pan-German tendencies, regardless of the fact that in Germany the nationalist regime has scornfully abolished these colours as remainders of former democratic ideals.

Ever since the "Away from Rome" cry had been raised by Herr von Schönerer,[1] the national conflict, especially in the mixed-linguistic areas, was fought out with violence in the religious field as well. It was a misfortune that the Catholic clergy in the German-speaking localities were generally of non-German origin, German candidates for the

---

[1] Georg von Schönerer (1842–1921) had tried to prepare the union of Austria's German-speaking parts with the German Empire by propagating a mass apostasy from the Catholic Church. This "Away from Rome" movement, which about 1900 had a considerable number of followers, was mainly directed against the Habsburg dynasty, the influence of which was supposed to rely principally upon the Catholic Church and its hold on the population.—TRANSLATOR.

priesthood being scarce. The Slovenian priests in the South
Styrian German towns certainly purposed to speak, preach
and pray in German, but naturally enough they could no
forget their own tongue. In effect some of them made very
little effort to forget it. Notwithstanding those conditions,
the vast majority of the Slovene clergy were perfectly loyal
to Austria, but nevertheless a ban upon the political activity
of priests might possibly have had happy results. Unfortunately there was never a question of that.

The tendency on the radical German-speaking side was
to oppose a German popular religion to the "ultramon-
tane," Catholic, and "anti-German" forces, as those were
often unscrupulously described. The evangelical Church
was at that time felt to provide some such popular religion
and it was hoped to defend with its help the German-speaking territory and to press back the Slovene influence. Thus
the German extremists exploited Protestantism for their
own political ends, a fact which must be set down bluntly
in the interest of historical truth and which, indeed, is confirmed a hundredfold in Pan-German polemical literature
of those days.

The assertion just made is by no means the outcome of
any denominational bias in the consideration of religious
problems. For more than a century all the churches had
absolutely equal rights in Austria, and even the occupants
of the very highest posts of the civil service and army were
never asked whether they were Catholics or Protestants.
Measures were never taken even against the political abuse
of religion. The State looked on while the mixed-linguistic
territories came to be regarded as political mission fields to
which pastors were drafted from Germany, for the purpose
of providing them with permanent domiciles in Austria.

Wherever there were Austrian pastors, complaints of political difficulties were rare.

Although the rival camps confronted each other in the fashion just described, there is no question that right up to the outbreak of the war the patriotic Austrian feeling was deeply rooted within the masses of the people and exercised among the nationalities an influence more potent than that of the anti-Austrian agitation carried on by bigoted nationalist "prophets" who had come, as often as not, from foreign countries.

But still there were storm warnings which should not have been overlooked. In rabid German national circles Austria and the debt to her were discounted as far as possible, especially throughout the intelligentsia of the small country towns, while on the other side Pan-Slavism, with its gymnastic societies and youth organizations, got more and more support from Prague and made itself increasingly noticeable in Slovene circles.

Yet when war broke out, there were only Austrians. In effect people, even in the disputed border districts, would have been ill advised to display an anti-Austrian attitude in the August days of 1914. I have a very clear recollection of the departure of the South Styrian troops for the front. According to his nationality each man wore either a black, red, and gold or a blue, white, and red ribbon in his buttonhole or in his cap; yet the Imperial black and yellow colours carried ahead of the marching regiment expressed the true spirit of the army.

Anybody who lived in our country could hardly fail to get the impression of the awakening of a nation, a nation positive and united in its patriotic feelings. Enthusiasm was real. The war was regarded as just and necessary. Everybody was ready to admit that the prestige of the Monarchy was at stake and that her influence would be seriously impaired, even at home, if what was universally felt to be a challenge were answered with another surrender and another diplomatic retreat. Popular sentiment and the general atmosphere were then directly opposed to a higher political wisdom, though what that wisdom should have consisted in, it was left to History to reveal.

And so destiny took its course, while I, an Austrian youth who had reached military age, supposed myself to be the witness of my country's rebirth. Thank God, I did not realize what was the tragic path in front of me. The world caught its breath and only a handful of people knew what was at stake. Thus has it ever been, thus it will be to the end. Whoever, hypocritically, clamours for the culprits is himself generally ready to shoulder the same guilt. Who actually opened the account, and for what ends the price was paid in blood by a whole generation, these questions lose their importance once the balance of profit and loss is struck. What cannot be changed is the ebb and flow of national destiny, history's repetitions, the fact that the many must pay for the tragic mistakes of the few at decisive moments. And there is the further consideration that the mechanism of destruction invariably forges ahead of the constructive purposes of mankind, purposes whose fulfilment is too frequently hindered by barren debates. For years on end the technics of armaments will provide thousands of people with their livelihood and will even seem to make a whole nation prosperous; and then it will let destruction loose upon the next generation.

In the matter of my own war experiences I have nothing outstanding to describe. My adventures and hardships were those of innumerable other young men who found it a natural thing that they should go to the front. Today I still hold the opinion that war experience provides an essential background for the political evolution of any man who in 1914–18 was physically fit and of military age. It may well have been that the young man with no responsibilities and nothing to lose saw things differently from the youth snatched by the war from home and career.

Beyond the naval port of Pola I got to know only the Italian front—namely, the part between Gorizia and the sea known as the Carso sector. With the exception of a leave granted me in connection with my studies in the early summer of 1918 I was in all the fighting on that front, from May 1916 to the end of the war, beginning with the sixth battle of the Isonzo. Doberdo, Monte San Michele, Jamiano, and Hermada have become for me vivid, unfading memories. Just as elsewhere in the Austro-Hungarian army, so, too, in my battery the men of the different nationalities got on well together, no noticeable friction occurring before the spring of 1918, and nowhere was there a clash of political or religious creeds. I believed with many others that the same spirit of union would continue. This was a mistake on my part, unfortunately, as otherwise the war would have had a deep meaning for us, despite its calamitous end.

I recall clearly how something like a tremor passed through groups of our non-commissioned officers when they learned the news of the Russian Revolution and grasped what it meant. Many a man grew reflective about this time and gave voice unchecked in quiet hours to a craving for peace. Discipline, however, did not suffer, and for a long time there was no alarming sign that the agitation in the rear of the armies was spreading to the front. But whoever possessed keen ears was able now and then to catch up some significant remark or other, whispered during talks arising out of the assassination of the Prime Minister Count Stürgkh at the hand of Friedrich Adler in the autumn of 1916.

Naturally enough, peace talk was readily listened to. The young Emperor was undoubtedly popular with the troops at the front and it was in the rear that his reputation was blasted, knowledge of the fact, like many another misfortune, reaching the trenches by way of the justly detested bases. Confidence in the Fatherland persisted until just before the end of the war, notwithstanding many a danger warning and the growing anxiety over the want and misery of people at home.

The end in November 1918, more particularly in the neighbourhood where I was—the middle Piave—must always remain an indelible memory. Without any noticeable pressure by the enemy the disintegration of the army set in quite clearly in the last October days. The withdrawal of mutinous regiments caused gaps in the front. Now and then reserves that had been called for refused to obey orders. At Sacile, towards six o'clock one morning, just before the guns were got ready for action, my own battery was called out and the officers had to ask the men whether they were ready to go on fighting or not and whether they wanted a Monarchy or a Republic. From that moment we were seized by a feeling of taciturn resignation. Everyone experienced the gloomy certitude that everything was lost. It was All Souls' Eve 1918.

A few days afterwards came news of the armistice, news received with relief by us all. Then there was the rounding up of prisoners, something quite incomprehensible to us all, for we had assumed the armistice to be a fact. We were ordered to move on in marching kit to the bridge over the Tagliamento at Dignano, and when we got near it Scots infantry unexpectedly ordered us to disarm. We obeyed, but it will not cause astonishment when I say the incident long left a nasty aftertaste. When, in distress, we sought an explanation for this, the story got about that the Emperor and the Government had purposely tricked us by prematurely announcing an armistice, in order to prevent the troops from returning home. It was not until long after that the veil was lifted from the tragic mistake, with its disastrous consequences for tens of thousands. What really happened in these days, no one will completely understand, but as one recognizes when one looks back across the years, our personal fate was not of great moment in view of the universal catastrophe.

Anyhow, on November 4, two thousand officers, with an escort of British troops, began a march inland towards Treviso which was to last for days. Physical discomforts were insignificant compared with the anguish of the Austrian who, on his way to the prison camp, slowly began to apprehend that he had a country no longer.

When after anxious weeks the first news came from home and there was a muster of prisoners, it was realized that the Austro-Hungarian army had ceased to exist in the prison camp as well. The German Austrians and the Hungarians had retained their uniforms, whereas members of the other nationalities, though not all of them, had substituted badges in their national colours for the Imperial cockade in their caps.

We had almost a year to ponder our future, and in the meantime Austria was carried to the grave while the world looked on indifferent and unsympathetic as the funeral procession passed. But even from home, where desperate want had obliterated every trace of reason, we heard no other voices than those crying: "Peace at last!" We saw, without understanding it, how the new epoch watched with relief the interment of the Fatherland.

In my diary at that time I wrote: "Why did Austria die? Only later will it be possible to name, by means of a careful historical inquiry, the many forces which for decades were sapping and destroying her life. At present we think it was a matter of weakness of will." Bitterness certainly accounts for such an opinion, which was extremely unjust, and yet it contained a particle of the truth.

Until shortly before the fatal hour the army was the living embodiment of Austria. It is a fact that a happy or even a less unhappy outcome of the war could have kept Austria alive in a new form. Unquestionably the evolution of Austrian domestic politics must have paralysed the faculty of the State to survive defeat, and finally hunger and want played their part. But there is no doubt that only since we have lost her altogether have we been able to realize what Austria meant for us, for the German people, and for the world.

CHAPTER THREE

Revolution

WHILE the Austro-Hungarian troops were still at the front and fighting, the die had been cast in the capitals of the Central Powers.

In effect, there had been no Austria-Hungary since the last week of October 1918, and those who stood under her colours were fighting for a shadow, though they knew it not. The iron curtain of History had been rung down—a tragedy was over!

With violent and senseless hammer-strokes the ingenious creative work of centuries, which had gone into the making of the Dual Monarchy, had been shattered within the space of a few days. Out of blood and fire, misery and the pangs of hunger, a lamentable peace had been born, and with this peace the new Austria underwent her labour-pains.

There is no use today in criticizing those events. Bitter and shameful as many of their details were, at any rate it must be recognized that Austria was spared the flames of civil war with all its incalculable consequences and new sacrifices in blood.

We need not go into the question of responsibility here. Greater insight on the part of the victors could, it is certain, have laid the foundations of a better peace; that is, a better peace from everybody's point of view. The hecatombs of victims, the price paid by all the participants in the war, the destruction of so much that was irreparable culturally or economically, more than anything the idealistic program of the victors, as outlined for an attentive world in Wilson's Fourteen Points, all this called aloud for the removal of the grounds and occasions of conflict. Instead, an order of things was finally established which has led, only fifteen years later, to another impending European crisis.

For a just peace two conditions would have been required: first, the victors should have realized that the German people's deprivation of rights and their condemnation to permanent disarmament must produce—and within a calculable period—fresh explosions; and, more important still, there should have been judicious and just treatment of all the issues involved in winding up the old Monarchy. In this respect a little geography and ethnological knowledge, a slight acquaintance with history, would have prevented many an ill; whereas an intensity of destructive purpose produced a field of ruins which was not the more reasonable because its inhabitants, intoxicated by excitement and in a state of complete exhaustion, carried self-laceration to the extreme.

The unprecedented waste of energy and nervous force coupled with the over-organization of the war gave way abruptly to an undisciplined release from all restraint.

Thus the storm of the initial weeks of the revolution swept over ill-fated Austria like a wild spook. People's only desire was to get food at once.

About this time there occurred a hunt for the culprits who could be sent into the wilderness, and from the psychological standpoint this is comprehensible and it is a characteristic of every revolution. Later on, the leaders tried to take the wind out of the extremists' sails by compromising with the undiscerning masses, although these masses were inclined to follow the noisiest, most unrestrained, and most brutal agitators, as they usually do.

"Liberty," "self-determination," "social advancement," the overcoming of the "political and social dungeons" to which the peoples of Europe were said to have been condemned, "economic reconstruction"—such were the slogans of those days. Bewildered, terrified, dispersed, and starved out, the former upholders of the State, the exponents of moderate-minded conservatism, the guardians of traditions and old practices, the adherents of the *ancien régime* seemed to have vanished. It is vain to ask whether that was necessary and unavoidable—it was a fact.

The Emperor was regarded as the culprit *par excellence.* He could not defend himself and he was to learn how a pitiless "Crucify him!" could follow within two years of his being met with cries of "Hosanna!" Certainly the favour of the people is fickle. And so it came about that the man who personified the monarchical idea and the Monarchy as a form of government were the first victims.

No ruler has experienced a fate so ill as that which befell the Emperor Charles. It was his tragic lot to find himself put into a position which, judged by human standards, was no longer to be defended. He accepted his fate with dignity, and the way he bore himself in a crucial test did him honour as man and Habsburg. Whether he was a great monarch, was wisely advised at all times, did the right thing always, is not the question here. To recognize that he was thoroughly good, brave, and honest and a true Austrian who wanted the best and in misfortune bore himself more worthily than many other men would have done is to assert the truth—and this truth has been suppressed far too long.

Charles was not the traitor or the coward persistently represented by a transparent political propaganda. He was certainly not the superhuman personality either, which excessive zeal tried to make out of him. It was altogether right that he should strive for peace at the appropriate moment, for peace was a well-recognized interest not only of his own country but of the German people. His methods may perhaps have been inadequate and his path mistaken, yet it is not to be gainsaid that in the year 1917 the last opportunity seemed to have come for obtaining an honourable peace for the Central Powers. Had the Emperor then succeeded in bringing about such a peace, the deceptive intoxication of freedom would have been spared us and probably endless sacrifices and misery as well.

That the Emperor should have remained on in the country after the revolution as long as it was possible showed that he felt united to his people by reason of his good conscience and by what he owed his own name.

Already on October 21, 1918 the National Assembly of the Austro-German deputies met in Vienna, members returned at the elections for the Reichsrat (Parliament) held in 1911 coming together in the debating chamber of the Lower Austrian Diet on the Herrengasse. There, in accordance with the Imperial manifesto, and following the example of the other nationalities, they constituted themselves a National Assembly.

Of the 232 seats (including those of the Sudeten Deutsch), 102 were held by the Union of German National Parties, 72 by the Christian Socialist (Catholic) Party, and only 42 by the Socialists. At this first sitting Dr. Waldner, the acting President, said optimistically that nothing could now stand in the way of the well-being and unity of the German people in Austria, "since the national spirit and the spirit of the people, the well-being of the State, and the welfare of the people will all be fused together in the new State, where, moreover, German particularism, the source of every past division, will vanish and never be heard of again."

Dr. Victor Adler, the veteran of the Socialists, answered him thus: "We come to meet you here, but we come as Socialists, with our flags flying." Victor Adler, then in the last weeks of his life, went on to discuss the two possibilities of Austria's future:

"Austria should unite with the neighbouring countries in a free league of nations, if the other peoples are ready. Should the others reject this idea or lay down conditions which do not take note of the economic and national needs of our country, then the Austrian State (which left to itself has no prospect of expanding economically) will be forced to join the German Reich as an additional federal state. For German Austria we demand entire liberty to choose between these two possible associations. German Austria must in any case be a democratic and genuine people's state."

The question of Austria's future constitution was not raised.

In the name of the Union of German National Parties Dr. Steinwender made the following declaration: "The force of events has brought the old State to an end. We Germans, without dissension, take our stand upon the platform of independence. We keep unsullied, thereby, our love of our country and remain convinced supporters of the constitutional and monarchical form of government. Inspired by the ideal of the close union of all Germans, the German-Austrian State will settle its relations with the German Reich and with the other neighbouring countries by the unfettered exercise of its sovereign rights. . . ."

The Provincial Governor of the Tyrol, Herr Schraffl, speaking on behalf of the Christian Socialist (Catholic) Party, stressed their adhesion to the monarchical form of government as a principle and expressed the wish for the speedy democratization of German Austria. This is how he ended his speech: "Do not forget the Germans of the south! Help the Tyroleans in the present emergency of Reich and nation!"

All that was on October 21, 1918.

But as early as October 30, at the second meeting of the Provisional National Assembly, the Socialist member Dr. Ellenbogen announced that "the Socialists regard the establishment of a republic as the people's only safeguard against dynastic and other pretensions."

The stenographic report mentions loud and prolonged cheers and handclapping as well as shouts of "Long live the Republic!"

The Provisional National Assembly at this sitting elected from their midst an executive committee, called the Council of State, which consisted of the three party chairmen, Dinghofer (Nationalist), Fink (Catholic), and Seitz (Socialist), and twenty other members.

For its part the Council of State designated as its representatives the State Government, each of whose members received the title of State Secretary.

That was what happened within the Parliament. Meanwhile the fire of revolution had been stoked up by the press and at public meetings and no one resisted the radicalization of the streets. The enactment of unrestricted liberty of the press was one of the first acquisitions of the new epoch, that liberty of which Goethe once remarked: "What have the Germans got with their delightful press freedom, save that everyone says things as base and vile as he likes about everyone else?"

By these means every violent instinct was gradually aroused and every restraint relaxed. The mobilization of the street had begun.

At that time and later there was much talk as to the "will of the working class." Let it be said at once that what took place in the year 1918 was at first not the doing of the workers. On the contrary, the workers have always realized that order and law generally guarantee them their jobs. While many grounds for dissatisfaction admittedly existed—the food shortage ought to be specially mentioned—things would certainly have taken a different course had the workers, through real labour leaders chosen from among themselves, taken charge of the situation. But, as it happened, the control passed into the hands of a Socialist intelligentsia who wanted to mobilize the masses at all costs and wherever they could get them, in order to lay the foundations for permanent Socialist domination, particularly in Vienna.

In the first days of the collapse unruly and hungry soldiers, then demobilized, and the mob of the towns were the elements most reliable from the Socialist standpoint, and round them tens of thousands of industrious folk gathered in good faith, convinced the Promised Land their leaders spoke of was at hand. Nearly everyone else stood aside, helpless and intimidated.

Among the Socialist leaders there existed a dangerous anxiety to prevent, by the display of truculent radicalism, a split in the party ranks, thus preserving a united Socialist front in Austria. In this way the seed was sown for the country's subsequent political evolution. In due course there grew up in Austrian Socialism two types of leaders, the moderates and the extremists, and in decisive moments agreements were usually come to on lines advocated by the latter. Although at first this had the advantage of preventing the growth of Communism and the formation of a Spartacus group,[1] afterwards the price had to be paid in the truculence of the movement which became known as Austro-Marxism.

In the course of history revolutions and upheavals, with their standardized forms and atmosphere of violence, regularly recur, and Goethe clearly perceived the eternal repetitions in history when he addressed the prophets of mob rule thus:

> *Heroes have often vanished,*
> *But who will protect the masses*
> *Against the masses?*
> *The Mass has become the masses' oppressor!*

Concerning the overrating of the majority Goethe displayed his scepticism in a conversation with his secretary, Eckermann, in this fashion: "All that is great and wise is to be found among the minority; discernment will always

[1] Spartacus, a Roman gladiator, was leader of a slave revolt, 73–71 B.C. In 1918 the German radical Communists took his name for their title (*Spartakisten-Bewegung*).—TRANSLATOR.

be the exclusive gift of the superior few. Nothing is more repugnant than the majority, since it consists of a few vigorous ringleaders, of knaves who accommodate themselves to circumstances, of the weak who allow themselves to be assimilated, and of the crowd which runs after, without in the least knowing what they want."

To Austria's extremists, the Socialist ascendancy in Germany of Ebert and Scheidemann appeared to be an ideal picture and they called loudly for *"Anschluss"* (union) with the Reich. On November 2, 1918 Vienna's leading Socialist daily, the *Arbeiter-Zeitung*, printed an editorial with the caption "The Party Congress," referring to a speech by Dr. Otto Bauer [1] in which he had said: "German Austria cannot exist by itself. It may live on as part of a federation, but not otherwise, for its territory is not self-contained and is too small for its large industry. That is why we must claim the right to seek for union where we can find it, where we belong by nature, from where we were ingeniously divided some two hundred years ago—to seek for union with the German Reich."

On November 3, 1918 the *Arbeiter-Zeitung* elaborated this point of view in an article headed "The Military Monarchy Ends," in which it made a violent onslaught upon the monarchical system. "So that is the end of the war started by Austria-Hungary out of arrogance!" it wrote. "That is the end of the Monarchy, a shameful end, yet one in keeping with its history and thoroughly deserved!"

With increasing violence the overthrow of the Monarchy was thus clamoured for, and as regards these two points of their program the Socialists first got their way. Motions de-

[1] Dr. Otto Bauer was the most radical leader of Austrian Socialists. He fled to Czechoslovakia when the Socialist revolt in February 1934 failed.— TRANSLATOR.

claring for union with Germany and also for the establishment of a Republic were adopted by the National Assembly
on November 12, 1918. Shouts of "They are firing at us
from the street!" interrupted this decisive session, the official stenographer records.

Alone the deputy Miklas, now the President of the Austrian Federation, found words of courage to question the
power of the National Assembly to decide so fundamental
an issue as Austria's new constitution. But simultaneously
the red flag was run up outside Parliament, replacing the
red, white, and red of the State, cut to pieces by demonstrators.

Thus the Republic had been set up.

It is beyond dispute that, together with the catastrophic
atmosphere of the time, Socialist influences accounted for
the young Republic and that the idea of *"Anschluss,"* put
forward with such boisterousness, came also from Socialist
quarters. Not national considerations but ambitions to establish a huge German, republican, and Socialist bloc were
determining their attitude.

To make the new era palatable to the Austrian people,
who, beyond the boundaries of Vienna, scarcely took any
part in events and did not even grasp what was taking place,
the Socialists—and here lay the tragic responsibility which
they rued bitterly in the year 1934—began to besmirch the
very conception of old Austria.

Everything that recalled Austria, her history, or her symbols was persecuted with demonic hatred. With inexorable
consistency the agitators overwhelmed dynasty, army, above
all the high command and corps of officers, with outrageous
abuse. Where it was possible to do so at all, the idea of Austria, the idea of patriotism, were snatched from the hearts

of schoolchildren. For all the ideals that young people had hitherto found noble and sacred there was now nothing but derision and ridicule, and every attempt was made to efface the very memory of them.

Over and beyond that—and here we come to the most absurd and most exasperating aspect of the Socialist campaign—there was the attempt to saddle Austria with the exclusive responsibility for the war, so that the enemy was able to call Austrian witnesses when the theory of the war-guilt of the Central Powers was required to justify their peace dictates.

At this time and afterwards the tone of political controversy was such that the indignation of those who saw their ideals persistently degraded spontaneously grew into effervescence. So the ground was prepared for the conflicts to come later.

To be sure, no virile people will allow its land, home, and symbols to be everlastingly insulted, repudiated, and destroyed, and that often by people who had settled in Austria from outside. After all, this work of disintegration was carried on for no other purpose than to increase the slogans at the service of a political party.

In an editorial of November 5, 1918 the *Arbeiter-Zeitung* said that "of the fifty-five million people who were condemned to form the grandeur of the Habsburgs, thirty-five millions at least wanted the defeat of Austria-Hungary and placed their hopes in the victory of the Entente. A State," it went on ironically, "in which the overwhelming majority want to have nothing to do with it, actually hate and abhor it—that this State should be able to endure! Moreover, this State had the criminal audacity to start a war. Modesty is the least that one might look for from such a State, yet it was arrogant enough to launch the World War! This was a challenge to fate, and fate now strikes back with an inexorability that is deserved."

This passage was written eight days previous to the armistice!

Again, the Socialist Karl Leuthner wrote in the *Arbeiter-Zeitung* of November 17, 1918: "You see them crowding together, the court parasites, the high officers and officials of the entire one-time Reich, like vermin scenting a wound. The counter-revolutionary material of an entire great power is concentrated in our diminutive land. At present these counter-revolutionary forces bow before the storm of the revolution, but they are crouched in ambush, ready to jump, should momentary hesitations of the people tempt them. The apartment of a fallen prince, be it ever so small, is a court—and what has a court to do in a Republic? In a Republic, moreover, *whose citizens are so lukewarm, who accept the Republic under compulsion only.* Who would not be ready to pay a reasonable sum in order to get rid of our beloved dynasty?"

A week later the editorial-writer of the *Arbeiter-Zeitung* deplored the "Republic without republicans" and demanded that the unintellectual swamp should be drained, the refuse of the past got rid of, and a settlement reached with all the elements of monarchist corruption.

Another editorial, of November 26, is addressed to "the guilty parties," the writer saying: "What an infamous exploit it was on the part of a country such as Austria to let loose a World War for the sake of her own miserable existence, which had exasperated the world! A couple of conscienceless rascals—a Berchtold and two or three of his abetters, Hötzendorf, Stürgkh, and Tisza—had all power in their hands and were able to unchain this wanton war of bravado which plunged mankind into inutterable grief and misery. The moral abhorrence of the universe must strike these wretches who conspired against the peace of the world."

Of "the leaders who made off" the same newspaper wrote in the same issue: "Are we to wonder at the moral rottenness and decadence displayed in the war by our former corps of officers? Austro-Hungarian officers lacked everything that helps men to rise above their lowest instincts. Neither the idea of a country, nor a unity of culture and language—not even the sentiment of freedom or any great tradition of victory—united these officers. They were merely in the service of their employer, real mercenaries by outlook and morals."

Still more significant was an editorial headed: "Not Heroes but Martyrs," which appeared on December 4, 1918. "We deplore," said the writer, "the irreparable losses and devastations of the war, we who stand amid the ruins of the Monarchy, whose heirs, worthy of commiseration, we are. *Yet its outcome, so far as it means the downfall of the Empire, gives us pleasure and we estimate the collapse of the Habsburg Reich as the only compensation for all we underwent, suffered, and lost.* The mere thought that the walls and chains of the people's prison which was the Empire of the Habsburgs might still persist, despite four years of mass slaughter, affronts our deepest feelings as being an insult to the law of nature. . . . For the peoples of Austria-Hungary —for them all—nothing could have been better or more desirable than that the Monarchy, swiftly overwhelmed, had been destroyed in the first year of the war and that the nations, without having to shed their blood in torrents and suffer economic ruin, should have shaken off the yoke of the Habsburgs which forced them together in so unnatural a fashion. Victories merely postponed the hour of deliverance for the peoples of Austria, prolonged their period of oppression and added to their griefs and hardships."

It goes without saying that propaganda of this sort was aimed at the Church also, her institutions and her ministers, and that in the end it came to regard nothing as sacred. In view of the fact that peace negotiations were about to begin and that national unity was more essential than ever, the unscrupulousness of such pathological excesses of hate can only be appreciated fully when studied in retrospect. The old French saying: "It is worse than a crime, it is a blunder," suggests itself in this connection.

As a result of this kind of agitation, unity among the people was out of the question for a long time. The agitators shortsightedly forgot that a harvest of violence would one day ripen from their sowing.

To anyone who knew Austria intimately it must have been clear that all these undignified contradictions must one day bring their own punishment. The hour had to come, inevitably, when everyone would recognize the outrage of trifling with sacred values and ideas, in order to obtain temporary political advantages. For, after all, that was what the Socialists had done.

The hour had to come when it would be plain that the revolution had not given workers, peasants, and soldiers what had been promised them. The country's power of resistance to crises and its economic structure were alike undermined, and after a relatively short time growing unemployment was the inevitable upshot, and young people, when they went into the world, found themselves before closed factory gates.

No one can deny that a great deal of good was achieved on the other hand. The extension of social legislation deserves praise, though, apart from unemployment benefits, the new system of social insurance was increasingly unable to meet the demands put upon it. Big business was by no means destroyed by revolutionary legislation. As a fact the reverse was the case, for it flourished as scarcely ever before, since in the quagmire of inflation speculation and inordinate desire for profits expanded.

The social order of other days was overthrown, including much that was rotten, over which no tears need be shed. Yet some of the new business magnates in their private and commercial activities behaved far more scandalously than was ever the case before. Sovereignty of the people had succeeded to the sovereignty of the Monarch; this would have been all right had not such sovereignty existed on paper only. There were no Privy Councillors of the Emperor any more, but often enough there was a cabal pulling the strings, without the representatives of the people, whose political credit was at stake, being aware of it or being even able to perceive it. Scarcely anything more had taken place than a change in labels. Instead of the political artistocrats there appeared the political bosses, who were soon as unpopular.

The broad middle class, who had for their part once been the source of work and profits to thousands, were broken on the wheel. The little man suffered more than anybody under the unkindness of the hour, and the most eloquent political oration or editorial in a revolutionary Socialist paper could not change the fact that his savings and the prospect of security in old age had gone for good.

And wordy warfare as to who were the responsible parties would break out again and again. Each party blamed the other, while new election struggles, waged under new slogans, showed that substantially nothing had changed.

All this one must have lived through, must have understood, not only to realize how the new Austria came into being, but also to know why there has since come a reaction against the enormities characterizing the revolutionary period. Out of the age of revolution there grew slowly and surely, in the course of fifteen stern years, the age of despair.

Now only did we recognize what we had lost when our country collapsed. The time was long, but then the scales did fall from people's eyes. There came sober thought, righteous judgment—and nostalgia. And thus we found our way back to Austria.

CHAPTER FOUR

The First Epoch of Revolutionary Austria

I RETURNED home from captivity in the autumn of 1919. It was a dismal homecoming.

Although I was overjoyed that the end had come to an imprisonment the senselessness of which I doubly felt in view of the war's end, and although my heart beat rapidly at the prospect of seeing home once more, the sense of dejection aroused in my mind by what I encountered everywhere was deep indeed.

Where was my country? Did she exist at all? Did there survive anything that, transcending the narrow meaning of home, was capable of appealing to the mind and heart? Even sober reason, which accepted the new State as such as a necessary element of order and guarantee of a regulated intercourse of men, was confronted by a hundred unsolved problems. All around there was dissolution. The State as such appeared to have lost all meaning and was only felt as

the expression of constraint, with all its unwelcome consequences.

Every reminder of other days was sternly proscribed. An
absurd iconoclasm, a state of mind which did not stop short
even of inscriptions as harmless as street-names, if they recalled historical characters or events, best characterized the
confusion of minds which then prevailed. Any impulse of
patriotism was alien to the spirit of the hour and was rejected offhand as the embodiment of reactionary opinions.

Many among us were too poor to get civilian clothes, and
so we had to go on wearing our uniforms. But woe betide
him who dared to wear his officer's distinctions or even war
decorations. No one was allowed to lift himself, no matter
how slightly, above anybody else. It was the typical revolutionary period, when to excel was an offence.

It was supposed then that the deification of Liberty and
Equality must be characteristic of any real revolution—anyhow, so it was taught in books and descriptions of the French
Revolution. But at the same time the general atmosphere
existing when the Austria of the débâcle had to take her
first tentative steps was far from being truly demonic and
elemental; it seemed a commonplace, dull, and superficial
copy, made to fit a lamentably miserable epoch.

Sometimes it would happen that the question of one's war
service would crop up. Whoever raised it with the authorities had to reckon with being called a fool.

"Why were you so silly as to join up?" I myself was asked
this question when I came before a demobilization board
and was unwise enough to ask for compensation for some
articles that had been lost.

The "Medal for Bravery" was watched out for especially
carefully at that time, and it was so long jeered at as a piece

of tin that men returning from the front were really persuaded, although for a short time only, to think wearing it a degradation. Still more was the wearing of the Imperial cockade in the cap treated as a demonstration against the State. Indeed, any reminder of the old times was feared as the plague.

All that would not have been so bad, for, after all, every revolution must have its growing-pains. But what did cause deep distress was that want of convictions and villainy itself had become the fashion in so many cases. Fortunately the years pass by and the lapse of time dims the memory, as otherwise many a man who nowadays wallows in patriotism and displays an exaggerated national zeal, perhaps even wears the crown of the Legitimists in his buttonhole (not finding red, white, and red Austrian enough), might feel ashamed of his own shadow—that is, if he possesses any sense of shame at all.

There were others—and they have not changed since—who found out with surprising rapidity that service to Emperor and country had been the fatal blunder of their lives and in conflict with their suddenly discovered national feelings. In those days, it is true, not much moral courage was required to hold your head up before a prince.

Yet, notwithstanding all these bitter memories, one thing in justice should not be lost sight of: there really was definite want in the land, and want and hunger deprive people of their senses.

Naturally enough, the new leaders were not able to conjure up a heaven on earth. Food-credits and relief organizations—the Americans, Swiss, Danes, Swedes, Dutch, and Belgians ought to be remembered gratefully in this connection—were a barrier indeed against starvation, but dur-

ing nearly two anxious years there was just a little too much
for people to die on, and not enough to live on, in our Austria. It was not astonishing that there should have been in
this air laden with the possibilities of explosion an un-
curbed agitation recalling the craziest periods of radicalism.

That was the time when the individual did not count and
the organization was everything. More and more did politicians seek to pander to the masses. Fear of the masses was
in the ascendant, the mobilization and the terror of the
street had become the final and conclusive argument.

The industrial workers were not to be blamed for becoming in special measure victims of mass psychosis. For them,
as for the peasants, the organization, in the one case the
trade union, in the other the peasants' union, was the surest
safeguard and the base from which they set out to win more
rights still. Obviously it was not so much the rank and file
of the movement as the leaders who really counted.

Let me admit in this place that there were many experienced and efficient trade-union leaders in Austria then. Disaster only set in when the political leaders outvoiced the
trade-unionists, who, as a rule, were men of soberer and
more practical outlook.

As was to be expected, Socialism and with it the trade
unions attached most importance to Vienna, the only big
city of new Austria, and from the capital the attempt was
made in increasing measure to centralize the movement
and, by means of standardized party cries, to get control of
the entire country.

It was otherwise with the peasants' organizations. With
them the federal tendencies were much in the ascendant
and hence their political power was firmly rooted in the
provinces. Wise and moderate leadership all the time not

only brought about a planned agrarian reconstruction, but in the political field put up an offensive resistance to the forces of Socialism, then surging forward impetuously.

In this manner these two political forces substantially counterbalanced during the first few years of the new Austria. This, looked at retrospectively, must no doubt be regarded as an advantage, because in all the excesses of a Left nature that were perpetrated an over-violent swing of the political pendulum in one direction, with all the convulsions which must have resulted from it, was for a long time averted. There was, to be sure, this disadvantage: that a sort of trench warfare set in, with the fronts becoming rigid, thereby preventing a really enterprising leadership from carrying anything through.

The most urgent problem facing the government was to assure the feeding of the population. A violent controversy raged round the abolishment of State food-subsidies. Just as it was difficult to push through reforms in this field which of necessity were bound to result in a further lowering of the standard of living, so, on the other hand, the problem of the continuous depreciation of the currency, which threatened to sink into the ocean of inflation, was a pressing one. That was the time, today incredible, when the value of money depreciated overnight, when a street-car ticket would first cost a thousand kronen and soon after ten thousand, when the starting wage of an auxiliary worker ran into millions.

Problems arising out of succession to the Monarchy played an important part in all this. Countless people must have felt it as a deep injustice that their hard-saved small change as well as the money they had invested in securities should appear all at once to be confiscated through inflation.

The problem of the small investor arose in this way. A similar fate befell the army of former pensioners. They all appealed to fairness and justice. They all felt it as a derision that they should receive the new paper krone instead of the gold krone, and as a fact justice and equity were on their side, and their allegation of legal robbery against the State was quite comprehensible.

As against that, the judicious person clearly recognized the limitations of the financial capacity of the new State, on which indeed the burdens of succession were imposed without any equivalent assets being placed at its disposal for meeting them. Through the so-called optants' regulations Austria was required to recognize as her citizens optants who decided for Austria and that meant a substantial additional burden for the Republic. The army of the dispossessed who had recourse to the most heterogeneous organizations, putting forward their claims in forms more and more violent, helped to increase the dissatisfaction in the country and to keep people, anxious on other grounds, in a state of constant bitterness.

Side by side with a situation at home the reverse of encouraging, the position as regards foreign politics was positively hopeless. With each of her neighbours Austria had some account or other to settle, either as regards the question of minorities or because territorial dismemberment had set up fresh sores in the country's mutilated frame. To that had to be added economic dismemberment, which tore asunder what had grown organically, and, further, there was the effort to make still more precarious, by the erection of customs walls, the already straitened existence of the Austrian State.

In this time, so shortly after the war, relations with the

victorious countries were naturally very much strained, while as to the former neutrals, they were but little concerned with a country which was now so uninteresting. Thus Austria became the object of assistance by the charitable, which to recall with thankfulness remains our obvious duty. Beyond that, Austria found herself more and more cast for the part of the international beggar—unjustly, to be sure, as those who had converted a flourishing land full of vitality into a cripple should also have assumed responsibility for giving her a chance to exist.

Then there was the German Reich, with which Austria felt herself united by the bond of the common stock and with which she had moreover passed through the tragedy of a common fate. Germany was still better off than Austria, thanks to the size of her territory and her natural riches, but the convulsions to which the Reich was exposed at home and the somewhat unclear position prevailing in various extremely important parts of her territory did not in any case conduce to an attempt to establish, over and above the natural partnership in fate, bonds of a constitutional character. Such bonds could have brought advantage neither to the Germans nor to us; from the standpoint of the German race as a whole, they were not of decisive importance either, quite apart from the fact that the constitutional structure of the two states differed fundamentally already at that period. Finally, the international situation forbade any radical changes.

Thus we had to bear the burden of the lost war—a burden which was heavy enough in all conscience, while, as far as human vision could foresee, an improvement seemed out of the question.

I had not a great deal of time for reflection. After the leave of a few weeks granted me in the last year of the war for purposes of study, I had two years only in which to complete my academic career. I took my degree in law at Innsbruck University and incidentally followed the matriculation course at the Academy of Commerce, so as to equip myself in every way for an economic career.

In the summer of 1921 I finished my examinations, by which time no real choice of a career existed for a young man in Austria. Each one had to see to it that he got on his own feet as quickly as possible to earn the minimum necessary to keep body and soul together.

At that time I did not interest myself very much in politics, even though the questions of organization attracted me greatly. A profound aversion for the political machine and unbounded pessimism characterized my state of mind at that period. Around us there was no sign of authority, yet authority and leadership are just what youth have always craved.

What took place then in Vienna seemed to us outside in the provinces entirely uninteresting. Indeed, it may have been that our view of the work of some of the men who, by the exertion of all their power, strove to prevent still worse from happening was somewhat unjust at first.

It was in this time of complete poverty of ideas and lack of ideals that the noted plebiscites upon union with Germany were held in different parts of Austria. Obviously, what took place in 1921 ought not to be used as a political argument subsequently, not only because of the way these plebiscites were organized—and, after all, that is a matter of great importance—but also because this political movement, which sprang from a private initiative, should not be treated as something isolated. To the Socialist "union" slogan in the year 1918, comprehensible only from the exclusive party standpoint, was now opposed a national avowal, in the course of which an impassioned protest was made against the war-guilt lie and the whole mentality of the revolutionary period.

With abundant subsidies from the Reich a daily news-paper called *Alpenland* was founded about this time at Innsbruck with Herr Gilbert In der Mauer [1] as editor. We come across the editor of this rigidly anti-clerical newspaper later on, in the capacity of a regular correspondent of the Centre (Catholic) *Germania* of Berlin. He was originally a major of dragoons in the Austro-Hungarian army.

I know something about the plebiscite in the Tyrol on the "union" issue as I was a counter on that occasion. Its political significance was doubtless considerable at the time, as the leaders of the State were then furnished with arguments of which they made effective use in due course.

A state without the ideal of patriotism and the definite will to exist is in effect not conceivable in the long run. As Austria was then, her purpose was no longer to be recognized and in no event could she have been able to fulfil her historic task. A summoner had to appear to arouse new life in Austria, to revive the idea of Austria, and to accomplish this task notwithstanding the state of affairs at home, the calamities of the hour, the wrangling of parties, the dire necessity of the land, the threatening Bolshevism, the desperate, hopeless inertia of nearly all classes of the population, notwithstanding despair of Austria herself.

This deliverer was Seipel.

---

[1] Later on, Gilbert In der Mauer became known as one of the leaders of National-Socialist agitation in Austria.—TRANSLATOR.

CHAPTER FIVE

Seipel

IN Ignaz Seipel,[1] there stepped forward to take the helm the statesman whose political profile was the most accentuated and original of the post-war epoch in Austria. Appealed to by his own friends as the last and most decisive reserve, when troubles had reached the point of utmost danger, and urged at the same time by his political opponents to take up the responsibility of power, he flung himself into the breach in May 1922, as Chancellor.

The holder of any responsible office, especially when he is called upon to achieve the extraordinary in exceptional times and when his personality surpasses the average, has a right to be considered as a man also; otherwise he runs the risk of not being appraised justly or judged rightly.

Rarely has there been another man of eminence in whom

1 Dr. Ignaz Seipel (1876–1932), Catholic priest and prelate, Professor of Moral Theology at the Vienna University, became Minister of Social Administration in Emperor Charles's last cabinet in 1918. After the revolution he was the leader of the Christian Socialist (Catholic) Party, 1922–4, and Chancellor of Austria, 1926–9.—TRANSLATOR.

practical achievement and personality combined in such compact harmony to form the sharply outlined portrait of a complete character.

Perhaps I shall be charged with lack of impartiality if I attempt to put into words my personal recollections of this truly great Austrian. Among much else it is, after all, to be accepted as a firmly established belief of the public that I was one of the favourite disciples of the master, that he looked on me as one especially worthy of his confidence.

In this case, too, as in most others, truth and fiction are to be found together. True it is that unqualified reverence and absolute attachment always linked me to Seipel, a man in whom we young men, from the first moment of his stepping into the political limelight, saw the reawakener of Austrian ideals.

True it is, too, that the modest political activity which I was able to develop from the year 1927, as a member of the Nationalrat (Chamber of Deputies), proceeded steadily along the lines laid down by the leadership of Seipel, whose experience and far-reaching vision, in my deep-rooted conviction, today held more strongly than ever, always divined the right thing with absolute assurance and pursued it logically and with all prudence.

Not well founded, on the other hand, was the opinion that this relationship had in some way been the outcome of a particularly close intercourse and had grown out of the personal exchange of ideas and views. That, unfortunately, was never the case. In all those years I had only on perhaps five different occasions an exchange of ideas exhaustively with Seipel, and on one of those occasions Seipel lay already on his death-bed—that was three days before his all too premature end.

There was, it is true, now and then a passing nod and a word from him, a friendly gesture, but as a rule without any particular relevance.

Why was that so? Seipel was not at all so reserved and taciturn as the superficial observer from a distance might perhaps have supposed. On the contrary, in spite of his astonishing capacity for work and his all-embracing activities, he always found time, day after day, to receive numerous callers, belonging to every walk of life, and wherever he might show himself, particularly in the Parliament buildings, he would be surrounded by friends, political and non-political, including those who belonged to the undying race of the busybody with their somewhat one-sided opinion of their importance and powers of conversation. Just on that account did I, who all my life had a horror of pushfulness and whose greatest anxiety was not to come under the suspicion of pushfulness myself, find it more than usually difficult to come near the much venerated master.

Seipel, I believe, knew very well that he could count on the unconditional and trustworthy support of myself and of those who thought as I did—especially the Tyrolean deputies—but he did nothing on his side to encourage a close personal relationship. I was a young assistant lawyer when I heard Chancellor Seipel speak for the first time. It was at a meeting at Innsbruck, just after his first journey abroad, when he had become an international figure. The lucid, quiet, convincing words in which he formulated his confession of faith in Austria moved us deeply. At last a man had come forward, courageously seized the helm, and without ifs and buts, without stipulations, recognized the ideal of the Fatherland. At the same time this man took his stand upon practical and realistic grounds, the maintenance of which was necessary if Austria's desperate economic problems were to be mastered. Thus he summoned us to share in his determination to re-create Austria.

One small incident I recall, for its artless inoffensiveness was significant—it might have occurred somewhat earlier or later. As Seipel left the town hall at Innsbruck after his speech, crowds of curious people from different ranks of life thronged round the door, for the Chancellor's presence aroused a great deal of real enthusiasm. Near me, in the middle of the crowd, a pert woman's voice exclaimed: "It's all very fine and maybe he is right, but he is still a clerical, and after all it's Frank who's doing everything!" (Dr. Frank was Seipel's very worthy collaborator and Vice-Chancellor, afterwards for many years Austrian minister in Berlin, a very capable and likable politician, who belonged, however, to the Pan-German Party, which were, as a rule, in contrast to the "black" Catholics, called "Blues.")

That was just the admirable and original characteristic of Seipel: What he stood for, he represented wholeheartedly and never denied or concealed. He was a politician through and through, to whom politics had become an essential part of life, yet he interpreted his task in the noblest and classical sense. Politics to him signified care for the *res publica,* in such a form that the State really was, as the Latin phrase has it, *res publica* and not, as Seipel once defined it in a speech at Heiligenkreuz Abbey, the *res privata,* the business of a clique.

He was a statesman and leader who served the cause to an extraordinary degree of self-sacrifice, to whom personal ambition was a quite alien consideration, who had no interest in mere formalities and needed no setting in order to achieve effects. Yet, for all this, in certain cases he knew how to keep people at an appropriate distance.

He was a savant who, despite all the labours of the day, found his way back to his original calling, acknowledging himself a professor. A minister of the Emperor, called upon when times were most difficult, he most emphatically took his oath seriously and never for one second varied in his established attitude towards Austria (though many people of shallow vision would no longer admit this). Still, he rejected the purely retrospective way of thinking as fruitless and emphasized that in the realm of historical development, too, the dead never rise again in the old form. Courageously he set about providing the undying spirit of Austria with new corporeal forms akin to the spirit of the age.

Above all and most of all, however, he was the priest who looked on everything earthly *sub specie æternitatis* and in the manner and style of his life and in every situation brought his actions and decisions into relation with the sanctity of his original calling. Therein lay his greatness and the source of his strength; therein also on occasion was to be found his most vulnerable spot.

Ignaz Seipel was the model of concentration, of order in thought, of discipline and control in action, the man of great perceptive concepts, of lucid political calculation.

Notwithstanding all the unequivocalness and absoluteness of his own intellectual outlook, he was conciliatory and full of understanding for anyone who thought differently, and serious people could never have taken umbrage at either his philosophy or his priestly habit. But the serious and deep-thinking are ever destined to be a minority, and for all too many others, when they wished to strike him, he was only too soon and too often merely the "prelate."

After his death, it is true, many also found all this out again who had been unable to understand him in his lifetime and, during his last years particularly, had rather troubled him by their determination to misinterpret his actions. Soon afterwards Seipel had suddenly become in their eyes the great protagonist of Nationalism. They now endeavoured to elucidate by extracts from his speeches and writings his national outlook, particularly in view of Austria's relations with Germany.

Now, it is notorious that anything can be proved by sentences torn from their context and especially can anything be explained by tricks of interpretation, the more so if one is not inclined to look at the context at all because it would refute the theory which one wishes to prove.

And in this connection I would remark here that not one sentence said by Seipel loses its force today in anything, especially with regard to Austria's national attitude and her relations with Germany. Now as then all his ideas are altogether valid, ideas deeply rooted in the traditions of Austrian thought. But such ideas ought not to be snatched forcibly from the organically constructed compact range of concepts, as otherwise one comes perilously near being a party to falsification.

The fact ought never to be ignored that Seipel was the exponent of the synthesis and harmony of German, Austrian, and Catholic culture. His life work consisted to a great degree in showing again and again, in the spoken word, in writing, and by actions, that it was necessary to find the right order of values, to examine into the different associations, and to bring into a proper relation race, culture, national sentiment, and the recognition of the State. He held that one must overcome that narrowness of mind

BREAD-LINES IN FRONT OF BAKERIES IN POST-WAR VIENNA

We do not believe that the State is alone able to give expression to the life of a nation. Our own national history has not been that of other nations. In fact I doubt whether the cause of harmony is served by leading our national ideal on to paths along which other nations have sought or found their ideals."

That is how Seipel thought.

When, in a desperate hour, he reached the head of the government, he regarded it as of the highest importance to create new confidence in the State at home and to offer proof of its ability to live.

In his first speech before the League Council at Geneva, in September 1922, he was able, by quoting a few figures, to shed light upon the gravity of Austria's situation.

On July 1, 1919, he pointed out, 100 Swiss francs were equal to 567 Austrian kronen; on July 1, 1920 they represented as much as 2,702 kronen; a year later, 12,200; and finally, on July 1, 1922, these 100 Swiss francs were worth 360,000 Austrian kronen. By this time a loaf of bread cost 6,600 kronen, a kilogram of Czechoslovak coal 700, a shirt 200,000.

The Chancellor raised alarm throughout the world and in that way he inaugurated a spell of activity in the field of foreign policy, in order to secure consideration for Austria. In the summer of 1922 he set out on the journey, which was to arouse such a stir, to Berlin, Prague, and Verona, in order to convince the powers that adequate help for Austria in the form of credits was indispensable. He pointed out that it was not the fault of Austria that then in the direst need she had to call for foreign assistance; rather was it through the peace treaty that the old economic structure had been torn asunder and great wealth lost thereby. The State found itself under the grim necessity of embarking on a root-and-branch reform of its civil administration, in order to balance the budget, a necessary condition for the attainment of economic stability.

But sweeping and trenchant measures of economy were neither feasible nor justifiable unless the definite restoration of the State were assured. Moreover, the credits were absolutely necessary if Austria was not to break up without the hope of recovery. For years the European chancelleries had been aware of that precarious state of things, but every step of the Austrian government had until then merely led to fair words, investigations and repeated postponements. Thus the time had to come when at length the hopelessness of the Austrian situation gave rise to rumours of an impending invasion by foreign troops, with the partitioning of Austria.

Seipel was able to return home with a triumph. A credit of 500,000,000 gold kronen was guaranteed. After that it became a matter of getting control of the situation at home.

In the Austrian Parliament of that day there was a non-Socialist majority, consisting of the Christian Socialists and the Pan-German Party, the Socialists being in opposition. In this hour of crisis parliamentary democracy in Austria was put to a crucial test, for no one could seriously question the necessity of the loan and no one could assert that he was in a position to get better and easier conditions for it. Thus not a problem of domestic politics which could be settled on the basis of party views and tactics was being debated, but the very existence of the State was at stake.

The course of the decisive sitting of the Nationalrat on September 14, 1922 reveals with clarity the grounds of subsequent political evolution during Seipel's term of office and fully discloses the factors in domestic policy which were bound to lead to a crisis.

With every sign of dramatic tension the Chancellor rose from the government bench and made his exhaustive plea for the loan, the bringing about of which depended on the consent of the Nationalrat. He referred to the disturbing rumours of an impending end of Austria, whose fate was to be decided by the invasion of foreign troops and her partitioning among her neighbours. Rejecting all these rumours, Seipel said:

"Nowhere is there any such intention, and certainly not among the great powers who have, after all, the last say, even where the policy of the small powers is in question. To be sure, I have been told everywhere that the firm intention to maintain our freedom and territorial integrity depends upon the way things turn out in our own land. Should something really unheard of occur" (here Seipel was referring to the possibility of disorders accompanying the political discussions) "or even should our neighbours suppose themselves justified in assuming that certain disorders in Austria might give rise to a situation menacing the peace of Europe, then, obviously, one cannot tell what might happen."

In solemn words Seipel went on to justify the need for the help of the League of Nations, help which depended on the Nationalrat's consent to financial control. He entreated the opposition, in the interest of the State, to set aside all considerations of mere agitation, since the rejection of the loan, together with the financial control, would do good to nobody. The threat to call out the masses could only cause a conflagration which would seal the fate of the State without putting an end to its want and misery.

The government parties, through their various speakers, supported the Chancellor and emphasized that it was by his extreme skill that the country had been saved, in the last hour, from a second collapse worse than anything that had gone before.

The Socialist opposition were adamant to all argument, not so much because they could offer another solution as merely because they would not help the Chancellor, so violently opposed, to obtain a triumph with their votes. At the same time they did not in the least think seriously of preventing this success, being shrewd enough to recognize that not a party matter was involved but the existence of the community itself.

Now, there would have been nothing to say against it if, following parliamentary tradition, the opposition had, from considerations of principle, refused their votes to the government, especially if that did not prevent the bill from passing. But the kind of argument used and the actual terms of the rejection deserve attention, for they are symptomatic of the bitterness of the opposition and their negative spirit.

The leader of the Socialists on their intellectual side, Dr. Otto Bauer, answered the Chancellor thus: "With high treason we do not enter into discussion. So long as it is harmless we treat it with contempt, and we crush it when it becomes a menace. . . ." The earlier Austrian Chancellor Dr. Renner, the next Socialist orator, said: "Of course we all know that as things are now, Austria has no future. We can keep ourselves alive just until the hour of liberation strikes; that is, until we as Germans can decide in favour of the State to which we belong by the nature of things." With this line of argument Dr. Renner opposed the government motion for the acceptance of the loan on the conditions agreed upon.

Since then, to be sure, sixteen years have gone by. I can hardly believe that the same arguments would be repeated by the same people today and especially I wonder whether the classes for which the speeches of 1922 were meant would regard it as an advantage in 1938 if the principles the orators expounded on that occasion had prevailed in subsequent policy.

A reflection such as this seems to me especially worth the attention of the people who today are in sympathy with the opinion of the Socialist opposition, but have long forgotten the attitude their own party then took up—of the people who now reproach the present Austrian regime with insisting too strongly, and to the supposed disadvantage of the workers, on a Germanophile policy.

The debate of September 14, 1922 was continued at later sittings of the Nationalrat. On October 12 of the same year Dr. Renner, proceeding with his attack upon the Chancellor, said: "I believe that present trust in the League of the Nations will get more questionable daily. In Protocol Number I" (which deals with the maintenance of Austria's independence) "you are bartering the hopes our people have in the future. You will understand me when I say we shall not go along with you. No, no, and again no! That path we shall never tread!"

Here too, again, in view of the situation of world politics today and the attitude of the different "ideologies" towards the League of Nations, a moment of reflection regarding the vicissitudes of events and opinions seems not to be out of place. How times do change indeed!

To the controversial remarks of the previous speakers of

his party, the deputy Karl Seitz, Socialist Mayor of Vienna, speaking on October 12, 1922, added this: "We hoped there would never be a Saint-Germain again. We do not believe and did not wish to believe that a man elected from among the German-Austrian people would be a party to the betrayal of his own nation. We Socialists cannot pardon this crime, the crime of high treason to people and land."

Finally the opposition moved a resolution voicing the Nationalrat's sternest disapproval of the Chancellor. That was done, too, despite the fact that the Pan-German Party, of whose political creed the *Anschluss* idea was a definite part, voted for the government, in which they had several representatives, for at that time they recognized quite clearly that no national advantage was to be derived by passing the sentence of death upon one's own land and that it was far more important to keep the country and its people alive and not close the way to a peaceful and fortunate future against them.

The motion of the government was accepted. This result evidently pleased the Socialist opposition, despite the violence with which they voiced their indignation, for, after all, they had still been left the platform upon which they could go on with their agitation. The whole controversy, however, was the signal for an even more violent attack upon the Chancellor and was characteristic of the way the conflict was to be fought out in the future. All this clearly shows how Austria's subsequent political evolution became inevitable.

Seipel has often been reproached with being a pedantic anti-Marxist, never able to rise above his own opinions so as to establish relations with the Socialists and in that way attain the concentration of all the forces of the country.

Seipel was often in favour of such a concentration of forces, and it was the others who did not want it. That was proved both in the year 1922 and eight years later, when Seipel, in another hour of crisis, appealed for the co-operation of all the constructive elements of the country. It is true that nothing was to be expected from Seipel beyond that. He would never have been prepared to ratify a political alliance in such a manner that, for the sake of peace, principles would have been sacrificed. Upon this matter Seipel always had his own opinion, an opinion that sometimes brought him into opposition with many leaders of the Centre (Catholic) Party in the German Reich. The course of events proved him right.

From the year 1922 onwards he fought a heroic fight with stubborn determination. His aim was to make Austria respected abroad, to arouse faith in Austria at home. For faith in one's own power to live, in one's capacity for achievement, is an essential condition even for economic recovery.

He, who had himself come from modest conditions, who had known want from personal experience, who was, moreover, free from any pretensions and ready for any sacrifice, was assuredly the last person against whom the charge of hostility to the working classes ought to have been brought. Social problems, even to the paramount notion of the reform of society, belonged to the kingly ideas of this life rich in labour. What he resented throughout his life was the identification of the interests of the workers with the struggle in behalf of Socialist doctrines. In that respect he seemed quite the reverse of antisocial, though certainly anti-Socialist in his outlook and actions. In those days, when Austrian Socialism would not even once co-operate with other parties in the interest of the State as a whole, Seipel from time to time addressed to them such words as "To give the loudest cheer for the Republic is not so important as to do more work for it."

Therefore it came about by necessity that Seipel should get his majority in Parliament by a coalition of the non-Socialist parties and that the Socialists should be driven into the position of an isolated opposition party. To preserve Austria and create the conditions needed for her future, Seipel decided to weld all the forces available into a front of defence against the Socialists, and by prematurely using up his strength in the process he paid for that policy by his far too early death. At the same time, however, he laid the foundations of the freedom and independence of his country. It was in this way that the "Bourgeois Bloc," round which so much controversy raged, was formed, though the title was a misnomer applied to the government coalition by its opponents.

In the government camp the coalition pact resulted in a truce among conflicting political creeds and it served to harmonize opposing outlooks. First the Pan-German, then the Agrarian League forwent the immediate achievement of their political aims, so far as they related to the *"Anschluss,"* and the Catholics on their side were obliged to respect the ideas of their political allies.

The essence of every parliamentary coalition is that all the parties must make sacrifices. In Austria it was always extremely difficult to bring opposing outlooks together for a specific purpose, and far too often people of shallow judgment would apportion blame and attribute responsibility wrongly, when the fulfilment of an aspiration, admirable in itself, had been frustrated by prevailing political conditions.

Thus it was that the party coalition of that day was compelled by the circumstances to restrict itself to a position of pure defence against the Socialist onslaught. This gave the opposition the chance of exploiting their own situation by means of unbounded promises and irresponsible demands.

Purposeful encouragement of the conception of Austria and of confidence in her destiny was rather neglected at that time, though Seipel himself on countless occasions insisted on the possibility—nay, the necessity—of harmonizing the national German with the patriotic Austrian outlook. It was never possible, for various considerations, to bring this idea to fruition systematically in the period of which I write. Later on we all found this a great misfortune, but it often happens that even high values must be put aside as long as the most vital elements of existence are in danger.

In this way, and as far as it was humanly possible, the Chancellor had obtained for himself the majority needed under a parliamentary system to do the work ahead of him, especially the difficult and complex task of economic reconstruction. Yet, on the other hand, the political struggle at home grew more and more violent and at last it created a tension which led to fierce outbursts.

Even when there was no election campaign in progress, the unbridled agitation of which the Chancellor was the target and which strove to hit him at the point where he was most sensitive—his priest's soutane—caused party passion to mount to fever-heat. The revolver-shots of June 1, 1924, which laid the Chancellor low with a dangerous wound,[1] were an outcome of this agitation, which caused many another disaster, to be discussed elsewhere.

Quite apart from the consequences of this attempt upon his life, Seipel was greatly handicapped in his work by lin-

[1] Karl Jaworek an unemployed worker, attempted to assassinate Seipel at the Vienna Southern Railway Terminus.—TRANSLATOR.

gering diabetes. Nevertheless he continued his march onwards, head erect, and imperturbable. Whether he was at
the head of the government or had given up the chancellorship, as during the period from November 1924 to October
1926, when Dr. Ramek [1] was at the head of the government,
and last of all in the time from April 1929 onwards, he continued to be looked on by foreign opinion and at home as
Austria's most respected political leader, the statesman who
represented her most worthily.

He was the epitome of superiority and wisdom. Whether
he spoke among a small group or down from the rostrum,
peculiar to himself was a purposeful, refined, slightly hesi-
tating delivery, and the contents and style of his speech, as
far as the final comma, were a harmonious entity never calling for the least modification. Hostile to dramatic gesture
and cheap pathos, Seipel achieved his effects through the
concentrated force of sober arguments, marshalled one after
another, and the subtle irony that was always a feature of
his private talk recurred also, though in a different form, in
the oratorical formulation of his ideas. This produced an
impression that was always to the point, yet never tedious
or wearisome. Quite the reverse of a mass orator in the current sense he captured the intellectuals above all, exercis-
ing over them permanent influence. But his aim was to address himself to all, and all were thrilled by the earnestness
and the compelling honesty which spoke from his crystal-
clear sentences.

Thus was Seipel, in his influence as an orator also, a
unique personality. Only very rarely have I seen him lose
his self-control. A colour a shade deeper than usual would

1 Dr. Karl Ramek, Christian Socialist deputy from Salzburg, was Chancellor during the two years when Dr. Seipel held no official position.—
TRANSLATOR.

spread across his face, there would be a sudden, hardly noticeable raising of the voice—infallible signs that to contradict him would be out of place. But very soon he would again display the iron calm which so decidedly belonged to his salient characteristics.

There is no doubt that Austria's subsequent evolution would not have been conceivable without Seipel. In his time it was the custom, in those cases where a debate was not thought desirable even among friends, to say what one wanted to be known in some public speech or other. Thus we in Austria sometimes heard Seipel's views upon questions of the hour in a lecture which he had arranged to deliver in Sweden or in the Reich, in a quite different connection. I have a particularly lively recollection of an unusually clever speech upon the essence of German federalism which Seipel once delivered at Munich. It is true that he seemed on that occasion to have before his mind the whole complex of Prussian-Bavarian rivalries; but we in the Tyrol, too, understood him quite well, for it was clear that much of what he said was meant for Austria.

Then there was that New Year's Eve speech in Vienna, when Seipel subjected the organization and administration of the Chamber of Agriculture to a critical analysis. That speech led to the first public contact between Seipel and Engelbert Dollfuss. Dollfuss, then treasurer of the Lower Austrian Chamber of Agriculture, a man full of the joy of work, charged with all the energies of youth, interpreted Seipel's words as a challenge and, on his side, criticized in public the all too academic professor.

Thus the two men whose fate became that of Austria as well, who wore themselves out for her, and who were destined to save her, were at first poles asunder in outlook, despite the fundamental political sympathies between them. Seipel was, after all, the conservative, while Dollfuss, rich in new ideas, hastened forward into the future. For years both followed the same path, side by side, but now and then also one would fail to understand the other.

History took its course: the pitiless law of nature exacted replacement. At this juncture the two men found each other. Dollfuss held Seipel in unqualified respect as soon as he himself was assuming political power, and Seipel followed with deep sympathy and entire approval the first steps of the new Chancellor, Engelbert Dollfuss, which he lived to see.

In Mariazell on one occasion Dollfuss told me of the deep impression he had just brought away from Pernitz [a health resort in Lower Austria], where he had visited Seipel, then weary unto death. I knew what he meant by that, as about the same time I myself had been received by Seipel in his sick-room. The recollection of Seipel was always with Dollfuss, and in that, too, I am like Dollfuss.

In a tired voice and struggling against shortness of breath, Seipel, after a brief discussion about the course of events in Germany (at that time Herr von Papen had been appointed Chancellor), uttered to me words something like these: "Thank God, Austria is on the right road!"

Barely a week later, on August 5, 1932, we bore Ignaz Seipel to the grave.

CHAPTER SIX

Years of Crisis

FOR years after the Austrian Monarchy had gone down in the thunder and lightning of the events of 1918, a thick and impenetrable pall of darkness—politically and economically speaking—lay over that unfortunate and conquered land. Hunger and despair spoke out of mournful eyes. There was a vacillating conception of politics which upset the Austrian, whether he lived in Vienna or beyond the Arlberg. The breakdown of self-control deadened the sense of spiritual values. There came the intoxicating, frantic speculation of the inflation period, with the inordinate desire to relish whatever the present had to give, for fear that the future might bring the loss of everything. Such were the outward signs of the crisis besetting Austria.

To overcome this state of things, at least on the economic and political side, Seipel had stepped forward and laid the foundations of a new Austria, which one might call the second phase of her existence. He spoke those words concerning the indispensable "reconstruction of souls"—words often quoted and criticized—and he put the general conception of the State into a sound and reasonable shape again.

This tireless and purposeful captain, moving along the channels of that parliamentary democracy which gave to the decade 1922–32 its most characteristic aspect, brought the ship of state round innumerable rocks. Adaptation of the administrative machinery to the reduced capacities of the country, reduction of officials, increase in taxation, reform and stabilization of the currency, balancing of the budget—those were the promontories round which he had to steer his course. At the same time he tried to revive memories of the past, in order to use them as a foundation for building up a new self-consciousness within the mind of the Austrian citizen.

To achieve all this it was essential to refute and overcome, step by step, the disruptive revolutionary outlook which had quickly run to waste in obviously futile plans and experiments. And so Austria's path led her to an increase of consideration abroad and a quite remarkable economic recovery at home.

This recovery, favoured by a boom which proved to be more apparent than real, looked very hopeful about the year 1927, and the upward trend continued until 1929. In the year 1927 there was even talk in the Nationalrat of the so-called prosperity index; and a law to deal with workers' insurance, which had been passed, was to be applied in its entirety once the number of unemployed on relief dropped below a yearly average of 100,000. Many people assumed such a position would be reached speedily, though, to be sure, there were industrial leaders who raised monitory

voices and pointed out the storm signal of the growing pas-
sivity of the trade balance, which had risen to a billion Austrian schillings by the year 1929. In 1927 an average over
the year of more than 200,000 unemployed was reported.
In the two following years this figure dropped, rose steadily
in 1930, was twice as high in 1933, and afterwards fell slowly.

From 1931 on, a second big crisis, this time involving the
entire world, broke over Austria and once more shook the
country to her foundations. The crash of the Credit-Anstalt, Austria's leading bank, necessitated the State's assumption of its liabilities, led to a general business slump, and
involved a dangerous fluctuation of the currency (which,
when the crisis was at its height, was dealt in abroad at a
discount of thirty per cent). A new trenchant and painful
reduction of the budget, owing to the financial catastrophe,
was a further characteristic of that melancholy period.

In the summer of 1932, when Seipel went from us, Austria stood at the parting of the ways again. The political
and economic foundations of the State rocked once more,
and the whole structure of Austria, put up after such immense effort, seemed in danger of collapsing. That was the
hour when Dollfuss rose up and flung himself into the
breach. He struggled first to find a new basis for the national economy, then to bring about the reconstitution of
State and society, and eventually he put us on the road leading to the third Austria.

I now propose to tell how this fateful decade separating
the rebirth of Austria under Seipel in 1922 from the advent
of the third Austria affected me, a man of the war generation, who during that period gradually entered into political life.

Immediately after the end of the war we all felt a strong and natural desire to enjoy our freedom, after years of service and captivity. Then there was the urgency of earning a modest living as quickly as possible. This explained the general rush to get employment in the banks, a rush which took place in the first post-war years. Soon afterwards the end of the inflation led to the inevitable collapse of the over-expanded Austrian banking system, and a large number of young men were faced with the tragic problem of beginning all over again for a second time. Many a man who had come through the war without mishap went under during these first years of the new order.

The general attitude of mind to the problems of the day was essentially subjective. Scepticism with regard to traditions and stale formulas, together with a general repudiation of the mass principle—those were the features which, as a rule, characterized the intellectual outlook of the young men then struggling with the exigencies of the hour. Others, it is true, were simply intoxicated by the feeling of freedom, embarked upon a wholly licentious life, and often completely ruined themselves.

Side by side with these people from twenty to thirty there had grown up in the meantime another generation who knew little about the war from personal experience and were naturally hostile to it. This younger generation searched for new forms of society and sometimes behaved as though they aspired to overthrow the philosophy of their elders, which they felt to be out of harmony with the times and lacking in discipline. There was a great deal that was valuable in the earnest endeavours of those young people. They inscribed a program of reform upon their banner, recognized frankly the inadequacies of the past, had a contempt for what was deterrent in the post-war period, and aspired to the pureness of a happier future world. Besides much that was commendable, presumption, too, undoubtedly characterized some of the different organizations of youth, which very soon embraced extremist ideas.

While we, as the result of war experience and its constraints, wished for freedom and repudiated every restraint, the younger generation, who had not benefited by the discipline of the uniform, started to struggle for a new form of collective organization. There was a general quest for new romanticism and the wish to overcome the summarily condemned past, especially all the earlier social and political forms. To return to nature was the universal cry, and it found an expression in the careful cultivation of new songs, dances, and games, in new forms of life, and also now and then in original and slovenly dress, meant to be a demonstration in favour of new and healthier communal ideals. Curiously enough, by this stressed neglect of traditional forms a new formalism resulted, and this sought to gain ground in a number of organizations, particularly those of a denominational character, organizations which worked side by side, yet never could get to know one another.

Among the determining factors was the perfectly healthy wish to overcome much that was antiquated and out of date. Many a bad practice among the traditional usages of university students, for example, was replaced by new forms. Even if this movement did not at first make great headway, Austria was soon influenced by the different organizations and leagues in Germany, where, particularly in the west, youth was in a ferment.

The generation which had served at the front argued that they should be given first place in the work of reconstructing the country and should on no account be overlooked. We were not in the least disposed to allow ourselves to be pushed into the background.

Thus the younger people in those years presented a motley picture, by no means uniform, but split up into manifold shades of colour. In common there was a desire to overcome the lost war's legacy of humiliation, a recognition of the deficiencies of the times, and a deep feeling of dissatisfaction with the conditions of society and State.

It soon became clear that neither the individualistic spirit nor the party formations, with their over-emphasis on distinctions, could open the way to a new community of work. Both the authority that unites and the knowledge that is needed to obey were wanting, though precisely in the youth organizations remarkable discussions about the need for leadership and the obligation to obey took place from time to time.

Out of this unsatisfactory state of things, which enabled unrivalled achievements to be performed by individuals without permitting a real triumph of the new ideals, there slowly came the time when military discipline revived and with it the desire for uniform acknowledgment of leadership, for the absorption of the individual in the community, for the revival of discipline in thought and conduct. Suddenly the pendulum approached the extreme after having reached the extreme in the opposite direction just after the war. Unity was on the way to being re-established, yet this way first led through an attitude of negation, refutation, and defence.

Associated with the economic crisis there was a very marked loss of confidence, on a large scale, and this led to mental turmoil among young people with regard to their concepts of State and society.

With the retrospective frame of mind, which looked on the restoration of the Monarchy as a supreme remedy, youth as a rule had at first neither sympathy nor understanding. At that period emotional factors almost always lay behind the monarchist idea, and only very rarely did considerations of reason contribute to it. The upshot was that there was far too much discussion about personal experiences and memories, far too little about the needs of the hour and the possibilities of the future; too much about what had happened yesterday, too little about what was happening then or might happen afterwards.

Now, it is evident that references, whether blunt or subtle, to the past—particularly in the form of sentimental glorification of "the good old days"—tend to exasperate young people into contradiction, because such references instinctively evoke with them a picture of sterile pettifoggery. Young people have always had a terror of being looked on as reactionaries. In times of instability the youth have invariably been opposed to any conservative, retrograde, or even merely prudent and immobile tendencies. What they are eager for is the dynamics of movement, and their hearts are glad, setting apart sober reflection, when they listen to talks of attack, progress, and revolution.

Thus the immobile aspects of parliamentary democracy in its typical expression—the municipal councils, provincial diets, and the central Parliament—together with its methods of government and administration very soon aroused the criticism and resistance of youth. It is not as though democracy in itself might not have been able to capture the imagination and goodwill of the young. In 1925 or so, Dr. Hellpach, the former President of the state of Baden (in Germany) wrote about "The Crisis of Democcracy," and what he said left a durable impression. Whenever parliamentary government reaches the zenith of power, he stated, and whenever political authority is concentrated in the hands of people's representatives, confidence is forfeited and diminution and then loss of power follow invariably. But as soon as the power of Parliament is broken, then its authority tends to revive and the demand for popular government again becomes a rallying cry.

Reactions such as these are quite natural. The *"panta rhei"* ("Everything is in a state of flux") of the old Greeks, the eternal ascent and descent, the alternations of the high and the low in human affairs, like the natural law of light and shade, are an essential part of political science too. No form of government is wholly perfect. After all, government is the handiwork of man and must display man's weaknesses. As times move on, flaws appear in the temporary forms, and the darker side of institutions or regimes reveals itself so clearly that remedies become necessary.

In times of intellectual, economic, and political crisis the rhythm of this alternate movement is bound to be shorter than in times of a level, undisturbed, and peaceful prosperity. That is why the mental attitude of a nation's youth is scarcely determined by anything else than by the accidental position this youth happens to take within this eternal rhythm. In 1848 our students mounted the barricades to fight for popular rights, for the paramount ideal of democracy, and for parliamentary institutions; while in 1930 they were equally ready to anathematize those ideals of yesterday, for in the meantime the overthrow of parliamentary democracy had become the popular remedy of the day. I wonder on which side the next generation will be found.

I am of the opinion that there is never finality in political forms or tendencies and I do not think it right to regard any system, no matter what it may be called, as wholly timeless and immune from error. Politicians would do well to remember the opinion of Hanslick [(1825–1904), renowned Viennese art critic, and adversary of Richard Wagner], who said he had "not the presumption to be infallible, but the courage to be sincere." Doubtless, too, it is right, as prominent modern exponents of new national systems assert sometimes, that their ideas should not be considered in the light of goods for export.

Precisely with regard to the practical political form of a state, the people's rights, its share in responsibility, and the attainment of a truly democratic order of thought, a great deal depends on the special atmosphere that has been created by historical experience and tradition. This atmosphere is further determined by natural conditions, by the general disposition and the particular gifts of a nation.

Let me refer to an anecdote current on the Continent. On the occasion of a great international entertainment in London a distinguished Continental personage asked an English dignitary in whose company he had been admiring the famous English lawn in front of some mansion or other: "What does one have to do to get such beautiful grass? I should like to introduce it into my own land!"

"Then you will need five hundred years to start with."

That was the Englishman's reply.

CHAPTER SEVEN

The Decline of Parliamentary Institutions

IN THE struggle against parliamentary democracy the political parties were chiefly struck at, as being the upholders of the "system." In many other countries as well the authority of parliament had been for a long time badly shaken, but there were three reasons why in Austria in particular these institutions were open to assault.

Firstly, Austria, unlike England, or even Hungary, had not the tradition of parliament. Already in pre-war Austria parliaments had had a problematical reputation. Their activities had often been futile; the repeated cases of obstruction, the pronounced centrifugal and disruptive tendencies, and the constant abuse of the privilege of parliamental immunity, besides various other features, had left an unpleasant aftertaste with all reflecting patriotic people.

Moreover, after the revolution the new Nationalrat was faced at once with the ungrateful task of winding up the old

92

system, besides having to support the odium of all the painful measures needed to meet the economic emergency, while the ratification of the Treaty of Saint-Germain, which had been forced upon Austria, was also a serious handicap on it.

It is true that no other authority or political body could have done differently or much better; but this consideration did not interest public opinion, which judged by results alone. On that account it was quite natural that the process of decay, against which no political system can be immune, should have set in rapidly.

Finally, the republican constitution had tried to satisfy the idea of full sovereignty of the people by saddling the Parliament with every power and responsibility. There was scarcely any other authority with competence to act effectively in times of crisis. More particularly the President of the Republic did not possess powers corresponding to his office, for up to the year 1929 he could not even exercise the right to dissolve the Nationalrat or to appoint the government. Limitations such as those clearly made responsible and far-seeing administration almost impossible.

Only someone who has himself lived through many fateful hours, when the existence of the State seemed in jeopardy, can fully appreciate what such conditions meant for Austria, a small country without the means possessed by large and wealthy nations for resisting a crisis.

The distribution of political forces within the country did not contribute towards the effective working of the parliamentary system either, for a kind of trench-warfare had set in and electoral fronts had become rigid.

Two great parties, the Christian Socialists and the Socialists, almost equal in strength, faced each other, one drawing its support mainly from the countryside, the other from Vienna and the industrial districts. Besides these there were the two "bourgeois" parties, the Pan-Germans and the Agricultural League. They were often able to turn the scale at divisions, but their numbers had not changed very much in the course of several elections held up to 1932.

As a result, the problem of securing a majority in the Nationalrat was always a delicate one, and this was particularly serious, since any constitutional change needed a two-thirds majority, and no government could count on getting such a qualified majority without great difficulties. Neither the French nor the Swiss constitution, to mention only two democracies, requires a two-thirds majority in Parliament to enact constitutional changes.

On the other hand the government parties who, in the critical years after 1920, had supported the responsibility of power without having a substantial majority, were shouldered with a one-sided responsibility which diminished their prestige with the masses.

Therefore, when in the spring of 1932 political trench-warfare gave way to general movement, it was the National Socialists who appeared to prosper by the new electoral activity. Their struggle to get into Parliament admittedly aimed at the destruction of parliamentary institutions altogether, and, moreover, in their campaign to seize the power of the State they had before their eyes, as the final goal, the effective surrender of Austria's sovereignty and the rejection of the idea of her national independence.

Of course the geographical position of Austria in itself favoured the spread, within her borders, of the order of ideas which had led to transformation of the State and the suppression of Parliament in Germany and Italy.

Parliamentary democracy in Austria has often been described as a democracy of form only, and this description was justified. From the first the reputed sovereignty of the people had existed on paper only and had never been anything but an anæmic fiction, a delusive façade of apparently democratic institutions.

The way of nominating the candidates for Parliament and, more particularly, the system of voting on lists of candidates instead of individuals had roused legitimate criticism. Under this system the broad masses had never the right to have a say in the choice of candidates, a right granted them in theory. They were bound to accept the proposals of the election committee, the members of which, in turn, were nominated by the different party committees. Lists got together on this principle had to be voted on as a whole, no alterations, erasures, or substitutions being allowed.

The upshot of this system was that not single candidates but parties presented themselves for election, an arrangement that need not necessarily have been unsound, provided that in addition to Parliament there had been some final instance, in the person of a President or Monarch, who enjoyed the nation's full confidence and was able, when the need arose, to make decisions on his own responsibility. An instance of the sort did not exist in Austria, where on the contrary the President of the Republic was elected by Parliament and, moreover, for a long time possessed no definite powers. That is why, for example, the standards of American democracy will not give a just idea of the conditions in Austria.

Besides, parliamentary democracy was greatly restricted in its scope. In times of crisis it was never in a position to solve really big problems with the speed required. Every political coalition exacts from each party represented in it the sacrifice of a part of its program, if the alliance is to be kept in being. This invariably led to the popular reproach against the parties of "bargaining," by which was meant the search for compromises resulting in half-solutions only, satisfactory to no one.

Precisely such methods were bound to exasperate the young and vigorous forces of the nation. A government responsible to Parliament only was evidently required to face very difficult problems and was never in a position to frame a policy of long view. The situation got especially dangerous whenever the government needed to obtain the consent of the opposition to a policy involving vital State interests. All too frequently such consent had to be paid for in concessions technically inadmissible. The upshot was that many political decisions were based on the principle of the choice of the smaller evil only.

I grant that the fight against the parliamentary system was also carried on with arguments as unsound as those employed in most day-by-day political conflicts. But as party democracy itself for years had offered the example of a demagogic agitation, it had not the right to complain when the poisoned arrows now flew in increasing numbers in its own direction.

From the first years after the revolution the possibility of getting a solid two-thirds majority, needed at any time to bring about a change in the constitution, was blocked, as the tactics of the Austrian Socialists, their procedure and attitude to the idea of the State, their scarcely veiled efforts to set up the "dictatorship of the working class" made political co-operation between them and the other parties out of the question. Indeed, that was why the crisis grew more acute and menacing, and in this connection it should never

be forgotten that if, at a fateful moment, the Socialist upholders of a jeopardized democracy went under, it was retri-
bution for the fact that they themselves had toyed with the
idea of dictatorship for years.

For too long a time did the Socialists persist, for purposes
of their own agitation, to assert that, after all, democracy
was only meant to be an ephemeral and transitory system;
too often did they announce in Austria, as they have done
elsewhere since then, that democracy was not an article of
faith with Marxists, but only a matter of political expedi-
ency, determined by the conditions of time. In other words,
they claimed that political systems depended on force and
that once they possessed power, there would be a change of
system and democratic trappings would go into the lumber-
room, there to accumulate dust with other "bourgeois"
prejudices.

I uphold this opinion of Austrian Socialist mentality notwithstanding the criticism which Lenin once levelled at
Otto Bauer's political tactics. "It is clear," wrote Lenin,
"that this man, ablest of the Socialist traitors, is nothing
more than a hopeless scholarly buffoon—a common example of the pedant and a bourgeois shopkeeper in his outlook."

As events afterwards revealed, there had been a difference
of opinion only regarding prospects of success and the time
when force was to be used to overthrow the "bourgeois"
and replace him by the "working class."

Among typical aspects of a "party democracy," disposed
to approach every problem from the standpoint of election
prospects, was this one also: that ideas, wise and necessary in
themselves, were resisted with bitterness if they should happen to be put forward by a rival party. Thus it happened

frequently that an essential or, at any rate, a reasonable measure was held up just because one party grudged the other a success. As a consequence endless harm was caused by this attitude, which tried to make party capital out of any important question, and that despite the fact that State or workers might have to foot the bill later on.

The prolonged and unscrupulous treatment of real or manufactured scandals in public, without any conscientious investigation, belongs also to the misdeeds of the Austrian parliamentary system. Under the mask of an injured sense of justice or a demand, which no one challenged, for fair play, there was too frequently an attempt to work up an attractive and useful slogan for the next elections. In the interest of public integrity and for the sake of swift justice the right course to adopt in such cases should have been, obviously, to get at the facts first, by means of an investigation in private, and then only to disclose the evidence, sum up, and deliver judgment in open court.

To this same chapter belonged the practice of addressing speeches not to Parliament itself so much as to the public outside its doors. Thus earnest work and frivolous agitation went on side by side, the last mentioned getting the upper hand far too frequently.

It must finally be considered that the parliamentary system, as it worked in Austria, meant that personal opinion could find expression in the political clubs [1] only, while each public action was just the outcome of discussions by a group of party leaders. Real debates, without prearranged views and attitude, took place at most in sittings of the different parliamentary committees, while the debates in Par-

[1] Not clubs in the English or American sense, primarily for social purposes, but purely political party organizations with their seat in the house of Parliament.—TRANSLATOR.

liament were just a piece of stagecraft, where only the absence by chance of some deputy or other might, on occasion,
lead to surprises on divisions. With conditions such as I
have described them it was clear that it required no particularly adroit knowledge of stagecraft to stir up public
opinion against Parliament and what Parliament stood for.

In those times of crisis, when the reputation of Parliament was declining, the members themselves naturally were
the chief sufferers. Often enough were they faced with
problems they were not able to solve, despite all the goodwill in the world.

The evil was in the system itself; even the choice of candidates depended not on merit or aptitude for the tasks of
Parliament but rather upon local considerations and party
interests.

Besides, every member was expected to be at home
equally in all questions that might come up for discussion
by the legislature. An industrial worker with a seat in the
Nationalrat had to take a part in discussions and decisions
on purely farming issues; the representative of an agricultural division had to concern himself with questions such
as the social rights of factory workers; the tradesman or
small business man was supposed to understand all about
the complicated regulations governing employment and
wages in the public services. The upshot was that the collaboration of members in debate, either at committee meetings or parliamentary sittings, was not of importance so
much as their sheer material presence, for that ensured that
the divisions corresponded to the relative powers of the parties.

Nevertheless, that might have been supportable had
members, whose votes, according to the constitution, were

of such vital importance, been able to devote themselves altogether to their parliamentary duties. Such duties were manifold, for besides actual assistance at debates members were expected to act as the intermediaries between their constituents and the authorities and to perform those other tasks which fell within the general description of "using influence." It was, for obvious reasons, never possible to stamp out the practice of "using influence," though the attempt was made often enough.

The member of Parliament, except when he was a public official who could claim leave of absence to attend to his parliamentary duties, had his own occupation to follow as before his election, for while his work in the Nationalrat might last a long time or a short, it could never, in the nature of things, be permanent.

Thus the deputy as a rule had to attend to his own profession or business as well, and if he did give it up, then he ran the risk of getting a reputation as a discredited "professional politician."

Clearly the best arrangement would have been for each member to forgo private work while in Parliament, but then there was the obstacle I have just referred to: the charge of being a professional politician has been a favourite and effective weapon of political controversy. To make a living out of politics has always been looked on as dishonourable, and the popular view is sound, should the politician abuse his position for personal profit.

Thus an almost insoluble dilemma arose. The only way out would have been to see that no candidate was elected who was dependent on the income from his profession or business. But since deputies could only receive a modest salary for their parliamentary activities, that would have meant in practice that only public officials, people on pension, or wealthy people could have got seats, a scheme which clearly ran counter to the whole conception of democracy.

On the other hand it was of importance that each social and economic class, more particularly the younger generation, should have their spokesmen in Parliament, and it was further necessary that persons with political capacity, a certain amount of oratorical gifts, and nerves to match should get seats. None of the political parties could get along without such spokesmen of the different stations in life, for each party in itself offered a fairly true picture of the entire nation. All parties were "people's parties," all had followers drawn from every occupation and social walk. Indeed, only political ideas and outlook distinguished one party from another.

The Socialists were just as little a sheer workers' party as was the National-Socialist German Workers' Party (N.S.D. A.P.), or as little as the Christian Socialists could be regarded as a party of peasants alone.

It is true that the Socialists began as the political organization of a very substantial part of the industrial workers and small employees, but those classes were never in their ranks to a man—the Christian and so-called national workers and employees had already found political asylum in other organizations. Moreover, in the ranks of the Socialists there were to be found public servants as well, including in a few instances the heads of ministry departments, just as there were business men and shopkeepers in that party too. That the N.S.D.A.P. never appealed to the workers exclusively was evident from the beginning, while the peasants were not by all means Christian Socialists—the liberal-minded peasants invariably adhered to the Agricultural Union.

Thus it came about that in political agitation all parties used to appeal to the nation as a whole and none of them addressed themselves to particular groups only. Still, it frequently happened on decisive occasions that the majority would overrule the minority in favour of some special advantage to be obtained by a small group. This was due to the rigid party discipline imposed on the deputies by the different clubs. If members did not respect this discipline, that would result in their being driven out of political life altogether.

This way of working practically led to the predominance of an all-powerful official class, although, according to the letter of the constitution, the Nationalrat was supposed to exercise supreme authority. In the course of this development even the army and the civil service got to be subservient to political influences. This was disturbing, but in the circumstances an inevitable development.

From time to time every parliament and party had to face the charge of corruption, another popular weapon in political controversy everywhere. In Austria as well there was a great deal of talk about the "corruption" of the system and the "corruption" of democracy. Like other countries Austria experienced scandals which threw a dark shadow upon political life, besides bringing to daylight many a personal and material failure and proving again how the greed of the individual can always contrive to secure personal profit by turning to account gaps in the existing system. As has been said, political marauders have always existed, and no party, no political philosophy, has ever been immune from their activities. But to blame democracy as such for this state of things would be a manifest injustice.

Constantly and with the utmost insistence Seipel had called for the divorce between business and politics. That it was never feasible to impose this distinction was due to the reasons, above mentioned, relating to the way candidates were nominated and to their activities afterwards as deputies. In acting as go-between and in "using influence" the member who took his tasks seriously spent a great deal of time on thankless tasks, besides being liable to be called a "door-knocker."

If, then, apart from a few cases, the sweeping reproach of personal corruption was rather unjust, it cannot be denied that the system, as such, necessarily led to something bordering on corruption for practical party ends. That was true of the bargaining so often needed to get vital measures through. As for this charge of bargaining, often brought publicly and with much ill feeling against Parliament, it was due to the impression, from the outset, that members took the easy middle line and did not stand up seriously for their principles or at most put up an irrelevant mock fight.

The necessities of government by coalition prevented the public from learning in every case on what conditions the different parties had agreed to give their support to one motion or another. This also gave rise to the suspicion of corruption, and the appointments to posts often led to similar reproaches.

It was a common event for the vote to run counter to the opinions previously voiced by deputies at public meetings. So it seemed natural to ask what some member or other, this or that group, had obtained in exchange for abandoning their opposition. Certainly they did not get any eco-

nomic advantage, yet, on the other hand, the prospect of
political openings in some greater or lesser field of responsibility was frequently made dependent on whether these
deputies were prepared to sacrifice in good time the need
for agitation to the exigencies of business.

And one might perhaps be allowed to add that the allegation levelled against the professional politician of graft and
clinging to office has invariably been voiced in loudest tones
by the very people who were most eager to get into Parliament themselves. Had they succeeded in this, even through
the overthrow of democracy and the substitution of the one-
party State for the parliamentary system, then the valiant
opponents of political professionalism might quickly have
remembered Plato, who in his *Republic* had described politicians as the privileged class. One might then have found a
lot of arguments in favour of educating a special class of professional politicians.

Austria chose a different path and on that account all this
discussion has merely a historical interest for us today. And
yet one thing is worth noting: the theory that the science of
politics is the only thing in the world that need not be
studied, that its secrets are to be fathomed and mastered by
everyone from the start as a matter of course, this theory is
surely as untrue today as it ever was. In this sense the rather
extravagant ideas on the rule of philosophers in Plato's classical State deserve consideration even nowadays, especially
if they help to correct J. J. Rousseau's teaching about the
sovereignty of the people.

Besides, there is in this respect no prescription which is
valid in every circumstance. Neither Plato nor Rousseau is
able to serve us as a guide today. Goethe has said the right

thing in one of his conversations with Eckermann: "What is good for a nation must spring from its own core and exigencies. Any attempt, therefore, to introduce reforms from outside, when the need of them is not rooted in the deep soul of the nation itself, is absurd."

In the ten years that lay between 1922 and 1932 there were constantly at work factors which anyone who surveyed the political conditions of the time must have interpreted as leading to an inevitable change, even though no one could quite say at first what form such change should take. A deep feeling of discontent had seized large parts of the nation, particularly the younger generation, and the craving for the new, for what was different, spread perceptibly. This tendency was not changed, because those who clung to tradition would not look facts in the face or distrusted the prophets of reform. Young people felt instinctively that the most dynamic force in Austria—Seipel—had ideas resembling their own.

In the spring of 1927 new elections for the Nationalrat were promulgated, and a group of young Tyroleans arranged to nominate me as a candidate of the Volkspartei, as the Tyrol Christian Socialists were called.

I myself was at first rather indifferent in the matter because, as it happened, I had had, since 1924, a happy home of my own, and the prospect of the repeated separations which political work in Vienna was bound to entail did not appeal to me very much. Moreover, I had been called to the bar a few months earlier and that imposed upon me a great deal of professional work, particularly at the outset. Finally, it was just about this time that a well-known writer on cultural questions, writing in a Catholic monthly, had said: "Politics are today the little-esteemed occupation of a little-esteemed body of men."

On the other hand, politics and the prospect of a political career were nevertheless alluring to a man at that time still young. Anyhow, I never had it in mind to become a politician by profession and to give up my own occupation. I fully realized from the start how difficult it would be to combine my legal work with my duties as a deputy. In this matter a disharmony could have arisen in my life, and that I was determined to prevent from the start.

In the Tyrol the advanced elements had got the upper hand in the ranks of the Volkspartei, and without there being any obvious grounds for it, an almost complete change in its representatives in Parliament was effectuated. By their self-sacrifice and integrity our Tyrolean predecessors in the Nationalrat had rendered excellent services, but the cry: "Youth to the fore!" proved itself stronger than any other consideration. Our constituents at once expected us to perform miracles, and when, naturally, the miracles were not performed, we soon found ourselves also criticized from various sides as mere "scrap iron."

Under the leadership of the well-proved peasant leader Haueis we newly elected members of the Volkspartei, together with the Pan-German Dr. Straffner and the Socialists Abram and Scheibein, entered the new Nationalrat as representatives of the Tyrol. In our own ranks there was Dr. Thaler, then Minister of Agriculture, whom destiny has since led to the young Austrian settlement in Brazil known as Dreizehnlinden, Franz Steiner, captain of the Landsturm [second reserve] in the World War and then industrial leader, Dr. Franz Kolb, priest, professor, and specialist in questions relating to the South Tyrol, and Dr. Kneussl, the local Governor of East Tyrol.

The years that followed brought much work and many anxieties and disappointments. At the best not more than three days in the week could be devoted to the home, and these were frequently interrupted by political expeditions in my constituency, Sundays being often taken up in this way.

Yet I would not readily have missed these years of my initiation into politics, for without them it would have been extremely difficult for me to have borne my responsibilities in after years. The Christian Socialist Party Club in those days was admirably led and offered ample opportunities for acquiring political knowledge and experience; and for that reason as well as others I must always be indebted to many of my fellow-members. We recognized especially that we had hitherto taken politics far too lightly—after all, politics should not be looked on as a form of sport—and we discovered that problems when seen from near are, as a rule, quite different from what they appear at a distance. Moreover, we grew acquainted with the background of all such problems.

In the government, and therefore in the Christian Socialist Club, Chancellor Seipel ruled, then full of energy and vigour. We "freshmen," in whom the Chancellor showed the keenest interest, did not always have an easy time and we soon discovered that the right of free speech was not quite what we had pictured it to be.

I remember how one attempt I made to stand up to Seipel ended in a complete fiasco, though, as it happened, the Chancellor, by his decision, acknowledged I had been right as to the facts. Even today I can recall exactly that the question had to do with the salary and pension rights of a small employee. Before the entire club I was given a stern lesson, thus learning how useful and indeed how necessary it is to control one's speech in public.

When I look back at that time, now more than ten years ago, the venerable image of Jodok Fink [senior of the Tyrolean Christian Socialist politicians, for several years Vice-Chancellor] rises up in memory. Even today his profile commands respect, as indeed does the whole personality of this truly great and pure-hearted democrat and peasant leader. His skill as a negotiator, his expert knowledge, and his authority were recognized without demur by every party, and everywhere there was respect for his exemplary personality.

Professor Alfred Gürtler, afterwards President of the Nationalrat, has also passed from us. He, too, was a democrat of a model kind, with astonishing gifts of intellect. Unsurpassed in the cut and thrust of satiric dialectics, and characterized by a certain wilfulness, this somewhat gruff, informal, and in many ways eccentric party leader was a thoroughly original personality, never to be replaced by anyone else.

Naturally, the members of the Seipel cabinet enjoyed particular esteem and each of them could at that time boast of achievements well above the average. Vaugoin,[1] the creator of the new Austrian army, ought to be mentioned here first. Then there was Kienböck, the Finance Minister of that time; Richard Schmitz, the Minister of Education; Resch, the Minister of Social Welfare; and many others.

In those times of great strain each of these men acted as a helpful counsellor to the recruits who were to be associated

[1] General Karl Vaugoin, for many years Minister of National Defence, in 1930 Chancellor, retired from active politics under Dollfuss.—TRANSLATOR.

with them in work for the nation. To Wilhelm Miklas, the President of the Nationalrat at that time, we were especially grateful, for he never neglected an opportunity of facilitating, through his vast experience, the tasks of his new colleagues, and when the need arose he would readily spur them on by a word of praise or encouragement.

The picture of the club in the days of which I write would not be complete if I did not recall the few surviving Lueger veterans. The actual portrait of the founder and first leader of the Christian Socialist Party dominated the club-room. Great memories and great deeds in the field of political conflict were embodied in the carefully tended Lueger tradition.

Of Lueger's associates, who did now grow weary even in that new epoch, Leopold Kunschak deserves to be mentioned first. Often attacked and often opposed, he has remained the unchallenged mentor of the Christian Socialist workers' movement in Austria. What Jodok Fink represented with the peasants, Leopold Kunschak was to the town workers, an upholder of democracy whose banner could be seen from afar, a man who was a little self-willed, yet gave proof, by his life's work, of capacity and earned for himself a reputation as a sincere and unflinching patriot. He was indeed a politician who by his integrity, extreme modesty, and the stainlessness of his life brought honour upon Austria.

Many another recollection of men and things keeps vivid the remembrance of those days. I very soon got into touch with Dr. Anton Rintelen, who as the Governor of Styria led his fellow Styrians into the Nationalrat. In long and exceedingly interesting conversations Rintelen in those days defined his attitude to the different contemporary issues and always defended himself in lively fashion against the very dissimilar attacks made on him personally by political opponents. In all his utterances Rintelen showed himself a vigorous anti-Socialist. He displayed, too, some antagonism to Seipel, though the two men differed only as regards methods and tactics.

Rintelen was always aware that I and my close friends were ranged unconditionally behind Seipel's leadership. Of the tragic events with which Rintelen became entangled afterwards there will be no mention here.[1] Undoubtedly the Governor of Styria ought to be numbered among the most interesting, striking, and mobile characters in Austria's domestic politics. By calling, a teacher of law in the University of Graz, he laid stress, in all circumstances, even when he was Minister, upon carrying out his tutorial duties and more especially his work as an examiner, for he did not want to lose touch with his proper sphere of activity. For the rest, very striking talents, a certain hastiness and unrest, with which was combined a marked desire to secure power, though entirely simple in his personal tastes, are among the conspicuous traits of his character as a politician. Many people in those days must have gained the impression that with him a delight in political tactics was sometimes keener than the clear vision of what was actually to come. At all events Rintelen was invariably the man of constant motion whose temperament knew no repose. With him the telephone was the most vital necessity of daily life.

[1] On July 25, 1934 the National-Socialists started their attempt to overthrow the government by proclaiming, over the radio, the resignation of Dollfuss and the establishment of a new government with Dr. Rintelen as Chancellor. Rintelen was immediately put under arrest, tried to commit suicide, was subsequently found guilty of high treason and sentenced to lifelong imprisonment. The amnesty of February 1938 set him free again. —TRANSLATOR.

Foremost in his interests, even when he was Minister of Education, were questions of trade policy. The tempo of his work was a quite unusual one. In the heavy, flowing drapery of a bygone classical age Anton Rintelen would have been the typical Peripatetic, to whom sitting at the table of negotiations or, indeed, staying in one spot for any length of time would seem a physical impossibility.

Whoever had a chance of observing this strange and assuredly, in his way, talented politician at close quarters could not have failed to remark the astonishing adaptation of his habits of life to the trend of his ideas and aims. During long sittings or conferences it was his practice to use up an uncanny number of matches, with which he set fire, in play, to notes, memoranda, or other scraps of paper he might happen to have in his possession at the time. On that account Dollfuss jokingly called him a pyromaniac.

To do justice to the full personality of Anton Rintelen, whose forebears came to Austria from the Rhineland and whose family have been responsible for great scientific achievements, some more peaceful epoch in the future will be needed. In the meantime present wounds must be scarred over, and afterwards it will be possible to discover the light and shade interwoven so intriguingly in his somewhat dæmonic character. Then perhaps it will become evident that much that one was accustomed to interpret politically represented in reality a psychological problem.

Besides colleagues in my own political club, work on parliamentary committees brought me into touch with members of other parties also. Veteran politicians of great merit in the Pan-German Party, like Dinghofer, Weber, Straffner, and others who had beyond question rendered great service to the country, did what they could to promote smooth and fruitful co-operation, particularly at the time of Seipel. Among the Socialists, too, though I met with them only in their role as members of the opposition, I got to know many men, more particularly those belonging to the trade-union wing, who not only did good work to the best of their ability for their cause, but who, as men, gave no occasion for attack. In this connection I think especially of my fellow-Tyrolean Wilhelm Scheibein, now dead.

In general men worked side by side, against each other, but scarcely ever together, and besides there was the established abuse of securing support from abroad, and that, too, when the existence of the country was at stake. This abuse was not the least among those which accounted for the irresistible and inevitable decline of democracy in Austria,

In this manner government and Parliament stood on opposite sides, despite the fact that the government was chosen from Parliament. Certainly there were, on both sides, a fund of goodwill and the desire to solve problems constantly growing more complex; nor can it be contested that there was much personal ability and enthusiasm for work at hand. If, nevertheless, effort was vain and the interludes of stagnation followed on each other ever more swiftly, if Parliament was not able to overcome the difficulties on whose overcoming the existence of the State depended, then such a condition of things could be interpreted only as a sign that the days of the system as such were numbered and that a new construction of the State, more particularly a fundamental reform of democracy and the parliamentary system, were urgently needed.

CHAPTER EIGHT

Schober

By a strange play of forces, Ignaz Seipel and Johannes Schober [1] both fell victim to disease within the same month of the year 1932, when both were in the prime of life. In days of crisis each had been at the helm of the State as head of the Austrian government. Each had sacrificed his powers in the fight for Austria, each struggled for years to recover his strength, shattered by this effort, before he succumbed under the strain. Patriots mourned their loss.

By another remarkable coincidence the deaths of these two men opened the way for their successor, Engelbert Dollfuss, enabling him to take the essential first steps in the creation of another Austria.

About this time Dollfuss was fighting hard to obtain a

---

[1] Dr. Johannes Schober (1874–1932), made a swift career as a police official before the war, was President of the Vienna police from 1918 on, became Chancellor in 1921 and, for a second time, in 1929, was Vice-Chancellor and Foreign Minister thereafter.—TRANSLATOR.

parliamentary majority which would be prepared to approve the reconstruction loan, the conditions of which had been elaborated during a conference of the great powers at Lausanne. Parliament's decision on this issue was vital for the existence of the government, and therefore for Dollfuss's work of reform.

Both Seipel and Schober were members of the Nationalrat, though they stood at that time on different sides. On Seipel's death his place in Parliament was taken by another supporter of the government, which got an additional vote as a consequence, for owing to his serious illness Seipel had not taken his seat in the House for some months. The death of Schober, too, created a parliamentary vacancy, but in his case the vacancy was filled by a member of the Agricultural League, a party loyal to the government, and not by a member of the Pan-Germans, who were then in opposition.

In this way these two statesmen, so totally opposed to each other in every way, by their death influenced for good the destiny of the Fatherland to which they had devoted their lives.[1]

No doubt Schober differed fundamentally in all questions of politics from Seipel, and one should not attempt to compare him with the latter, if his portrait and the appraisement of his character are not to suffer. The essential distinction between the two men lay in the fact that Schober was a government official through and through, whereas Seipel was the authentic statesman, though in the soutane of a priest. Schober approached the tasks of government

---

[1] In both cases to which the author refers, the division of votes and thus the destiny of the Dollfuss cabinet depended on *one* vote in the Nationalrat. Thus the government was saved successively by the death of Seipel, and then of Schober.—TRANSLATOR.

DR. JOHANNES SCHOBER

NAZIS HELD BACK BY POLICE

During Celebration of the Anniversary of Austrian Liberation from Turkey,
May 23, 1933

as a practical man, whereas Seipel's attitude was always that of the man of science. Schober never recognized any hard and fast principles existing above the fluctuations and tactical requirements of a situation, whereas Seipel stood for a more dogmatic attitude even in politics. Schober, having been a police official, would stress the factors of power, authority, and order, while Seipel, on the other hand, attached more importance to the organic forms and sociological values of a properly constituted State and society.

Both men had in common the readiness to sacrifice themselves in the service of the people and country, and though their outlooks and emotional reactions differed as well as their practical opinions, their hearts beat in the same Austrian rhythm. As a result their ideas on national issues were not at all so dissimilar as the public was often inclined to think. Seipel put greater emphasis on Austria's mission for Germanism, Schober on the mission of Germanism for Austria.

Johannes Schober had won an international reputation as a police expert. The outset of his career was marked, as he liked to tell, by a particularly delicate task that took him, in the days of the Emperor Francis Joseph, as a young police officer on the staff of the Vienna police headquarters, to Marienbad, where King Edward VII of England was staying. His thorough knowledge of the English language proved then, as often later, useful to the young police official, who achieved promotion rapidly. At the time of the revolution he held the difficult and responsible position of President of the Vienna police, in which capacity he was taken over by the young Republic. In those critical days Schober rendered great service to the State.

As successor to the Chancellor Michael Mayr he became

the head of the government himself for the first time in the
year 1921, but after one year of office he was defeated on a
question of foreign policy in May 1922 (on account of having concluded the Treaty of Lana, with Czechoslovakia),
when the Pan-Germans carried a vote of no confidence, on
the ground of national considerations.

Seven years later, in the autumn of 1929, Schober became
Chancellor again and he held office as head of the government for a year, afterwards serving for another year as Vice-
Chancellor and Foreign Minister under the Chancellors
Ender and Buresch, who held office in succession. This was
the time when the tide was turning and when it had become
clear that democracy and parliamentary government were
approaching a deadlock.

Schober felt himself to be, above all, a servant of the State,
and this he frequently emphasized. With his urbane ways,
his affability, and his untiring zeal for work, while not lacking in ambition for achievement, the head of the Vienna
police was the model of an Austrian official of the old school.
It would be unjust to reproach him for wishing the public
to recognize his good work; and his strong susceptibility to
criticize was nothing else than the equivalent of his own
meticulously correct manner of thinking and speaking, for
he expected everyone to be as conscientious in his judg-
ments as he himself was.

His position as head of the police gave him no little
knowledge and understanding of men. His winning manners secured him respect and love on all sides. He was devoted to the public service and regarded the police, of which
he was the head, as the very apple of his eye. They owe him
a deep debt of gratitude, for not only was he a jealous
guardian of the traditions and efficiency of the force, but he

extended their influence and activities and was always deeply concerned with the personal welfare of even the lowest subordinate.

He was never really at home in politics or with politicians, this being particularly clear in the last years of his life. During his second term of office as Chancellor he strongly emphasized the distance separating him from parties and partisanship and he showed the importance he attached to being looked on as the official who had become a statesman, and not as a politician. His contacts with the parties in Parliament were limited to the strictly necessary. In his cabinet there was only one representative of each majority party and he liked to underline the fact that he was the head of a ministry not of politicians but of experts, which had been announced to the public as a non-political cabinet of personalities.

My own activity as a member of the Nationalrat brought me into personal touch with him on two occasions entirely different, yet in some ways related. Our first meeting was of a casual nature and took place in the stormy days of July 1927, when, on the second day of the grave disorders in Vienna, I went with Dr. Rintelen to the Police Presidency on the Schottenring.

The tragic events of those days are still vivid in my memory, despite all that has happened since. In a trial by a jury prisoners had been acquitted who had, during a parade of ex-soldiers at Schattendorf in the Burgenland, fired at some counter-demonstrators. There had been two fatalities, one being a member of the Socialist Schutzbund.[1] The prisoners had pleaded self-defence, and the jurymen acquitted

[1] Republikanischer Schutzbund was the name of the Austrian Socialist armed formations which later on, in February 1934, waged an open fight against the government forces.—TRANSLATOR.

them, just as they did, earlier and later, in dozens of non-political cases. The outcome of this trial set afoot a demand, which was justified, for the reform of Austrian criminal procedure and the question came to be raised again and again, for a series of miscarriages of justice committed by juries had offended the country's sense of justice. But, as it happened, the Socialists opposed this demand on purely formal and orthodox grounds and it was not possible to carry through the reform in a parliamentary fashion.

The verdict of acquittal in July 1927, afterwards known as the "Schattendorf Verdict," was given by the Vienna Criminal Court on the Alserstrasse, and by way of revenge an angry mob set fire to the Civil Law Court building on the Schmerlingplatz, which had nothing whatever to do with the trial.

From the House of Parliament, which faces the Law Court, I was an eyewitness of what happened and I am able to confirm from personal experience that the disaster, which might have become even graver than it was, could have apparently been avoided if the government had acted in time and opposed its armed forces to the raging mob. But such intervention was not allowed by the laws then in force, for the police was under the direct control of the Socialist Mayor of Vienna, who refused to give the necessary orders. Police action, when it did occur, was belated—a fact which resulted in heavy loss on both sides. Had the authorities been able, in good time, to make it clear how grave the situation was, most of those demonstrators who eventually paid with their lives for the folly of their leaders might have escaped. The police acted with great energy and paid a heavy toll in blood, thus saving the capital from consequences that might have been incalculable.

Although the Socialist leaders had by no means wished
or encouraged the tumult, they did their best to protect
the fanatics guilty of the excesses. They imagined the time
was come when they could drive Seipel and his detested government from power. So they called a general transport
strike. In particular the Socialists swore revenge against
Schober, then Police President and responsible for the energetic action of the armed forces. He was denounced in huge
headlines in the Socialist evening newspapers as a "blood-
stained tyrant" and "assassinator of the workers." Here
again the style of some of the newspapers of that day must
be borne in mind if the reform, afterwards, of the Austrian
press law is to be understood.

In an editorial published on July 18, 1927, the Socialist
Arbeiter-Zeitung violently attacked Chancellor Seipel on
the ground that his regime "was to blame for the explosion
of resentment by the workers" and because "his administration was responsible for the orgy of police atrocities."

The Socialist party leaders and the leaders of the trade
unions, in an appeal which they issued, first admitted there
had been mob elements among the demonstrators. "We do
not deny," they wrote, "that some hundreds of rowdies
mingled among the big crowds of demonstrators and contributed to the great catastrophe. Were we not compelled
to see how undisciplined, reckless boys dared to offer violent
resistance even to our Schutzbund when they were perform-
ing their duties with immense self-sacrifice? We do not
deny that these several hundred youths committed actions
unworthy of the aims and methods of the working class."
The appeal ended thus: "The strength of the proletariat
lies in their economic power, in the fact that all wheels must
come to a standstill when our strong arm wants it. The

power to hold up the transport of the nation is labour's strongest weapon. This is the means of resistance we shall make use of first."

Finally, in an editorial of August 2, 1927, the *Arbeiter-Zeitung* proclaimed its new "Away from Rome" movement. In an attack upon Seipel these words occur: "The people have lived to see a Catholic priest having unarmed citizens shot down and women and children killed in the streets of the city. . . ."

In this fashion the Socialists, who were bent upon securing a political success, committed the fatal mistake of putting the workers on a level with mob elements they themselves had denounced. They further adopted the tactics, always popular in Austria and always employed when political emotions are at fever heat, though under a variety of pretexts, of launching a movement against the Church.

Well, on that July 16, while Vienna was still trembling with horror and fear and every means of transport was at a standstill, I had two meetings which I still recall with vividness. Together with Rintelen I had walked first to the Chancellery on the Ballhausplatz, and leaving there, we met Count Lerchenfeld, the German Minister in Vienna, a man who enjoyed great popularity in political quarters. The Minister expressed his apprehension as to the situation and urged us not to make political capital out of the tragic happenings. It was, he said, clearly not a prearranged political outbreak, but rather a regrettable incident, the importance of which should not be exaggerated or misrepresented.

But just then the leaders of the Socialist Party had called upon the Chancellor to resign because it was impossible in any other way, they claimed, to restore order and calm. . . .

At the office of the President of police afterwards we

found Schober at his desk going over reports he had just received on the situation. He was working with his habitual self-reliance and calm. He viewed the situation hopefully, but showed himself very embittered at the attacks which newspapers were making on him personally. Upon the whole I got the impression that he was in control of the situation and that, very definitely, the right man was in the right place.

Two years later my political work brought me into closer and more extended touch with him, then Chancellor. The events of the year 1927 had continued to work upon the public mind and had given an impetus to the forces determined to do away with the system of parliamentary democracy, in which they no longer saw a suitable type of State organization. A thorough reform of the constitution was the first stage contemplated. Under Chancellor Streeruwitz, Schober's predecessor in office, a comprehensive law for the reform of the constitution had been drafted. Schober took over the measure and, after making a few alterations, placed it before the Nationalrat. In his speech introducing the bill he pointed out that Parliament was faced, in a critical hour, with a task of paramount importance. Public opinion as a whole, he said, imperatively demanded the reform of the constitution, the purpose of which was to create a real and healthy democracy and to open new ways for parliamentary action.

I was appointed to draw up the report on this motion and so was in a position to watch at close quarters what happened to the bill. Its aim, in short, was on one hand to promote the systematic reform of the parliamentary system and on the other to strengthen in decisive fashion the authority of the State by rendering the government less dependent upon the political situation of the moment. Therefore the President of the Republic was in future not to be elected by the Nationalrat but by a general plebiscite. He was to be given far-reaching rights, among them the right to dissolve the Nationalrat, and to appoint the government, and the supreme command of the army. Further, the right of promulgating emergency decrees was to be put into the hands of the President, within clearly defined limitations and for exceptional cases only. Special regulations were proposed for a "state of emergency" and it was also intended to centralize the administration of the police. The law courts were to be made wholly free of political influences and, finally, the constitutional position of the city of Vienna was to be changed, the reform of the jury system undertaken, and the press laws amended. Moreover, the measure gave expression, for the first time, to the idea of corporative representation. Thus the Federal Council, which consisted of representatives of the provinces, was to be replaced by a council representing the "provinces and corporations." The bill did not include the details about the future structure of this new legislative body, but limited itself to the formulation of principles.

From the start it was obvious that this measure would cause a keen fight in Parliament. On the one side the extra-parliamentary forces, the Home Defence League (Heimatwehr), very popular since 1927, were pressing for a speedy and extreme solution, claiming that Schober had made them binding promises in the matter, while on the other side the Socialists were defending their political position and seemed (more particularly as regards Vienna) unwilling to yield so much as an inch of their power.

Still, it was a sign of general recognition of the necessities

and changes of the time that the Socialists should enter into
negotiations with the government at all, for it would have
been impossible to get this constitutional law through without a two-thirds majority; for the Chancellor, in his conversations with the party leaders, had definitely repudiated the
idea of applying force for the purpose. Nor, indeed, would
there have been a majority on the government side for any
solution based on force.

The discussions on the bill, left to a parliamentary committee, were difficult and prolonged, lasting for weeks.
Every day brought a new situation, for besides the discussions in committee, negotiations took place between the
Chancellor and the spokesman of the Socialists, Dr. Danneberg, a politician who fought hard against the more drastic
aspects of the government's proposals.

At length both sides met at a middle point of compromise.
A few important clauses of the government bill were carried, the Socialists being ready to let their votes go towards
the two-thirds majority needed, but for other equally important clauses no such majority could be got and the law
as originally projected by the government had to be given
up.

Upon the whole the debate left the Socialist political
strongholds unshaken, more particularly as regards their
domination over the city of Vienna, though it should be
added in justice that no other result was to be reached by
parliamentary methods, and that a non-parliamentary solution was out of the question. On the whole, therefore, the
Chancellor had done his best to bring about what was, after
all, a fairly satisfactory solution.

On neither side, however, did the result give much pleasure. The forces outside Parliament showed themselves

rather disappointed, and within Parliament itself opinions differed greatly. The outcome of the reform was that the Austrian constitution had in its chief aspects become assimilated to the Weimar constitution of the German Reich —to be sure, an advance compared with the previous state of affairs, characterized by that peculiar Austrian feature of an overemphasized and exclusive parliamentary rule.

From this dramatic political period I have retained in memory two incidents, unimportant in themselves, but in their way not without significance.

At the height of the controversy in committee a retired military officer of high rank whom I knew during the war came to see me in my private room at the House, having first rung me up. He has been dead several years, this ardent patriot, a gentleman to his fingertips, who had never been in direct contact with politics. When he saw me he explained that his visit was of great importance and obtained my word that I would treat it as strictly confidential.

He informed me that several hundred men, all ex-soldiers and now members of the Home Defence movement, were ready to occupy at any moment the House of Parliament, eliminate the political parties, and thereby bring about a change of constitution by force. He added that they were waiting for a hint from me as to when they should strike.

I pointed out to him, of course, that I thought the plan a pure fantasy, that they could expect no assistance from me, and finally I got his promise that he and his friends would undertake nothing without my knowledge. As a result no attempt whatever was made to interfere with the work of Parliament.

I mention this incident not because I regarded it as very important at the time, but as illustrating the excitement then prevailing among many sections of the population, which would have led to rash acts had the parliamentary debates been protracted. The incident occurred in the late autumn of 1929.

The second episode also throws an effective light upon the situation at that time and related to the plan to eliminate, while the constitution was being revised, the so-called "Habsburg laws." One remembers how, in the first wild extravagances of revolution, the estates of the Imperial house had been expropriated by means of a constitutional law, not only property belonging to the Crown, but also property that belonged to the Imperial family in their private capacity being seized.

On the ground of the various expert opinions which justified my doubts as to the legality of those laws, and with the support of several political friends, I had tried to get the law in question rescinded.

At first I informed the Chancellor of my plan when I visited him one night in his office. Chancellor Schober, who had been in conference throughout the afternoon, listened kindly to what I said and then suddenly he took me by the arm and led me from his office to an adjoining room. There he showed me a photograph of the Imperial family with their signatures and remarked: "Her Majesty sent me this photograph as a token of remembrance when I was appointed Chancellor."

He added that he showed it to me in order that I might see how he, an old official of the Dual Monarchy, felt on the point under discussion and what his general attitude to the monarchist question was. He said I should strive to get the consent of the other parties of the coalition to the proposal to rescind the law. But the effort failed, since at a subsequent conference of representatives of the majority parties the idea was rejected, without the government expressing any official opinion.

I readily admit that the words of the Chancellor made a deep impression upon me. I personally would have liked the matter to be raised, at least by the coalition parties, during the debate on the revision of the constitution; after ten years of republican rule the two aspects—the political and the judicial—of the question relating to the property rights of the Imperial house should no longer have been confused.

Still, I shall always hold in grateful remembrance my time of collaboration with Chancellor Schober. I came to esteem him as a man and as an Austrian, and the events which occurred after the year 1930 could not affect this feeling. Ex-Chancellor Schober, annoyed at certain political developments, then became the leader of the "National Economic Bloc" and opposed Chancellor Vaugoin, his successor. In that, too, he was animated, I do not doubt, by the best intentions. It is my conviction that he felt his position as a political leader alien to his nature and that he was anxious, at times, to end his contract as a "star performer" in the House of Parliament, a part which did not suit his character and urged him on other courses which easily might have been lost in twilight.

CHAPTER NINE

Forces Outside Parliament

A LONG time before the declining influence of Parliament had clearly manifested itself and the crisis of democracy had become a favourite topic of conversation—indeed, very soon after the upheaval—those extra-parliamentary elements had become active which many years later grew into a powerful political force.

A number of causes go to explain the self-defence movement, at whose cradle the ex-combatants stood, as far as Vienna was concerned, while in the provinces the "Heimwehr" became its nucleus numerically and with regard to political influence.

First of all, quite apart from considerations of domestic policy in the narrow sense, it was a military consideration that brought into being these formations of armed volunteers. By the peace treaty, compulsory service was forbidden and the military forces of the State were reduced to a level that was scarcely adequate. Nevertheless the desire for military preparedness, more particularly in the Alpine lands, was deeply rooted in the character of the people. In the end this desire led to the formation of home-defence formations in the different provinces. Then there was the necessity of calling up volunteers to take part in the defence of the frontiers in the various conflicts which broke out in the first post-war years, as in Carinthia, where the armed volunteers protected the threatened border under the military command of the then Governor, now General Hülgerth, later on Commander in Chief of the militia and Vice-Chancellor.

The "Heimatschutz" of Carinthia had thus been one of the first and most reliable pillars of the genuine self-defence movement, and even during the first years of its existence it had earned the gratitude of the country—gratitude that could not be exaggerated.

The second reason for the strengthening of this movement had to do with considerations of home policy. There had come an inevitable reaction to new institutions such as Workers' and Soldiers' Councils with their suspicious resemblance to Communist ideology, a reaction to the Socialist claim to control the streets, as it was boisterously voiced in the first years after the revolution, more particularly in the big cities. There was a feeling of revolt against the systematic derision and uprooting of everything that suggested the traditional, against the constant mobilization of the Socialist masses.

The situation, after all, was not such that everyone who thought on lines different from the prevailing fashion of the revolutionary period could be condemned to lasting silence. Rather did the more conservative elements learn to realize that speeches and newspaper articles would not suffice to

resist at length the pressure from the Left. So they closed
the ranks and began to march, though at first these demonstrations generally took place without the demonstrators'
carrying arms.

In the course of time another reason which increased the
need for a self-defence movement came into prominence,
and that was a consideration of a more sociological nature.
To overcome the class struggle and the disruptive influence
of the trade-union movement in the factories, a number of
big industrialists, more particularly the Alpine Montan-
Gesellschaft [Austria's biggest mining and steel-producing
concern], began to organize their workers and clerical staffs
into works branches of the Heimatschutz, the aim being
thus to promote political unity within the factory. In order
to attain this end independent trade unions were afterwards
started, which met with the bitterest resistance from the
Social Democrats and also from other workers' organizations, as "yellow" or "company" unions.

There is no doubt that the Heimwehr or Heimatschutz
movement—the two terms were eventually used in the same
sense and adopted indiscriminately by the different provinces—embodied a really sane idea. The movement was
necessary and indispensable and, notwithstanding that it
had its shady side, rendered great service to people and
country. Every Austrian will arrive at this conclusion, if
he views the political evolution with impartiality and
avoids the temptation to lose his sound judgment over a
great mass of accompanying details, omissions, and defects.
Above all, it should not be forgotten that this movement,
like every other form of political organization, was the expression of the age in which it arose. Therefore, when it
committed the error of supposing that it was an end in it-

self, it betrayed the fact that it had passed the zenith of its power and influence. That this is true of every political organization has been proved most eloquently by the history of Austrian Socialism.

It is surely idle today to ask to whom belongs the palm for having recognized first the compelling necessity of the hour, who, with respect to the home-defence movement, first raised the rallying cry, whether the Carinthians, Styrians, or Tyroleans. The creation of the Heimwehr had everywhere a special local importance, but in the end it was, after all, the outcome of a situation and development common to all, and this brought the various territorial groups of the movement together in the course of time.

In the measure that the Socialist Schutzbund came to the fore as an instrument of brutal force, so, on the other side, did the Heimwehr movement loom ever larger as a political factor. Thus the time came, regrettably, yet in the nature of things inevitably, when the armed political groups of the country faced each other, each animated by the determination at all costs to be the stronger and better armed, so as to remain masters of the battlefield in the hour of decision.

From the moment when these two armed camps existed, it was only a question of time before a spark would set fire to the accumulated explosives of long excited passions. All this was part of the tragedy of a lost war; yet the self-defence movement was also, despite everything, a chapter in the heroic history of a nation which, notwithstanding economic need and misery, in spite of exaggerated political antagonisms, and lacking for a long time in any real patriotic feeling for the new State, still fought for its independence and the freedom of its soil.

Thus the profound motivations, political and psychological, of the Austrian self-defence movement are clear, as well as the inevitable course of its subsequent history, and the ups and downs of its varying importance and significance to the country.

In what I am going to say, I have avoided a critical attitude or judgment as not being in harmony with the frame of this book. In particular, I have set myself the task of going into the complex history of the movement, with its often heterogeneous tendencies and dramatic episodes, only in so far as such an investigation is required for a proper understanding of the movement's political significance. I purposely avoid taking up an attitude in the question of leadership, as I regard it as unimportant in the long run, considering the problem as a whole. The significance of the self-defence movement for Austria, its influence and successes, are, when the movement is contemplated in its entirety, not lessened by any attendant circumstances.

It was at Innsbruck that soon after the revolution the "Einwohnerwehren" (Citizens' Defence Corps) were started in the first instance, with Dr. Richard Steidle as their leader. Their task was to ensure the restoration of order in the event of plunderings and demonstrations with violence, apt to occur from time to time even as late as in the year 1920; for the army could scarcely be used in such cases and the police were too weak numerically and not adequately armed.

These "Einwohnerwehren" afterwards grew into the Tyrol Heimwehr, which had a big following in town and countryside and in whose ranks all those came together without exception who were not Socialist in outlook. I have still in my possession the green-white armlet I wore at that time as a member of the organization.

Richard Steidle was then a member of the Tyrol provincial government and played a prominent part in the Peasants' League. In the critical times after the war he had displayed dauntless energy on repeated occasions and remarkable courage besides, so that he had an assured body of supporters throughout the Tyrol and more particularly among the peasants. Richard Steidle was a fiery and unusually forceful mass-orator, who in due course became one of the best and most successful political agitators the non-Socialist parties have ever had in Austria.

I heard him for the first time a few years after the war, just at the start of his public career, at a meeting at Innsbruck, where he was the chief speaker. In particular he counted university students among his adherents, while ex-soldiers and Tyrolese sharpshooters also obeyed his call.

In the critical year of 1927 the Heimwehr of the Tyrol, which had made headway slowly and steadily and had, from an earlier day, been in close contact with the Bavarian Einwohnerwehr, had reached quite remarkable strength. There were as a rule no squabbles within the movement; its character as an organization for self-defence was maintained and a strictly non-party attitude was adhered to.

The events of July 1927 put a practical task before the Heimwehr for the first time, and this task was performed without any serious friction occurring. It involved taking measures against the transport strike, in the course of which the Heimwehr, co-operating with the military and gendarmes, had to occupy some important railway stations in the Austrian provinces. The measures taken met with complete success, and the transport strike, which might have caused immeasurable damage to the whole of the national industry, besides aggravating the political tension, collapsed almost at once.

After that, the self-defence movement entered upon a fresh and decisive phase of its history, for, in the course of the years that followed, it took part in political controversy more openly and with a very definite program. It had served the State in an hour of crisis and it now came forward as a political force.

That was the time when Chancellor Seipel, too, began to occupy himself closely with this forceful, active, and increasing movement, and he did so the more readily because he had always been on terms of sympathy with its leaders. The grounds for such sympathy were obvious. Seipel recognized in the deliverance of the land from the dangers of Bolshevism the task of the hour. I, personally, do not believe that the great mass of the Socialist workers, more particularly in the provinces, were really to be won for Bolshevism, but their leaders then, as previously, played with fire and outbid one another in growing extremism—a policy to which they had been true since the revolution of 1918.

The constant state of crisis within the Parliament turned out to be a crisis of the parliamentary system as such and led to a complete lack of confidence among those parts of the population who had been dissatisfied with prevailing political conditions. Curiously, National-Socialism at that time played hardly any part at all in Austria, despite the fact that our country had given birth to the movement.

Thus the government saw itself compelled to reckon with the fresh and growing forces gathered together in the home-defence movement, and, in turn, the government extended to this movement a great deal of moral support.

The word "anti-terror" was then coined, and by it was meant that the use of violence in politics could no longer be tolerated without protest, but had to be met, should the need arise, with the threat of counter-violence. The claim of the Socialists to the exclusive possession of the street, their pretension to the monopoly of public demonstrations, had to be broken, so that in this way expression might be found for the real state of political power in Austria. The idea was to destroy, once and for all, the false impression of Austria being "Red" through and through, an impression which had until then been created by the method of answering the Socialist mailed-fist policy only with smooth words and a perpetual readiness to compromise.

In Parliament, regardless of all differences in outlook, Christian Socialists, Pan-Germans, and Agricultural League had come to an agreement among themselves for the sake of the defence of their common political aims; correspondingly, the extra-parliamentary movement of the Heimatschutz tried to co-ordinate the anti-Socialist forces in the different camps and to bring them under a common leadership. This movement, however, had a definitely offensive purpose in view.

It was, then, all a question whether it would be possible, despite the differences of opinion existing, to get a common front upon an essential issue, to put aside divisions and agree upon a common rallying cry. At this point difficulties cropped up almost at once, difficulties which later on caused repeated splits in the movement.

In justice it must be admitted that the task of maintaining unity was very difficult and became constantly more so as the movement spread. I even doubt whether the problem was to be solved at all on the basis of the volunteer system and the free play of political forces. It depended on whether convinced monarchists and equally convinced extreme nationalists, devout Catholics and aggressive anti-clericals, enthusiastic believers in the corporative system and equally convinced upholders of individualism, people with a Fascist outlook and anti-Fascists could be kept in line together.

Even if this was possible in the case of the rank and file, difficulties were bound to arise soon among the leaders. While the high command of the movement, according to the state of things then prevailing, adopted the watchword of unqualified unity and repeatedly insisted on the urgency of unconditional discipline, among leaders of the middle and subordinate ranks and in various district branches temperaments frequently clashed. Very often, as is naturally the case with every movement of volunteers, personal ambition also played a prominent part. Further, in many departments there was a certain political inexperience which sought to settle every problem in a purely military way. Finally, inability to manage people may also have been, now and then, the cause of unnecessary friction.

The stronger the determination of the Heimwehr became to take the offensive politically and the more frequently they expressed their intention to capture the power of the State, the more did the political parties begin to fear for their own position. The cleavage grew all the more pronounced with the promulgation, in 1929, of the "Korneuburg program," with its clear pretensions to totality. Later, in the elections of 1930, a part of the Heimwehr decided to put forward their own candidates as a political party, and thus the movement entered into open competition with the parliamentary parties.

Symptomatic of the situation of that time was the effort

to promote an alliance between the Heimwehr and the N.S.D.A.P., a plan which broke down on the excessive demands of the National-Socialists, who from the start claimed three quarters of the seats that might result from running joint candidates for Parliament. The National-Socialists then went to the poll with their own candidates, but did not gain a single seat; and even the Heimatblock, as the political party of the Heimwehr was called, was only able to win eight seats in all.

Opinions must differ as to whether it was wise or useful, from their own standpoint, for the self-defence movement to put up their own candidates for Parliament. For the time being, that decision doubtless meant a split in the "bourgeois" camp, but it became evident afterwards that the presence of the Heimwehr in the Nationalrat was of decisive importance at critical times. Indeed, without that group Engelbert Dollfuss would probably never have been able to form his cabinet. This, of course, is only true under the assumption that not all the seats of the Heimatblock had been won at the expense of the other government parties.

Anyhow, in the petty warfare of domestic politics the difficulties were at that time considerable, and action in the interest of compromise and appeasement, more particularly by Seipel and his friends, was needed again and again to overcome the excitement which bubbled up whenever a Heimwehr speaker impetuously threw down the gauntlet or made a speech, as was sometimes the case, in the form of personal attacks. On the other hand it was unavoidable that if some small local agitator or other of the movement let himself go on clericalism, the whole Heimwehr should be suspected of anti-clericalism, though its leaders were at great pains to avoid every appearance of taking up a one-sided attitude. At the same time, if some Christian Socialist party speaker went off the rails, that was enough to inflame minds on the Heimwehr side.

More particularly in working-class circles did controversy more and more assume violent forms, and as is usual in political debate, each side was in the right to a certain extent. The Christian workers were justified when they insisted that the claim of the self-defence movement to have fought the fight against Bolshevism alone could not be maintained historically, since from the critical times following the revolution onwards the Christian labour organizations, often enough at personal and material sacrifice, had defended their positions against oncoming Socialism. The Heimwehr, on their side, were not at fault when they pointed out that this fight had not met with success and that the Christian labour organizations alone were not in a position to defeat Socialism decisively.

If one adds to this the consideration that various influences and interests were at work behind the scenes, then it is easy to understand how the public must have gained an impression of disunity and lack of definite aims.

But all that did not alter the fact that the Heimwehr was the first movement to refer to an overthrow of the pretence of democracy in Austria and, further, to inscribe on its banners the determination to wage war upon an exaggerated parliamentarism. They even represented with considerable vigour the idea of a corporate state, though that idea had not been clearly thought out or put into definite shape.

Precisely as regards the reform of society the Heimwehr found an eloquent advocate in Ignaz Seipel, who dedicated the last years of his life to working for this reform along the lines laid down in the Papal encyclical *"Quadragesimo anno,"* [1] though he never implied he was prepared to enter into political partnership with the home-defence movement.

At the turn of the year 1930 the difficulties in the movement, in the Tyrol as well as in other provinces, came to a head. The "ideological" differences found vent, a one-sided increase of influence on the part of prominent industrialists occurred, while, in addition, the movement, at least in the towns, became split into different tendencies as the result of rival leadership.

That was why a certain lethargy spread among valuable parts of the population, particularly among the youth, who had the idea of self-defence greatly at heart, but wanted to separate it from the squabbles of parties and leaders.

This led to the establishment of several other organizations, which only in the course of the following years again came together with the Heimatschutz.

In the first instance the "Ostmärkische Sturmscharen" [2] were founded, to whom I myself stood godfather and whose task it was to assemble young, active Austrians, sharing the same religious creed, in order to wage an uncompromising fight for an exclusively Austrian policy. The first leaflet of the new movement bore the double eagle,[3] long years be-

[1] Encyclical letter by Pope Pius XI, issued in 1931, establishing the attitude of the Catholic Church towards the social problems of the present time, according to the principles laid down forty years earlier by Leo XIII in his encyclical *"Novarum rerum."*—TRANSLATOR.

[2] Literally translated "Storm-Troops of the Eastern Marches," a militant organization of Catholic youths, founded by Kurt Schuschnigg. It played an important part in the stormy events of 1934, as the most reliable volunteer force on the side of the government. Like all the other volunteer formations the Sturmscharen were also dissolved later on as an independent organization and embodied in the Fatherland Front.—TRANSLATOR.

[3] The double eagle, symbol of the Austrian Monarchy, was abolished by the Republic in 1918, but subsequently re-established by the Dollfuss government as the arms of the Federal State.—TRANSLATOR.

fore this symbol became the arms of the State again.

The creation of the Sturmscharen took place at a time when it was urgent to bring about an unequivocal and clear Young Austria movement which would resolutely oppose Pan-German tendencies and repudiate all idea of concessions. Had the Heimwehr at that time given these ideas any useful support in the Tyrol, or at least not abandoned its former non-party attitude; if it had unanimously and unequivocally stood for the Austrian front, as a result there would have been no more Sturmscharen.

It was not until the chancellorship of Dollfuss, much later, that the Heimwehr returned to its former Austrian policy. The critical phase of its evolution was over by that time, but as other organizations had been started in the meantime and had gained strength, complete uniformity was unfortunately never to be achieved again.

An interesting history lies behind the idea of the Sturmscharen movement in Austria. On the occasion of a canvassing trip made by young Tyrolean theatre players in the Rhineland, the leader, a war invalid and schoolmaster, Hans Bator by name, recipient of the golden medal for bravery, was taken with the idea of organizing in Austria, on the lines of the Catholic youth organizations he had just seen in western Germany, activist groups whom he proposed to call Sturmscharen.

When he returned home we decided first of all to work out his plan on a small scale. The idea first met with scant sympathy, even among our own friends. I remember very well how, on the occasion of a sports meeting of Catholic youth at Innsbruck, a Vienna official to whom I spoke of the Sturmscharen, emphasizing the necessity of infusing new life in the old historic Imperial idea of Austria and carrying out a pronounced Austrian policy, answered me with a pitying chuckle to the effect that we ought not to lose ourselves in an eccentric romanticism, out of tune with the times. This remark was made as recently as the year 1930.

Among young people, however, the Storm-Troop movement caught on rapidly. After a relatively short time it underwent its baptism of fire. That was when rival student bands tried to break up a meeting of the Storm-Troops in the Innsbruck Town Hall, the pretext for the irruption being that the Storm-Troops were alleged to display a monarchist and therefore anti-national tendency (anti-national in the Pan-German sense).

I was the speaker on that occasion and my subject was: "Is there a legitimist danger in Austria?" In my address I argued that there could be no question of any such danger and that one must at last get rid of the theory that there was necessarily a conflict between the idea of Austria and the German national idea. I maintained that it was the duty of the young generation in Austria to serve German culture by stressing its Austrian aspect, and that the new movement must continue to strive for a peaceful union of monarchists and non-monarchists within its ranks. This should be achieved by generally acknowledging and understanding the great history and valuable traditions of Austria.

The failure of this attempt to break up our meeting did our movement a great deal of good, though it made real headway only when in the Dollfuss regime, later on, political conflicts brought together all those Austrians who were conscious of their traditions, and when the self-defence organizations had been enlisted in the service of the State as assistant militia and gendarmerie.

Apart from a few cases of friction, there was, at the time of which I write, complete harmony among the organizations of the defence movement, and to preserve that harmony was always my deepest concern.

While the Storm-Troops were composed to an overwhelming extent of young workers and clerks, another self-defence organization grew up by its side which in the main came from the Christian trade unions and as the League of Liberty made great headway. This organization, too, did its duty fully in days of difficulty, thereby rendering incalculable service to the country. Storm-Troops and the League of Liberty always got on well together, but there was friction from time to time between the League and the Heimwehr corps. The chief cause of such friction was the fact that the League, being connected with the Christian trade unions, rejected the Fascist tendencies within the Heimwehr movement, whereas the Heimwehr saw in the League an organization in sympathy with the Left and devoted to the parliamentary and democratic order of ideas.

Later on, all these organizations reproached each other with making their respective memberships unduly accessible, and whereas the Heimwehr were suspected, more particularly, of accepting as members unreliable elements from the Right, the others were accused of admitting similar elements from the Left into their ranks. In reality no one organization had the right to reproach the others on this point, since in their heyday all the voluntary organizations had been slack in admitting new members, the result being that in course of time they all suffered through lack of consistency. That was equally true of the Ostmärkische Sturmscharen, who, since the year 1934, had gone beyond their original limits and in different parts of Austria had become a frank rival to the Heimwehr movement, which was certainly not their original purpose.

Besides the organizations already referred to, the Christian German Athletes and the Sharpshooters, an association restricted to the province of the Burgenland, were among the props of the Fatherland in the hour of trial. Both these groups were wisely led and thus managed to limit the tasks they set before themselves; by this they avoided many a dangerous pitfall which caused great damage to the other self-defence organizations.

Opinions may differ regarding the entire self-defence movement and more particularly the Heimwehr, yet they achieved their tasks and did their duty in the fullest measure. Every Austrian has ground to recall with gratitude the sacrifices these voluntary organizations made in blood and substance on behalf of the harassed country. There is no doubt that the way to the new Austria would not have been thinkable without these self-defence organizations, more especially without the Heimwehr corps.

But it is equally beyond dispute that the existence, side by side, of these rival associations could not continue indefinitely. For one thing, the dangers which must result from clashes that were inevitable, particularly in the tranquil periods, were too great to be risked. Then, in the moment when controversial issues of domestic policy had to be settled, the solid front of all individuals and parties who had rallied to the support of the Fatherland was needed. Thus the concentration of the voluntary defence organizations had to be the next political aim.

The first step in such a development was partial co-ordination under a uniform leadership, so that the Heimwehr would stand side by side with the organizations, such as the Sturmscharen, which were under the direct command of the Chancellor.

The next step in this direction consisted in the establishment of a "United Defence Front," in which it was decided that all the leagues should take up their position under a common leadership. Out of this "Defence Front" there grew by degrees the "Front Militia," and this in turn was required to place itself as part of the army under the ordinary military command.

The purpose of the voluntary military formations, with their own leadership, had been achieved when military conscription was reintroduced, and at the same moment the *raison d'être* which had existed when they were created now disappeared.

But the country could certainly be taxed with ingratitude if it were ever to forget the services of the different defence organizations, their members and their leaders. Not only are they entitled to continued respect, but they have won for themselves the right to continue their co-operation and to share in responsibility within the framework of the community as a whole. No one, indeed, could ever think of challenging that right. The self-defence movement, and more especially the Heimwehr organization, would not have been thinkable without the selfless obedience of the men who were ready to line up when called for, or without the devotion and self-sacrificing spirit of the leaders, who worked in the full conviction that their cause was a just one.

The striking soldierly head of Major Emil Fey is familiar, through numberless pictures, to every Austrian who lived through the difficult years since 1931. Destiny confronted him with particularly irksome and difficult tasks and he resolved them by the exercise of his own inherent, steadfast, and purposeful sense of duty. Many members of the one-time Vienna Home-Defence Corps and many home-defenders in the provinces as well see in him the leader of merit who was sincerely solicitous for the welfare of those who had accepted his leadership.

The former federal leader of the Home-Defence movement, Ernst Rüdiger, Prince Starhemberg, was for long years the prime upholder of the Heimwehr idea in Austria; he, by great personal sacrifice, put the movement on the right road.

Although our ways separated, now as formerly I see in Prince Starhemberg not only a man of winning character who in all practical and personal matters always thought and acted with great propriety, but also the Austrian who in times of crisis, without ever concealing his German sentiments, did service to our country. Perhaps he could have done better, now and then, had he been assisted by a suitable chief of staff, as many of his decisions have evidently been dictated not so much by calm deliberation as by exuberant and impulsive temperament. But in the end it is the rounded picture and the sum of achievement that count, and in this point Starhemberg performed everything his name promised. We never differed as to fundamentals, and on only the question of methods did my opinion and his not coincide.

The self-defence movement first came into the foreground in the time to which Engelbert Dollfuss gave a determining character.

CHAPTER TEN

Engelbert Dollfuss

LET me begin with the memory of a day in the late autumn of 1934, in the Vienna Opera House.

Dark-garbed, breathless expectancy weighed down the splendid auditorium, where every seat was full. The black-clad sea stretched out beyond the orchestra and up to the stage, where the black-clad chorus stood waiting. Above and behind it, lonely in space and over life-size, towered a death-mask. In the mind, a memory, more living than life itself: Engelbert Dollfuss. And the knowledge of how it happened.

Over the whole splendid space, vast in height and depth, and over its ancient festal pomp of red and gold, rested like a veil an atmosphere of mourning, an All Souls' Day mood. It took command of the proceedings; the audience saw, heard, and felt as one, in a rare natural harmony, a communion of souls, even before Arturo Toscanini tapped

twice with his baton, then lifted it for the first notes of
Verdi's *Requiem.*

And then the vast hall, with its thousands of individual
souls, passed beyond the individual, passed beyond time.
There was nothing of the prearranged or artificial, not a
banner, not a drapery. Not a soul thought of politics, or
demonstrations, or artificial pomp. Yet in each one of those
round Dollfuss burned red and white like a flame the
thought: *et lux perpetua luceat ei.* Then, almost as in defiant yearning the *Kyrie eleison* bursts forth and fills the
whole gleaming, swimming, red, black, and golden space.

Red, black, and gold have significant meaning in Austria.
It is a tragedy of history that the symbolic tricolour has
been too often misused in the land, and hence also too often
misunderstood. But in this tragic hour of national mourning, Austria mourning for her most patriotic son, all colour
and sound were blended into that one natural, inevitable
melody which is the immortal language of our cultural
heritage, and from which, at each fresh confrontation, one
draws new life. It is the confession of faith in Austria, in its
German genius, in the imperishable content of the Catholic
mystery, which bursts all too-confining limits to strive after
understanding of the ideal of pure humanity; and despite
all its own narrownesses, its hard-pressed distresses, remains
with head proudly erect, a friend to the world and open to
the world. All this, in that solemn hour, emerged as scarcely
ever before, with startling elemental force into the consciousness. The brooding tension held, throughout the
Dies iræ, throughout the frightful depiction of the Last
Judgment, to the *Libera,* which with dramatic abruptness
makes to gape anew the awful abyss which to our human
minds lies between life and death. No use, it says, to strug-

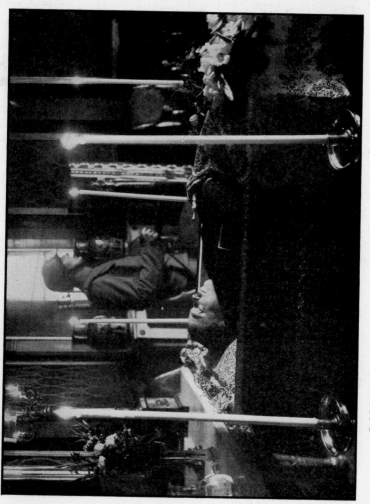

DOLLFUSS LYING IN STATE AT THE CHANCELLERY

REQUIEM FOR DOLLFUSS AT THE STATE OPERA
HOUSE, NOVEMBER 1, 1934

gle against that which to us is meaningless. At the end sounds the reconciling chord, the issue of all is peace. We must be able to believe and understand—and preserve the clarity of our understanding.

A mass for the dead, by the Italian composer, given in the Opera House at Vienna, rendered by the master whose name comes first among those magicians who interpret to us the realm of music, and played by the artists of our native land; a unique experience, a memorial service in the red, black, and gold atmosphere of an incomparable setting—such was the great hour when, mindful of the spiritual continuance of the idea of the sacred Reich, we bore witness for Austria. Such was the transfiguration of Engelbert Dollfuss.

His biographers have told us who Engelbert Dollfuss was; what he did stands before our eyes and needs no further explanation. Seeing him only at a distance, without opportunity for closer contact, one might easily get a superficial, distorted impression. His firm, deliberate hand-clasp, a glance from his cordial, laughing eyes, a friendly word or two, have disarmed many an opponent; they won him many friends and often accomplished more than hundreds of others could by hours of debate. An energy bordering on the impossible made him able to ignore time limits when at work—as his fellow-workers often knew to their cost. A conference with the Chancellor might be fixed for five o'clock, begin at seven, and end long after midnight. There were ministerial councils which began in the morning, lasted all day and all night, and only came to a close at eight in the morning. And then the Chancellor was always the freshest of them all. His frequent lack of a sense of time and appointments was often commented on, and with some justice: you would seldom or never see him watch in hand. He was governed by a lively and instinctive working rhythm. He would have no unsolved problems; all day long he would be confronted by hundreds of most various matters, and never dropped them until he came to a clear personal decision. Thus a rigid division of his time became impossible—always the unforeseen and the moment triumphed.

But here we encounter another striking characteristic of his personality. Dollfuss was no man of a political system; he constructed no far-reaching plans for the future. He was masterly at guiding situations as they came on and developed; never in any calculation did he rely upon a preconceived opinion, preferring to trust to his direct eyesight and his gift of understanding; with these he approached all things and they never failed him. Engelbert Dollfuss came from the business sphere; all economic questions were of the greatest interest to him. If Austria was not crushed, if the country could hold out through the hardest times, that is most of all thanks to the tireless, clear-headed intellect of the Chancellor, forever seeking new expedients, never for a moment losing his freedom of initiative. For a long time his one-sided agrarian policy met with suspicion. But with the skilled and experienced support of his Minister of Commerce, Fritz Stockinger, he dissipated all prejudice and enabled Austrian economics to turn the corner and establish dealings with the rest of the world.

In all his economic thinking, all his unemotional, practical attitude towards the encircling problems of daily life, which often enough demand a heavy hand, without much chance for softness or yielding, with all his emphasis upon logical deliberation and purely rational decision, Engelbert

Dollfuss had a great heart and took no trouble to hide the fact.

That was why he so easily found his way to the human beings whose destinies he shared; because he was so well aware that the best economic policy is not self-seeking, that it does not float in a void, sufficient to itself, but is intended to serve human beings—not a few privileged human beings, but as far as possible the entire community. It was Dollfuss's greatest pride and satisfaction to be able to help. He held with Conrad von Hötzendorf, who says in his memoirs that he "considered all men to be good until they convinced him of the contrary." On such a basis, disappointments are scarcely to be avoided. Thus the impressionable, impulsive, good-hearted Dollfuss often made mistakes. When he saw them he had it in for them; and whoever showed himself vacillating or unworthy had small chance of recovering Dollfuss's esteem. That might at most happen when the man was an old defender of the Fatherland, when the Chancellor's highly developed spirit of comradeship might triumph, which he acquired at the front and held in high honour.

Simple, homely, without demands on life, highly intelligent, with absolute integrity as a fundamental of his character, social, jolly, always on the move, swift—sometimes too swift—in decision, a foe to all pose or ostentation, yet carefully mindful for the respect due his office of representing the Fatherland; direct and courageous, effective by reason of his personality, which needed to put no distance between himself and his surroundings to carry his purpose—and this despite the fact that his actual person was certainly not impressive—all these he was. A loyal friend to companions and fellow-workers, always ready to be helpful; a man of faith and ideals, a true son of the German people, yet a fanatical believer in his Austria—as such we have seen and known him, we who were privileged to be at his side at the height of his activity, from the beginning of his public life, along that path of success and fortune, and up to the hour of departure—we who now bear witness, and will so long as life is granted us, for Engelbert Dollfuss and his Austria.

CHAPTER ELEVEN

Storm Signals

THE collapse of the Credit-Anstalt made 1931 a catastrophic year for Austria. The heavy shadow of economic crisis fell upon the country, and darkened the scene very much throughout the ensuing years. Unemployment rose steeply, international trade came to a standstill. Currency regulations acted as a check on the free movement and the exchange relations of trade. The stabilized schilling, bought at such heavy cost, was in great danger, and poverty, which since 1922 had gradually lapsed and been thankfully forgotten, stood once more threateningly at the door. All this was the frightful consequence and event of a time when political conflicts were emerging more and more sharply and burningly, in which dissatisfaction with the constituted boundaries of states grew ever wider and deeper, and in which there was less and less serious idea either of a genuine consciousness of a unified state or of honest self-assertion prepared for sacrifice.

Economic catastrophes are always a sign of confusion.
But few have courage or talent for keeping a clear view; the
great majority surrender all too easily to demagogic slogans.
At the same time, periods of catastrophe are often the signal
for parliaments to turn the tribune into a tribunal. The
effort is not so much or so pre-eminently to set limits to the
evil and cast about for rational means of salvation as for
the busy accumulation of evidence in order to level vehe-
ment complaints against actually or assumedly guilty parties. But from such accusations—even though they may be
justified—there can come no solution of burning problems,
which meanwhile press for solution lest the evil spread.
They are much more likely to add fuel to the popular mood,
which is, at least for the time, led away from the real concern
and inclines to clamour: Who is to blame? rather than:
Who will pay the debts? Likewise, in all times of crisis,
there arises a host of experts, genuine or self-styled; and
these pour out a flood of panaceas, disinterested or otherwise, practical or fantastic. All that gets mirrored in the
interests of parliamentary deputies and gives back a picture
doubly distorted by the sensational reports of those who for
various reasons find that the blacker the picture the more
it suits their book. Then there are those who actually earn
their bread by increasing the confusion and spreading
prophecies of evil; who are paid by somebody or other for
doing their utmost to make confusion worse confounded.
This somebody may live inside or outside the country;
whichever it is, he is mostly not to be got hold of.

So it was in this crisis in the Austrian Parliament. Instead
of forgetting their quarrels in the hour of need and uniting
their efforts in the common task, the opposed camps attacked more violently than ever. That at the decisive mo-

ment there was a consciousness that things must not be
pushed to extremes does not avail to change the picture
very much. For when a majority of votes seemed secured
and the opposition at last was quite clear that its theatrical
thundering meant nothing more than a tactical manœuvre,
it was none the less true that large parts of the population
either took seriously the long wrangle and the negative
votes, and thus the popular disaffection was increased, or
else in growing disgust they turned their backs more and
more on the parliamentary idea itself, because their years
of experience had convinced them of the inner dishonesty
of all those duels in words. For again and again it was
clearly shown that even in those cases where no two opinions were possible and there was but one single, imperative
way out, the opposition stuck by its rigid negative, without
going so far as to block the decree of the majority; obviously
because it was actually on the affirmative side, but out of
self-interest would simply not admit it; they were unwilling
to further the success of those of different political faith,
and, finally, they did not want to take the responsibility of
saying either no or yes. This parliamentary rigidity, which
made free decisions impossible, and forced every debate
and division into prearranged grooves, was one of the chief
causes of the growing unpopularity of the Austrian parliamentary system. It is true that in the provincial diets and
assemblies this was much less apparent, for the reason that
these much smaller groups preserved—as a rule, that is,
though not always and everywhere—a certain freedom of
opinion. The refusal to grant a success to a political opponent often went so far that a proposal would be shelved or
not brought forward, not because of its demerits, but simply
because it was sponsored by the other side.

All these weaknesses and bitternesses found abundant expression in the Austrian Parliament of 1931 and 1932. This was true of the Credit-Anstalt debate as well as of the question of the dissolution of the National Council and the promulgation of fresh elections and finally of the treatment of the bill dealing with the promotion of a foreign loan. Out of this hotly debated point of order grew, as is well known, the decisive struggle over the acceptance or rejection of the Lausanne Protocol.

Until June 1931 the shrewd and cautious Chancellor, Dr. Ender, had led the government. He had brought from his activities as Governor-General of the Vorarlberg a high reputation for special technical competence and an upright democratic attitude. To him fell the task of confining within limits the economic conflagration which broke out after the affair of the Credit-Anstalt, with all its unforeseeable consequences, and of preventing its further spread. He went to work self-sacrificingly and painstakingly, rather hindered than helped in his task by the forces of Parliament. In the end there was a government majority of proportions unheard-of in Austria until that time. It was much easier to criticize the measure than to put a more workable one in its place. In any case, many heavy burdens and sacrifices had now become unavoidable, and sometimes it seemed as though Austria had become too weak to bear them. The situation was not at all improved by the fact that before the great banking crash, which, moreover, occurred in much the same way and at about the same time in many other and larger countries, the project for a German-Austrian customs union emerged into publicity. Complete lack of preparation was the most essential defect of that measure. That cannot be laid at the door of the Chancellor, who had not personally charged himself with the responsibility of the Foreign Office. Nor was the Foreign Minister, Schober, at all clear over the meaning and intent of a publicity which came about entirely without his assistance.

The reconstruction of the Credit-Anstalt laid increasing burdens on the State and led of necessity to a very difficult, fundamental, and innovating reform of the government economy, with all the important consequences it brought in its train. The democratic Chancellor declared that he could not take the responsibility unless Parliament granted him extraordinary powers. Certainly his demand was not exaggerated, nor was he in the least aiming at a dictatorship. But he did need freedom of action and decision in crucial matters; it seemed to him clearly inequitable and dangerous to assume with his hands tied the responsibility of so serious an hour; even a moment of hesitation might easily bring about disaster.

Parliament had not grasped the seriousness of the situation. This would have been perhaps its last chance to rescue its reputation; a prudent restraint might have opened the way to renewed authority. Instead of which it simply acted to make its own ruin more inevitable.

Seipel, who had been in the background, now came forward and undertook what, after all that had happened, was a really sensational attempt: he tried to form a cabinet of all the parties, even the Socialist. His efforts failed. And with it government by parties definitively broke down. What followed was merely the slow, inevitable process of its death-agony.

Dr. Karl Buresch, Governor-General of Lower Austria and president of the Christian Socialist Club in the National Assembly, now tried to form a cabinet of the Centre, composed of the old party groups: the Christian Socialists, the Pan-German Party and the Landbund, or Agricultural League. It received the opposition fire on both flanks, from left and right: the Social Democrats and the Heimat bloc. The first were by now more moderate in their tone but strongly dissentient in fact; the second talked fiercely, but were rather more reserved in practice.

During this time, from June 1931 until January 1932, when the first Buresch cabinet was in office, storm signals of an impending economic and political crisis multiplied. By rallying all available forces, however, it was possible to get the law for the revision of the budget through Parliament, a law which by increased taxes exacted fresh sacrifices, in particular from the employees of the State.

The necessity of such sacrifices could be hidden to no one who had eyes for facts. There had been a deficit of 300,000,-000 schillings (about 44,100,000 dollars at the old par of exchange) in the budget for 1932, while the total sum of the bank notes in circulation had reached the billion-schilling level (147,000,000 dollars). At the same time unemployment was steadily rising and the ever increasing amounts necessary for unemployment relief made any calculations as to the future budget altogether questionable.

Such being the situation, the urgent necessity of the hour was to put on the brake and check the ever accelerating downward movement, if the State, if industry, were not to collapse inevitably.

What had been found to be the necessary course for Austria to follow in 1922 had to be repeated ten years later. In 1932 the Chancellor of Austria turned to the League of Nations again, but this time not like a petitioner who had, first of all, to furnish evidence of his reliability before claiming a little confidence on account. Ten years during which Seipel's work of reconstruction had been carried on lay between, and Austria could point out that she had kept all her promises, had a long record of self-sacrificing work to her credit, had invariably acknowledged her debts, and, political difficulties at home notwithstanding, had never repudiated the moral code of the borrower. But now she found herself battling with a gale of catastrophic force, which did not spare bigger and wealthier countries either. Austria's plea was, indeed, not the plea of a beggar in despair, for she was in a position to put forward reasoned proposals which could be worked out in the interests of creditor and debtor alike.

These proposals raised issues of trade policy first and then issues of financial policy. Only the modification (it was argued) of the rigid "Favoured-Nation Clause," as laid down in the peace treaty, together with the granting of mutual preferences, could open up new markets, revive international trade, and in that way save Austrian industrial production from the collapse threatening it—a collapse the consequences of which would not be limited to Austria. From the standpoint of financial policy, the efforts to obtain another international loan were comprehensible, as otherwise it would not have been possible to continue the interest of the old loan nor keep up the currency—and again Austria would not have been the only sufferer.

Certainly it would have been easy to take up the attitude that all transfers of payment abroad should simply be blocked on the plea that a state of emergency existed in Austria. Political propaganda later on made great play with this idea and there was, as a fact, much in it that might have proved attractive to persons who did not perceive its implications or take the trouble to contemplate the problem as a whole. After all, the popular comparison between Austria and other countries merely led to confusion. It is true that many another country in a situation similar to our own at that time decided for the drastic measure of suspending all payments abroad; but the law of nature that unequal sizes are not to be compared with one another holds true of nations as of individual objects.

There are countries which are able in essentials to support their own people by their proper resources or have to make no legal provision for their unemployed, either because industrial production, and therefore the labour question, do not have a decisive part in their economy, or because they have no reason to fear, on other grounds, that unemployment might endanger the budget and the State itself. There are countries as well whose foreign tourist industry is of no importance and which do not attach great weight to international trade and free and undisturbed communications. Countries, in a word, which live in a quite different political and economic atmosphere from Austria's might perhaps decide on the total suspension of foreign payments with a lighter heart.

But in Austria things were essentially otherwise, quite apart from the mortgage rights which encumbered the revenues from specific monopolies, safeguarding the interest service in respect of earlier international loans. Hundreds of reasons spoke for the honouring of the obligations that had been assumed as far as the limits of the possible; and that not only because of considerations of prestige and because the national credit was at stake. There were many other reasons why Austria should refrain from the step of suspending foreign payments, and not only on account of the general ethical rule which requires integrity from the State as well as from individuals.

Austria had to consider that for the feeding of her population and the maintenance of employment she had to rely upon harmonious relations with other lands, that tourist traffic was in increasing measure of economic importance for large areas of a country so rich in natural beauties and charm. The last but not the least consideration influencing the government's attitude in this matter was that, by reason of the high cultural and educational level of Austria's population and her social and political institutions, she required from the State a certain amount of financial support which in no circumstances could be substantially reduced if grave political convulsions leading to a general conflagration were to be avoided. And when a conflagration does break out, it is notoriously difficult to prevent it from spreading.

For that reason a comparison between the year 1922 and the year 1932, in connection with Austria's appeal to the League, is not in the least far-fetched. On each occasion everything was at stake—the preservation of the State, the maintenance of a minimum standard of living for all classes, the laying of foundations for the reconstruction of the country, and for a gradual improvement of the condition of the population.

The contrast between the way the political parties treated the appeal to the League in 1922 and the similar step in 1932 furnished convincing evidence of the lack of objectivity and therefore the inadequacy displayed by Parliament. To be or not to be was the issue on each occasion. The deputies who should have looked after the interests, not of the political parties, but of the nation as a whole, should assuredly have felt themselves impelled to forgo agitation and suspend the struggle for power in order to rally to the idea of saving the State itself, an idea which should have taken precedence of every other consideration. This attitude, clearly, would have been encouraged had the conception "Fatherland" been substituted for the conception "State," but until the year 1932 this word "Fatherland" had no great vogue in Austria.

Thus from the way in which Parliament handled on different occasions the vital bills dealing with international loans—the one arranged at Geneva, the other of Lausanne —the following considerations suggest themselves:

In the year 1922 the Socialists were hostile to the idea of a loan and denounced Seipel as a traitor for (as they alleged) bartering away the liberty of the land and accepting a bondage insufferable for a people of German race. The Pan-Germans, who at that time were on the side of the government, entertained no national misgivings regarding the loan and supported Chancellor Seipel.

In the year 1932 the Socialists again opposed the new loan, but on this occasion only because the rules of the parliamentary game required their opposition. The reproach that the government was betraying national interests was put forward with the same arguments as in 1922, but this time it came from the Pan-German benches in Parliament. The Pan-Germans, indeed, now sponsored exactly the same reproaches which had been uttered to satiety in speeches from the Socialist benches ten years earlier.

Nevertheless a difference was to be noted: In May 1932 the Socialists were doubtless in their hearts in favour of the bill, because for them, too, as masters of the municipality of Vienna, too much was at stake for a different line to be favoured. Similarly, the indignation they had displayed in the year 1922 had not been altogether genuine and was regarded as means to an end only, for, after all, though the debate in Parliament turned out to be an extremely shabby business, the passage of the bill was not prevented. On the other hand, the indignation of the Pan-Germans in 1932 was undoubtedly sincere and they left no weapon unused to defeat the bill.

But it was not quite clear why the 640,000,000 gold kronen involved in the year 1922 should have been, from the national standpoint, judged differently from the 300,-000,000 schillings of which there was question in the year 1932, unless it was that the attitude in each case reflected the political atmosphere which prevailed in Berlin.

The Austrian government announced in 1932, as it had announced in 1922, and as it had proved during the toilsome years of labour and development, that Austria's attitude in the fundamental issue of her cultural relations with Germany would never change. The difference in outlook lay in this: that we held not only that the German feeling and the promotion of the national idea in Austria were in harmony with the affirmation of the idea of the Fatherland, but that the maintenance of the State and the improvement of the conditions of life of our people were an essential condition for such a feeling.

The efforts of Chancellor Buresch to open up new ways in the fields of trade and financial policy alike did not at first meet with success. Tension in the country grew, crippling the action of the government; and so, towards the end of January 1932, a reconstruction of the cabinet took place.

The Pan-Germans insisted that Schober, until then Vice-Chancellor, should remain on at the Foreign Office. Chancellor Buresch resisted this plan, for in the circumstances he saw no way out of difficulties nor prospects of success. As a consequence the Pan-Germans went into opposition, and their action shattered the disposition of forces dominating the parliamentary picture since Seipel's day. A new phase of political development had begun.

On January 27, 1932 the Chancellor surprised me by asking whether I would be prepared to take the Ministry of Justice in his cabinet. I hesitated in the first instance, for I regarded it as important to get into touch with my political friends in the Tyrol, since without their express consent it would have been futile to accept the Chancellor's offer, more particularly as it was clear to me from the outset that work in a "minority cabinet" neither held out great promise of success nor was likely to be of long duration. I begged the Chancellor to get in touch himself with Innsbruck and assured him I would be at his disposition if the leaders of my party in the Tyrol approved of the proposal. Precisely this party had taken up, just previously, a somewhat critical attitude to the government and to the Chancellor personally.

Two conversations had led me to take up the position I have just explained. The first was with Seipel, who at that time was about to start on his trip to the south, where he hoped for relaxation and the restoration of his health. Seipel counselled me to take the Ministry of Justice, saying it meant a fine task and that I was well able to master the problems it presented. It was, he said, of the utmost importance to keep a straight political course just now.

The second conversation was with Dr. Dollfuss, then Minister of Agriculture, whom I had known from former days, but with whom I was not in close touch, though we were on good terms personally. In his impulsive way he dispersed my doubts; and I had, besides, the impression very

clearly that he wished, through me, to tie the Alpine provinces of the west closer to the government, more particularly the Tyroleans so readily disposed to restlessness. Dollfuss was then taken up with the new ideas and plans which
were to lead to the opening up of agrarian and trade ways
hitherto untrod and to the alleviation of the misery of the
peasants; and he tackled his work with the energy and great
sense of responsibility that were all his own. As an expert
in agrarian questions and as an economist he had long had
an international reputation.

From that day onwards our common path bound me to
Engelbert Dollfuss, whom I valued as man, comrade, and
leader equally and who stood by me just as I followed him
unconditionally and in many places as a loyal comrade-in-
arms. This relationship was never influenced by the efforts
of people to divide us. To those people he, like myself, always turned deaf ears.

Work in the Ministry of Justice was arduous, for difficulties arose in all departments there and sometimes I wondered whether it was worth while going on with the work.

I was still animated by the idea that my activities at the
Ministry would be but provisional and I counted so little
on any prolonged stay in Vienna that I did not take a permanent apartment there nor give up my home in Innsbruck.

In the Ministry of Justice at that time two main problems
had come to the foreground. Of these the first was the
assimilation of the Austrian legal code to that of Germany.
To this problem I devoted great attention, more particularly as I have always held the view that the common foundations of culture and the same racial stock should, wherever it was possible, also find expression in a common

written legal code. The second problem involved the reform of penal law, a task which had for generations been on the agenda in Austria, but the solution of which had always been prevented by one political difficulty or another.

Moreover, the continual discoveries of hoards of hidden arms then occupied the mind of the public to an increasing extent. It was a question not only of concealed stocks of rifles and machine-guns but also of quantities of explosives, the existence of which, more especially in a large city such as Vienna, was a constant source of danger.

The statement of policy of the reconstituted Buresch government (which no longer had a majority in Parliament) furnished no sensations, and the debate on it in the Nationalrat was equally colourless. Dr. Robert Danneberg, who spoke for the Socialists, dealt in detail with, among other matters, the political implications of my membership in the government. Controverting the view of a Christian Socialist newspaper, he said that "the confidential man of Professor Seipel" had joined the second Buresch cabinet and that he had been invited to do so in order to prevent the plan of disarming the Heimatschutz being carried through. Dr. Danneberg further complained that the new Minister "had quite frankly acknowledged it as a sacred obligation to annul the laws of expropriation against the Habsburgs"; and further that "he had asserted that the Monarchy was better than the present constitution, and that he would leave the Christian Socialist Party if monarchists were to be debarred from membership." These fears of the Minister, the Socialist spokesman went on ironically, were altogether groundless; for not only did the Christian Socialist Party not debar monarchists, but it even put them on the government bench and made them custodians of the republican laws. Because the Minister had taken a degree in law the government had made him Minister of Justice, although he did not fit that post in any way.

It was to be foreseen that the prospects of work for a "minority cabinet" would be limited as to time; and in effect this government was not in a position to get the better of the steadily growing domestic antagonisms, although it was at pains, in the spirit of complete impartiality, to deal with misdeeds and excesses, whether of the Right or of the Left, in accordance with precisely the same standards.

These infractions steadily increased in number, and incidents which had been unknown since the days of the revolution again became almost part of the day's cares. There were clashes in which opposing parties faced one another weapons in hand, and here and there loss of life had to be deplored. More and more violent did the methods of political controversy become among the extreme wings, one of which was the rising National-Socialist movement, the other the republican Schutzbund of the Socialist Party. Both were provided with weapons, and in addition the Schutzbund had regular military leadership. To an extent that aroused anxiety, the influences of political extremism grew in the administration, in the army, and in the police as well. For that reason the clamour to ban politics from within the armed forces and to carry through the long promised reform of the civil service would not abate.

In the spring of 1932, in the midst of an atmosphere charged with tension, the Vienna municipal elections were held, with the result that a group of fifteen National-Socialists entered the municipal council. The elections for the provincial diets in Salzburg and Lower Austria, in which the National-Socialists gained isolated successes, together with the new composition of the Vienna municipality, led to a change in the state of parties in the Bundesrat, then the representation of the provinces.

In the Nationalrat Dr. Otto Bauer, the Socialist leader, then ostentatiously proposed the dissolution of Parliament and the holding of new elections. The Pan-Germans brought forward a motion in the same sense and eventually the Heimat bloc declared themselves in agreement with it. On May 6 Chancellor Buresch handed in the resignation of the government—a step which caused political tension to reach the highest pitch.

On the one hand the aggressive National-Socialists, supported by a majority in the Nationalrat, pressed for the immediate holding of new elections, elections which in the circumstances then prevailing would have caused convulsions of the gravest character. Such convulsions, indeed, must have meant the downfall of the State. The game which was to be played was clear. Public opinion was to be worn down as the result of successive motions in favour of a dissolution, by a series of actual elections, by the exploitation of the industrial depression and the general dissatisfaction. In all this, naturally, there was no thought of economic reconstruction, of a foreign loan, or of the conclusion of trade treaties. Admittedly the National-Socialists in clamouring for democratic and parliamentary rights only regarded democracy as a means to an end, for their program postulated the disappearance of democracy and Parliament, once they gained power.

The alternative was to give free scope to the struggle of the political forces, and that would probably have meant civil war or, at least, the certainty of economic collapse; or, on the other hand, to postpone the settlement of the political controversies, to establish a firm and responsible government, and to set about the work of reconstruction. If the preservation of Austria were the aim in view, then, clearly, the second solution had to be decided for. Whoever stood for the first course premeditated the end of Austria or was too short-sighted to perceive the inevitable consequences.

At this moment the President of the Republic commissioned Engelbert Dollfuss with the difficult task of forming the new government. Dollfuss had come from the so-called National Catholic camp. As a young man he himself had studied in Berlin, and in Catholic academic circles he was always looked on as the spokesman of intimate co-operation with Germany. The idea that Austria and Germany were bound together by a common destiny was part of his flesh and blood to such an extent that Austrians of conservative disposition sometimes fancied him to be among their opponents.

He came of Lower Austrian peasant stock, and sound democratic instincts were therefore natural to him. At the moment when he was summoned to assume the highest responsibility, no doubts beset him. Despite his race-consciousness as a German, he was an Austrian and he saw in the preservation of Austria the purpose, and the fulfilment, of his task.

Fourteen anxious days long lasted his efforts to get together a government that would be viable. I was a party, together with Carl Vaugoin, Minister and chairman of the Christian Socialists, to almost all those day-and-night negotiations. I am convinced that the persevering resolution of Dollfuss alone prevented the failure of his mission. I can recall very clearly how I thought more than once in those days that, had I been in Dollfuss's place, I would long before have gone back to the President to explain my inability to fulfil the mission I had been entrusted with. Until that hour I had valued Dollfuss, but after that I marvelled at him.

Dollfuss, in his first effort, set about forming a government of the four non-Socialist parties—Christian Socialists, Agricultural League, Pan-Germans, and Heimat bloc. The consent of the Christian Socialists and the Agrarians was soon forthcoming, and the Heimat bloc, under Starhemberg's leadership, were also won over to co-operate. On the other hand, serious difficulties were met from the outset during the negotiations with the Pan-Germans. More than once it seemed as though an agreement had already been reached and yet a few hours later there would come a refusal together with new and unacceptable proposals. Finally a pause was agreed upon, during which Dollfuss still thought of persisting in his efforts to persuade the Pan-Germans to co-operate.

On May 12 the *Neues Wiener Journal* published an editorial which attracted great attention. Therein it was maintained that it was impossible for Dollfuss to form a government and that there could only be a question of a cabinet with Dr. Rintelen as Chancellor. The editor-in-chief of the *Neues Wiener Journal* at that time was Dr. Nagelstock, a personal friend of Dr. Rintelen.

Disregarding the different cross-shots aimed at him from all sides, Dollfuss went on negotiating, and after some ten days he had almost reached an arrangement, when, in the early hours of May 19, a new and unexpected crisis suddenly broke out.

The editorial of the *Neues Wiener Journal* had not been

written by chance. In a letter the Heimat bloc in effect put
forward the demand for the chancellorship of Dr. Rintelen,
with the remark that otherwise there could be no question
of political co-operation. This unexpected issue was due to
the threat of a group of Heimwehr organizations in Styria
to resign from the general association. This group had two
representatives in Parliament, upon whom the government's majority might depend. In the course of subsequent
events this Styrian group of the Heimwehr went over to
National-Socialism.

The crisis was got over in the sense that Dollfuss declared
himself ready to take Rintelen into the cabinet, and the
question of what office he should hold was left over for decision later. In the first instance it was intended that Rintelen should have the Ministry of Justice, but his advisers
asserted that this Ministry did not offer Rintelen, who had
formerly been Minister of Education, sufficient scope for
his powers; and so he was appointed again to the latter post,
keeping at the same time, as he had stipulated, his position
as Governor of Styria.

Until the last minute the situation seemed uncertain, yet
Dollfuss was determined, cost what it might, to achieve his
goal. In effect he was able at length—on May 21, after fourteen days' efforts—to form a government. This government
found itself confronted, at the very outset, with tasks of the
utmost difficulty. The crisis came to an end just in time,
for its persistence must have had incalculable consequences
to Austria's economic system.

On May 27, 1932 Chancellor Dollfuss presented his cabinet to the Nationalrat and on this occasion he made his
first appearance before the great public with a striking
declaration of government policy. In his speech he ex-

pressed regret first of all that he had not been able in an hour of crisis to associate all the non-Socialist parties in Parliament in a common task. While deploring that fact, he promised to continue his efforts to the same end.

"Austria," continued the Chancellor, "judged by the spirit of her people and her modest military equipment, is one of the most pacific countries in the world. She has striven and will continue to strive to live in peace and friendship with all her neighbours, with other European states, and with the world in general. At the same time the world must and will recognize that we, as an independent German state, conditioned by our blood, history, and geographical position, are conscious of our links and friendship with the German Reich. That friendship gives us rights as well as duties."

Later in his declaration the Chancellor dealt with the urgent economic questions and in particular he discussed concrete proposals of trade policy, in the course of which he broke a lance in favour of granting preferences in the central European area. In lucid phrases he made it plain that in no circumstances would the government relapse into the abuse of the bank-note printing-press and that the maintenance of an absolutely balanced budget was to be regarded as supreme law. At the same time he laid special stress upon the government's concern for the workers, manual and "white-collar," which concern, more particularly as regards unemployment, he characterized as among the State's most vital problems. Dollfuss on this occasion spoke almost extempore. Not without emotion can one read today the sentences with which he closed his first great speech in Parliament:

"Thus I stand before you, ladies [1] and gentlemen, in the name of the government, resolutely determined to shirk no personal sacrifice of time and labour, conscious of the oath I have taken before the President of the Republic, conscious also of the grave responsibility the present government bears in a time when everything depends on our economic recovery—our home affairs as well as our destiny with regard to foreign relations. Not only to our friends but to you all, honourable members of this House, do I address this appeal: Recognize with us the gravity of the hour and cooperate with us. Otherwise I fear the fate of our country has reached a crucial point."

Dr. Otto Bauer, the Socialist, as first opposition speaker, gave the answer to the Chancellor's appeal. He ended his speech thus: "We are ready to work that this land may be saved from the terrible economic fate still threatening it. But for this task, for the task of facilitating the formation of a government which could really assemble all the great and vital forces of the country, we regard as an essential condition a bitter, decisive, and ruthless struggle against this government, which is, in our eyes, an obstacle to Austria's recovery. On that account I beg to propose this resolution: That the Nationalrat refuses its confidence to the federal government."

Dr. Straffner, who spoke for the Pan-Germans, frankly admitted that the Chancellor's declaration of policy deviated from the usual form which in general suggested the compilation from different ministries. The government's statement, he said, was in a way a homogeneous whole which

---

[1] The Austrian election laws allowed women to vote and to have seats in Parliament. There were women deputies in almost every party represented in the Nationalrat.—TRANSLATOR.

through and through, from beginning to end, expressed a marked personality. He hoped the Chancellor would impose his program upon his own followers. The orator was bound to say that he heard the news, but so far he did not believe that the Chancellor would succeed in carrying through his program with his own party.

But Engelbert Dollfuss was bent, all difficulties notwithstanding, on pushing through his policy. In a conversation I had with him on one occasion during his first months as Chancellor he told me he always relied on his instinct, which rarely deceived him. He had from the first the feeling that he would be Chancellor for either a very short or a very long time. He was quite confident of being able to overcome all difficulties, though he could not say how it would work out in each individual case. This conversation took place in the middle of the fight over the "Lausanne loan."

Why that loan was necessary has been discussed in an earlier chapter. That, in view of the circumstances of the time, the loan could be obtained at all was a personal success for the Chancellor, who, in common with Dr. Kienböck, the president of the National Bank, had made every effort to bring it about.

In the course of the struggle over the loan the cleavage among the non-Socialist parties deepened rapidly. Already in June the Pan-Germans tabled a motion of no confidence in the government. A series of most remarkable coincidences enabled Dollfuss to overcome this and subsequent parliamentary difficulties, despite the utmost danger.

In the early hours of the day of the vote in Parliament, August 2, 1932, Seipel died, and in the afternoon the division on the "no-confidence" resolution took place in the Nationalrat. Had Seipel still been alive, his vote would have been wanting and there would, in all probability, have been a majority for the resolution of "no confidence." But in the last minute Dr. Seipel's successor [1] in the Nationalrat was called in, the division resulted in a tie—81 to 81—and according to the rules of the Austrian Parliament the resolution was declared lost and the resignation of the government avoided. It is deeply moving to recall how the one-time leader had by his own death in a decisive hour intervened as a deliverer.

The division on the vital "Lausanne Agreement" in the Nationalrat took an equally dramatic form. On August 17 the Nationalrat had ratified the Agreement by 81 votes to 80. The ayes were made up of 66 Christian Socialists, 9 members of the Agricultural League, and 6 members of the Heimat bloc; the two other members of the Heimat bloc, who belonged to the Styrian movement, voted on this occasion with the opposition. Subsequently the Bundesrat, where the government had no majority, had made use of its constitutional powers and imposed a veto against the ratification of the Lausanne Agreement by the Nationalrat. In the Bundesrat there were 22 Christian Socialists, 22 Socialists, 3 National-Socialists, 1 Pan-German, 1 representative of the Agricultural League, and 1 of the Heimat bloc.

The Socialist speaker recognized in principle the usefulness of the Lausanne Agreement, but the decision of his party to vote against the motion had already been taken. The veto of the Bundesrat had no great importance, as by the terms of the constitution the bill had to go back to the Nationalrat, which then had the opportunity of passing a

---

[1] Under the Austrian parliamentary law, when a seat in Parliament became vacant, it was automatically taken by the candidate of the same party next on the party electoral list.—TRANSLATOR.

resolution overriding the veto and giving definite legal sanction to its own previous vote.

The second sitting of the Nationalrat took place on August 23. In the meantime all forces had been mobilized by the opposition in order to prevent the passing of the overriding resolution. Influences from all sides, from within Austria and from beyond her frontiers, were brought into play, and their task it was, at all costs, to stamp the Lausanne Agreement as a national perjury.

The *Frankfurter Zeitung* and the *Berliner Tageblatt,* which even before had spread the most malicious reports about the schilling currency, then published from their correspondents in Vienna extremely bitter and misleading reports; and in this connection it may be remarked that long before the National-Socialists attained power, both these newspapers, though clearly not on "ideological" grounds, had taken up a pronounced anti-Austrian attitude. Their Vienna representatives then expounded a political standpoint diametrically opposed to the one they are now required by their country to champion.

The following incident throws a very effective light upon the methods adopted in this conflict: In a series of public demonstrations and resolutions the biggest and most esteemed economic bodies in Austria came forward, on comprehensive grounds, to insist on the necessity of the Lausanne loan. One of these organizations had in their employ a press officer who incidentally also had a post at the Vienna offices of an important German newspaper and book-publishing concern, besides being the correspondent of a dozen or so German newspapers. This industrial organization came out in favour of the Lausanne Agreement at an imposing public demonstration which it organized, whereas their press officer, who himself may have arranged that very demonstration, at the same time published in his German newspapers violent articles against the same Agreement. The indignation over the "Dictate of Lausanne" was thus obviously a worked-up piece of tactics and had no solid foundation whatever. The decisive vote resulted in 82 ayes and 80 noes, thus assuring a majority for the Lausanne Agreement.

Another suggestive incident deserves to be mentioned in this connection because it throws effective light upon the difficulties confronting the Chancellor at that time. Ex-Chancellor Schober had, for a time, united under his leadership the Pan-Germans and the Agricultural League. A deputy belonging to this Schober group, Vinzl by name, held a considerable position in the business world, being chairman of the Merchants' Association of Vienna. This deputy was sick and had gone to a sanatorium outside Vienna. He was in an extremely awkward position, for while the Merchants' Association which he represented was, for sound business reasons, in favour of the Lausanne Agreement, he, as a member of the Pan-German Party, to whom the Agreement was as a red rag to a bull, was required to vote against the motion for its ratification. By his absence from Vienna he hoped to extricate himself from the dilemma. The nature of his sickness alone, according to the general practice, would scarcely have excused his absence from Parliament on the occasion of the vote and he was pressed by his party to resign his seat so that his successor might vote with the opposition against the motion. In fact Herr Vinzl was induced to write a letter of resignation, and even before it reached its destination, his parliamentary substitute was called to Vienna. But when the Merchants'

Association heard of the affair, they intervened with their chairman to withdraw his resignation. In fact the deputy did so by telephone. The Pan-Germans, whose plan had thus been foiled, at once took the field against the Chancellor, whom they made responsible for the deputy's withdrawal of his resignation. Dollfuss, however, announced publicly that he learned of both the original offer to resign and its subsequent withdrawal only afterwards.

This incident might be regarded as evidence of how incompetent formalistic parliamentarism had become in Austria. But apart from this, an extraordinary hazard—others might call it a higher dispensation—played a part in those fateful days.

On August 19, 1932 Schober died. Four days afterwards the overriding resolution came up in the Nationalrat, the parliamentary successor of the deceased being among the deputies. But according to an arrangement made at an earlier date between the two parties which Schober had succeeded in uniting, this successor was a member, not of the Pan-Germans, but of the Agricultural League. Since in the meantime the League had been won over by Dollfuss to co-operate, his presence in Parliament meant an additional vote for the government.

By the way, this sitting of the Nationalrat furnished clear evidence that the Socialists were, from the outset, not very serious in their opposition to the loan. Under the terms of the constitution the presence of at least fifty per cent of the deputies was required for the Nationalrat to pass the overriding resolution. As there were 165 members in all, 83 would have to be present. The government disposed of 82 votes only and so it would have been possible for the Socialists, by absenting themselves from the Chamber, to prevent a quorum and therefore to frustrate the overriding resolution.

On the other hand, the Elections Appeal Board had decreed that there was no reason for a decision against Herr Vinzl's membership (on account of his resignation, immediately withdrawn) and so, after all the conceivable obstacles raised by the opposition in the path of the Chancellor had been surmounted, the much contested loan was assured.

Its rejection would have been, without any doubt, a disaster for our country. Whoever wanted such rejection was clearly quite determined to bring about the destruction of Austria. I do not doubt that grounds of idealism were behind this standpoint also; yet not all ideals are simultaneously wise and reasonable. One thing is beyond dispute— had the loan been rejected, no national interest would have been by any means served, for the inevitable consequence would have been the progressive misery of the country, oppressive dependence on foreign countries and, indeed, by no means on the German Reich alone. One of the chief reasons for the loan was to consolidate a short-term credit of 100,000,000 schillings (14,700,000 dollars at the old par), to be paid back to the Bank of England. Moreover, the rejection of the loan must have led to a further curtailment of national expenditure to the amount of 150,000,000 schillings (22,050,000 dollars), and that postulated new economies, additional taxes, and more dismissals and cuts in wages. The closing down of factories and the increase in unemployment—inevitable consequences of the rejection of the loan, too—would even have brought into the zone of insolvency the whole ingeniously constructed edifice of social welfare. Besides all that, the maintenance of the most rigid exchange control would have been unavoidable, and that must have had a withering effect not only on trade in general, but, more particularly, upon Austria's foreign tourist industry.

Subsequent events showed that the ratification of the Lausanne Agreement not only was unavoidable and justified, but was of decisive importance and advantage for Austria's development. Even if nothing more than the strengthening and stabilization of the currency had been attained and the foundations laid for the floating of an internal loan to finance provision-of-work schemes, then its purpose must be regarded as completely achieved.

The conditions of the loan were altogether acceptable and could not be compared with those required from us for the loan arranged at Geneva in 1922. We were required to balance the budget, to make outgoings and incomings tally in the administration of the federal railways, to assure the stability of the currency, to complete the reconstruction of the Credit-Anstalt, to agree to the accrediting of a representative of the League of Nations with the Austrian government, and an adviser to the National Bank, to give a stipulation that new loans would have the approval of the Control Committee of the League. Further, the Austrian government had to promise that provinces and municipalities would balance their budgets, and, lastly, there was the obligation to report to the National Bank any private credit transaction abroad exceeding one million schillings.

As regards the financial conditions, they must be described as pronouncedly favourable in view of the position at the time. The reproach that by signing the Lausanne Agreement we forfeited our national liberty, because this Agreement renewed the recognition of the Geneva Protocol of the year 1922 and the stipulation that Austria must enter into no agreements endangering her economic independence, is beyond doubt misleading. The very people who make this approach realize only too well that the question of Austria's independence is not so much a matter of treaties and legal obligations as one of political power and will. Quite apart from that, the assertion that by the Agreement of Lausanne a political obligation more far-reaching than the Protocol of Geneva had been taken over by Austria is materially false and not to be maintained theoretically or practically.

With the settlement of this thorny problem Engelbert Dollfuss opened the way leading to economic reconstruction. The first and most vital foundation stone of his burdensome and decisive work had been laid with success. Now it was a question, in the carefully thought-out work of economic reconstruction, to rebuild the economic foundations of the country. This had to be done at a moment when the industrial world crisis had just passed its climax. At the same time the government had to confront, with energy and decisive action, the general excitement prevailing in domestic politics.

When the year 1932 came to its end, it could be clearly seen that the conflict which had arisen in Austria surpassed by far the limits of discussions about the preponderance of this or that party, about parliamentarism and its merits or demerits, about a possible reform of the democratic system. The issue of this conflict was the existence of Austria as a state, as a nation.

CHAPTER TWELVE

Trips to Germany

THUS the first months of the Dollfuss government had been characterized by a continuous struggle to get the better of the difficulties in Parliament. Again and again did the cabinet only just succeed in overcoming dangers which might have been fatal; sometimes, indeed, it did so as the result of events which had not been anticipated and had to be looked on, as it were, as acts of providence. The Chancellor's perseverance in negotiating, which bordered on the incredible, contributed not least to that success.

Had the battle been given up prematurely, had the way to office thus been opened for other political parties, this would, first of all, have meant giving up the Lausanne loan once and for all. That, in turn, would have led to chaos in the economic field, and no doubt in the political field also. The blame would certainly have been put on those who had offered unbending opposition to the idea of reconstruction, contrary to sound sense, but it would also have been extended to those who deserted their posts in the hour of danger.

Dollfuss knew that, and that was why he remained on. He allowed himself to be called now a traitor, now a leech; to have his name besmirched in a manner hitherto unheard of; to have his intentions and convictions misinterpreted. That was why he embarked on the fight which was sure to seem hopeless, both at home and abroad. What gave him the necessary strength was his thorough conviction of the rightness of the way he had chosen and his determination to save Austria, his belief in his country and her mission of freedom. The more violently the waves of assault rolled up against the pillars of his activities, the clearer he felt within him the sense of an inescapable mission to accomplish, in a decisive hour, a historical task.

"The country must live, though we must die!" This intuition, meaning more to him than a mere rhetorical axiom, represented his deepest feeling and recurred repeatedly in his speeches as early as the second half of the year 1932.

Some members of his cabinet, too, were soon confronted with fundamental issues beyond the narrow range of their departmental duties, issues the solution of which was exacted by the new time in conditions quite different from those prevailing in the past.

At the outset the government had, of course, preserved the distinctive character of a coalition and it often proved difficult to get unanimity at cabinet meetings. Nobody thought at that time of eliminating Parliament or of attempting equally drastic solutions of the crisis of democracy; to appeal to the parties, not to get rid of them, was the catchword first raised.

But everyone recognized that the country, bleeding as it was with a hundred recent gashes, could not afford the luxury of continued electoral conflicts without incurring heavy damage; and that, besides, the epoch of governmental crises had to come to an end, at least temporarily. Since the resignation of Seipel in the spring of 1929 (that is, just three years before) there had been six changes in the chancellorship, and each time the change occurred in a state of imminent danger.

In addition to parliamentary combats, Dollfuss had thus to keep up a common front within the cabinet, and this he could only achieve by frequent shifts and bargains. That common front within the cabinet was menaced by clashes not only between Heimat bloc and Agrarian League, but also between these and various groups of the Christian Socialists. But on one question at any rate there was no divergence of opinion in the cabinet—on the necessity and importance of keeping as good and close relations with the German Reich as possible. Not a single voice was raised to advocate any other kind of foreign policy, and in particular it was the Chancellor's view that the "German course" was self-evident and must be beyond debate.

A thousand ties, some of a purely sentimental nature, bound Dollfuss to the Reich. Though he was free of the Austrian tendency to lack self-confidence and to be apt to extol everything existing beyond the borders, still he was bound up with the idea and conviction of a common German destiny and culture.

In fact, with the cultivation of the idea last mentioned I, too, was repeatedly concerned, both in my official capacity and unofficially. Even at the risk of being misunderstood in my own country by the over-timid, I had spoken over and over again on the problems of "all-German" thought, spirit, and cultural ties.

At one time repeated trips had led me into neighbouring Bavaria, where I had personal friends among the younger generation who had been in the war and were then active politicians. Even these relations with members of the Bavarian People's Party (Bayrische Volkspartei) were sometimes viewed with suspicion on different sides.

There is one thing I wish to stress: Not in a single instance did I come across separatist plans or wishes. There have been differences between the Prussian and Bavarian standpoints as to constitutional rights or State finances, but on the part of all the people I met, absolute loyalty to the Reich was axiomatic and beyond debate.

Especially the so-called "Main-Danube Line" danger,[1] which was occasionally trotted out in the course of political controversy in order to cast suspicion upon an opponent, is in my opinion nothing but the malicious invention of some political visionaries who made it their task to insinuate into natural personal relations a political program. Such trends of thought, on mature consideration, can only be dismissed as ridiculous. The charge of disloyalty seems to be particularly unjust when it is applied to German Catholicism. Still less, of course, has a plan ever existed in Austria for what has been termed the "Catholic South German" solution of the German question at the expense of the Reich. Nor have I ever found anyone who took such an idea seriously or thought it worth discussing.

[1] The rivers Main and Danube indicate a sort of spiritual border between the southern, mostly Catholic, and the northern, mostly Protestant, parts of Germany. There had been tendencies, from time to time, within German and particularly within foreign political circles to set up a southern Reich.— TRANSLATOR.

During the Lausanne negotiations Dollfuss had met Herr von Papen, then German Chancellor, and both of us had met him a year before at the Congress of the Christian Socialist Party at Klagenfurt, where von Papen had represented the German Centre Party. The two men seemed to get on well together.

Dollfuss attached the utmost importance to personal relations, to man-to-man talks, to spontaneous impressions. This spontaneity went so far that he, impulsive, eager, and decisive, was apt at times to resort to improvisation.

The German Catholic Congress had been arranged for Essen in September 1932, and I gladly accepted an invitation to deliver an address at one of the great meetings of this Congress. I did so with the utmost pleasure because the impression of the Catholic Congress at Frankfurt am Main, in 1921, which I was privileged to attend immediately on finishing my university studies, was still vivid with me; and further because I was particularly interested in visiting the Ruhr district, hitherto quite new to me. Incidentally, I thought it very desirable to get into touch with Catholic circles in Germany, more particularly as inarticulate divergencies of opinion had aroused interest among Austrian Catholics, and enlightenment on the point was needed by a personal exchange of views.

For all the similarity in the great questions involving world outlook and for all the self-evident recognition of a common race, the feeling among Catholics in Austria differed markedly from that which prevailed in the Catholic centres of western Germany. Precisely because of that, it was important to take susceptibilities into account if misunderstandings and defective judgment were to be avoided. I remember very well how in earlier years, when arranging gatherings of a joint religious and general outlook, the "Baroque Catholicism" of Austria was at times severely handled. Bruckner's Mass, sung at a meeting of the German-Catholic Academic Union at Innsbruck, was regarded by the clergy who had come from the north and west of Germany as a profanation of the ecclesiastical spirit and as a mere item in a concert program. That being so, it was not to be wondered at if we were anxious about our Haydn, Mozart, or Schubert, without whom Catholicism in Austria was not to be thought of.

Even our special prayers in May, with devotion to the Blessed Virgin as their outstanding feature, one of the most tender religious traditions of our Alpine provinces and deeply rooted in the soul of the nation, were apt to meet with doubts and objections on the part of the Germans. A young priest, one of the members of the Congress, assured me that we Austrians were too superficial, given too much to sensual impressions, and therefore dangerously near the world of heathen ideas. Naturally I contradicted him vehemently.

With all the keener expectation, therefore, did I look forward to the great Catholic Congress in the Rhineland. The subjects to be debated were exclusively religious, and great pains were taken to avoid references to politics. My own task was to speak on "Christ in the Modern Metropolis."

A few days before setting out for the Congress the Chancellor let me know that he, too, proposed to go to Essen. Dollfuss was going there, he explained, not as head of the Austrian government, but as a Catholic who made a point of being present at this, the greatest manifestation of faith on the part of the German people. He asked me whether I was ready to travel with him by plane, and of course I agreed, though I was not particularly pleased with the idea, for I had been looking forward to the journey by train. Besides, flying at that time in Austria was not considered everybody's pleasure. A small single-engined machine, seating four people, and later on used by the Chancellor in his flights across the Alps to Rome, took us by way of Munich and Frankfurt am Main to Essen, where we were given a hearty reception.

The following days were such as to impress us deeply; indeed, they were really unforgettable days. From the spiritual and technical standpoints alike the Congress was marvellously organized. There was not the least friction; all the differences I have referred to already as jarring upon our minds in Innsbruck seemed to have vanished; there was one deep harmony of the Catholic spirit, satisfying to mind and heart alike.

Behind the scenes, it is true, here and there faint shadows were to be perceived. Thus an address by Dr. Brüning, the former Chancellor, had been announced, and Herr von Papen, then Chancellor, himself a Westphalian Catholic, had also been invited to be present. Thereupon Brüning, we were told, refused to appear if the Chancellor was to come, while Herr von Papen declared that he was not prepared to take instructions from anybody. Whatever may have really happened, the upshot was that neither Brüning nor von Papen turned up.

Dollfuss was warmly welcomed among the circles of Catholic university people, and he, in his turn, seized the opportunity of emphasizing the ties that bound him to the German people. He spoke of Vienna as of the second German city and invited the German Catholics to hold their next congress there. This suggestion met with enthusiasm and when we Austrians left the Congress, in excellent spirits, our friends expressed the hope to see us again in the following year.

Another deep impression left on my mind by this trip to Essen was a visit to the Krupp works, which I was shown over in a most courteous manner. I saw the Ruhr coalfields and took a drive by car to Cologne, that memorable and marvellous city.

Scarcely more than three months later I travelled to Germany again; that was the time when we still thought it possible to complete the reform of our criminal law and at the same time establish a penal code common to Germany and Austria. On the invitation of the German Legal Society I had undertaken to deliver in the German capital on January 14, 1933 a lecture on the assimilation of the German and Austrian penal codes.

I carried out this engagement and after the lecture paid a call on Dr. Gürtner, the German Minister of Justice, who received me cordially. After luncheon the Minister held a reception, inviting a number of prominent German lawyers, practical and theoretical experts alike, together with the more important members of the Penal Law Committee of the Reichstag. Among the last-mentioned was Dr. Frank, a National-Socialist deputy from Bavaria who afterwards became Minister. At the time, if I remember rightly, Dr. Frank was the chairman of the Reichstag's Penal Law Committee.

I gathered from the talk I had with Dr. Frank on that occasion that no obstacles would be put by his own parliamentary group in the way of the assimilation of the penal law of the two countries and that he considered the results

hitherto attained by the two parliamentary committees—
one in Berlin, the other in Vienna—as a suitable basis for
the completion of the work. On this occasion and in the
presence of Dr. Frank I extended to the Minister of Justice
of the Reich an invitation to define, in his turn, the German attitude on the question of a common penal code in a
lecture to the Vienna jurists. Dr. Gürtner promised to do
so, remarking that he had planned for some time to visit
Vienna.

I recall this episode because, later on, Dr. Frank referred
to this Berlin conversation when he, as a Bavarian Minister,
wrote a letter to me, as the Austrian Minister of Justice, announcing his visit to Vienna, which took place on the invitation of the Vienna committee of the N.S.D.A.P. and which
led to very disagreeable incidents.[1]

As a member of the Austrian government I had applied,
while in Berlin, for an audience with the highest authority
in the Reich, President von Hindenburg, and it was with
great pleasure and keen expectation that I received through
our Minister in Berlin the intimation that the President
was ready to receive me.

I had been advised that the Field-Marshal was wont to
begin any conversation with a question about the war record of the visitor. The audience was fixed for twelve o'clock
noon and we pulled up at the Presidential Palace punctually
to the minute. A few moments later I stood in the study of
the head of the German Reich.

The President, a living awe-inspiring monument of a
man, was standing upright at his desk, near a high window

[1] Dr. Frank's visit to Vienna, in the spring of 1933, was officially considered by the Austrian government as "not asked for and unwelcome." The
National-Socialists profited by the occasion to organize turbulent demonstrations in Vienna.—TRANSLATOR.

through which one could see the wintry garden. Naturally this meeting with the great Field-Marshal, so familiar to us Austrians also, made a deep impression on me. The expressive head of this leader in the World War, chiseled out of stone, as it were, will never be forgotten by anyone who had the privilege of meeting him face to face.

Hindenburg began to talk immediately about the Tyrol and the Tyrol front in the war, more especially of Lake Garda and the neighbouring mountains, with an astonishing memory for details dating from days long past when he was still a Captain. He asked in words of warm sympathy about Austria and her anxieties, and he assured me, in particular, of his deep-rooted appreciation and sympathy for the Austrian army. The utmost care, of course, was taken to avoid touching on anything that might be open to a political interpretation.

This meeting with Hindenburg, though short, remains one of the lasting memories of my life.

From the Presidential Palace I was conducted to the Chancellery of the Reich, where a reception was being held by the Chancellor, General von Schleicher. The Chancellor behaved towards me as a man of most urbane manners, but with a friendliness that was kept a little in check. At first we spoke of different topical questions not exactly of a political nature. The appointment of a new Austrian Minister to Berlin was under discussion and I had been given certain instructions regarding it. Our previous experiences had suggested that the Chancellor did not concern himself to any extent with Austria, nor did he take a personal interest in our country. Accordingly, our conversation did not more than touch questions particularly Austrian. Instead, General von Schleicher showed himself rather hopeful of the German situation, of which, more particularly in its economic and political aspects, he spoke in vivid terms.

Without my making any suggestions in this sense, he then directed the conversation to the evolution of German domestic politics. I still precisely recall the words he used in that connection. He was, he said, about to establish some connections with the trade-union movement and he hoped to find in that way a new and suitable platform by which to ensure a pacific and beneficial development for the country.

Herr Hitler, he went on, was no longer a problem; the question of Hitler had been settled; his movement did not connote any political danger, it being numbered among the cares of yesterday. Then the Chancellor added something to the effect—though I cannot pledge myself as to the exact words—that the question of a possible co-operation with National-Socialists had been discussed, but that they had demanded from him the Ministry of Defence, evidently on purpose, because they knew he would never concede it to them.

It is easy to understand that this conversation, one of whose participants is no longer alive, was of the greatest interest to me. Its date has remained fixed in my memory —it was January 15, 1933.

The same forenoon had brought me an invitation to luncheon with Herr von Papen. My companions informed me that Herr von Papen, General von Schleicher's predecessor as Chancellor, was still occupying an apartment in the Chancellery, so that this third interview did not make it necessary for us to go very far.

Herr von Papen received me in a friendly fashion. We talked a great deal about Austria, which he knew from personal experience, and about Seipel and Dollfuss. Alto-

gether we seemed to get on very well. It was a big surprise
for me, though, to be asked in a casual way whether I had
met that day Emperor Otto. Answering negatively, I
learned from him that Otto von Habsburg had actually
arrived that morning in Berlin for the purpose of his studies.
Neither the Austrian legation nor I had the slightest idea
of his presence and not until the following day was it announced in the newspapers. By that time I had left Berlin.
I felt somewhat uneasy at the time, because situations like
that are apt to give rise to extravagant and baseless specu-
lations.

The afternoon of January 15 found me in the Reichstag,
where I visited the well-known Centre Party deputy and
leader of the Union of German Catholics Abroad, Prelate
Schreiber. I was surprised to find here, too, a great deal of
optimism regarding both the political and the economic
situation, optimism which impressed me deeply, more especially as I found no reason to doubt the statements made.

I also talked to Prelate Schreiber about the plan for an
all-German Catholic university at Salzburg. Prelate Schreiber we valued as a good judge, friend and supporter of many
an Austrian movement; but as regards the Salzburg plan,
he struck me as rather a sceptic.

I wound up the day with a brief call upon the Foreign
Minister, Baron von Neurath, who said he favoured an early
appointment, still open, of the next Austrian minister to
Berlin.

In the evening we went on to Cologne, where, on the invitation of the Catholic Academic Society, I was to deliver
another address, this time on "Austria and the Idea of the
Reich." There my views, which had found a ready response
before, when lecturing in Bavaria, met with surprising op-

position. My thesis that one should not speak of *"Anschluss,"* which implied something mechanical, but of *"Zusammenschluss,"* which had a spiritual and cultural significance, drew the retort from leading Catholic journalists that they failed to see why there should, all at once, be no more talk of *Anschluss*. That, they argued, was obviously an example of Austrian particularism, which was of recent date and which Catholic quarters in Germany were unable to sympathize with. I tried to refute that view, which came from people connected with the *Kölnische Volkszeitung*,[1] but I did not feel I had succeeded. None of us appreciated at that moment that the day of fundamental changes was approaching for the *Kölnische Volkszeitung* too.

Hardly had I got back to Vienna before the impressions I had formed in Berlin and Cologne were, for a great part, made valueless by the actual events in Germany. Scarcely a fortnight after my departure from Berlin Adolf Hitler, leader of the N.S.D.A.P., took over the Chancellorship of the Reich.

Two months later, in the middle of March, a lecture tour arranged for at an earlier period led me once again to Germany, this time to Weimar.

The Committee of Co-operation among German administrative legal officers had convened a business meeting, and as in former years, so this time, too, high officials of the staff of Austrian ministries, with me as leader, were invited to attend. I had to speak about constitutional evolution in the

---

[1] Having been one of the leading Catholic newspapers in Germany, the *Kölnische Volkszeitung* was seized by the National-Socialists very soon after the establishment of their regime.—TRANSLATOR.

Reich and in Austria. I find the following sentence in the manuscript of my lecture:

"Even before the World War the constitutional structures of the states in central Europe were in their fundamentals similar. Whereas the world saw in the republics and monarchies of the west of Europe outspoken democratic ideas in the foreground and while the east and south-east were looked upon as being near to absolutism, one had become accustomed to seeing in the centre of Europe authoritarian states. These were characterized by the firmly established and dominant position which the Crown held, partly equal to, partly above parliaments. This centre of Europe was and still is the 'German space,' and Austria was even then part of it."

I am grateful for those days passed in Weimar, for they enabled me to have talks with a number of interesting men about the new State, the outlines of which became gradually visible in the Third Reich—talks which furnished me with a host of new ideas. The determination to attain national union, to overcome old differences, and to achieve new forms found clear expression there. From time to time the closed doors of a newspaper office or a poster with some appeal or other were the only signs one saw of the political transformation that had taken place.

But the unique, the timeless, and the unchangeable made a deeper impression on me at Weimar than the mere discussion of contemporary questions. A visit to the Wittumspalais or to the Mausoleum, with its hushed and reverent awe in front of the tombs of Goethe and Schiller—that is included in the unique and imperishable that Weimar has to offer. To have been at Weimar must remain an unforgettable experience for anyone who has learned, as we in

Austria have done, to proclaim his pride in the cultural treasure of the German spirit and in the permanent ideals of mankind.

Singular in its development and vast in its spiritual range is our world. A strange thing it is, too, how this world, for all its manifold variety of conceptions, thoughts, and forms, meets again in a few culminating foci, even though a century lies between, as at Weimar.

There Goethe died in 1832 and Nietzsche in 1900—Goethe who has in the perfect harmony of his life's work given to the German people and to the world the sublime and eternal song of Man; Nietzsche who prophesies, with heroic fanfare, Man's conquest by the Superman.

Something, though, is common to the two, apart from their genius. Goethe says rather mildly in the *Xenien:*

Let not yourself be robbed of your own mind—
It is easy to believe what the crowd believes in!

This, Nietzsche, too, might have said.

I will speak in another connection of a second journey to Munich, which I took seven months later.

CHAPTER THIRTEEN

The Struggle for Austria

WITH the turn of the year from 1933 to 1934, we already lay in the shadow of coming events, the period of those preliminary skirmishes which led up more and more rapidly to the decisive moment. As already so often in its history, Austria's hour had struck. The heads of the State were faced with the alternative of yielding to pressure, hauling down the red and white banner, and giving up our existence as a free country—in other words, of giving up Austria —or of preserving her.

Those who decided on the latter knew that it was a life-and-death struggle. They had to realize the historical responsibility which lay in accepting battle even while its issue was still greatly uncertain; they must be clear as to the economic possibilities which existed for our country; they must above all take cognizance of her European position and her significance in the realm of German culture; they must be resolved, they must bend all their powers and their absolutely unconditional loyalty towards the fundamental principle and keep before their eyes the single aim of preserving Austria and upholding the Fatherland Front against every attack, no matter whence it came.

Some of the events of the years 1933 and 1934, in particular the sacrifices in which they resulted on all sides, were certainly not welcomed by Dollfuss and his co-workers. They were neither intentionally nor negligently provoked; and everything that could humanly be done was done to avert the evils that ensued. Throughout 1933 Dollfuss had made countless speeches, going every Sunday to different parts of the country to explain, to win over, to show the danger, explain his purposes and the measures he was taking; to point out the way which was open to every Austrian to walk, if he was willing to declare himself for the Fatherland. But with the revolts of February and July 1934 no choice was left; in the struggle for Austria we must conquer or be conquered. Success would have the same meaning as the defeat of the putschists. Defeat would have multiplied the sacrifices tenfold; six and a half million human beings, including those who had taken up arms against the Fatherland, would have been condemned to poverty and misery, a firebrand would have been kindled in the heart of Europe, which all too easily might cause a repetition of all that which since July 1914 was engraved in horror on the hearts and minds of all thinking and responsible men.

The first and indispensable thing was the summons to unity. No struggle for the existence of a state can be carried on when forces are dissipated and strive against each other with divided political aims and in the interest of party. The next necessity was to appeal to the will and power of self-defence. Not to threaten or attack—such an attitude, in that posture of affairs, was never even thought of. No, the question was exclusively one of self-defence. The peace treaties had reduced the armed power of the State to a minimum in both numbers and technique; that was why the voluntary organizations had come into being, and they served the State in a crucial hour. A third necessity was to secure the possibility of economic existence; the opening of new avenues to new markets, in order to meet and counter any boycotts which might force Austria to her knees. Hence the conclusion of the Rome protocols with Italy and Hungary, and the tireless efforts to stimulate trade by the conclusion of preferential treaties.

The fourth compelling necessity was the energetic suppression of every countermine laid to shake, to intimidate and wreck our purposes, whether in the field of economics or internal politics. Thus the necessities of State had to be met with legislation and administration, as in the time of war. The task was doubly hard, because there was no doubt from the first that, despite all the extraordinary measures that had to be taken, we must avoid all appearance of arbitrariness and keep in force the fundamentals of justice. There had to be an end of everybody doing as he liked, especially when he was an official and as such responsible to the State. There may have been cases of hardship and unfairness, such as cannot be avoided in such exceptional times. But comparatively speaking, Austria, even in the time of her hardest struggle, undoubtedly had far and away the mildest methods, the most far-reaching possibilities for checking and supervising by influences outside the government; and despite everything, reckoned in numbers, the fewest sacrifices!

But of course things did not proceed according to a previously thought-out plan. It was not the struggle for power within the State that made Dollfuss strike out new paths. It was a battle, mounting to ever higher dramatic climaxes, for the preservation, not of the regime, but of the Fatherland—a battle in which the quenching of mad, ill-founded, and fruitless revolts had led to the Austrian revolution. There has sometimes been talk of the so-called reactionary forces, which supposedly overthrew democracy in Austria. But democracy in Austria, at least in its previous forms, had been condemned to death since the hour when it became clear that all too many of its supporters had in reality no will to Austria, and, sometimes with help from outside, from this or that quarter, sought to carry out their own programs. It had been compromised some years since by the well-known declaration of responsible Socialist leaders that democracy is only a transitional stage to the dictatorship of the proletariat. It may be that this formulation was made on tactical grounds, as a counterweight to Communist agitation, which has never found a foothold in this country. But it is sometimes dangerous to use too much tactics in dealing with fundamentals; it shrouds the real purposes in a fog.

When we speak of reaction, we can only refer to that against the events of 1918—the revolution, the collapse of the old Fatherland, the peace treaties and all their consequences. The revolution of that time went under amid the convulsions of the years 1933 and 1934. But the new one had as its aim and goal one thing above all else, and that its opponents certainly never intended or even thought of: the reawakening of feeling for the Fatherland, for the recognition of the State, and, arising out of that, faith in Austria.

It was not the political parties that discovered this anew and rooted it in the mass of the people; nor was it the powers of science, economics, or religion working on the country; just as little was it that conservative section whose primary interest lay in the form the State should take, unthinking that its preservation was the first and fundamental premise of every later progress. To be the first herald of the new idea, its standard-bearer and martyr, remains the heroic achievement of Engelbert Dollfuss. The struggle for Austria mounted, from the last months of 1932, in swift succession to its dramatic climax.

First the fight in Parliament and in the Austrian press; from irrelevant criticism, cynical distortion of all that was involved, down to the foulest personal insults and slanders —no means were rejected which lay to hand in the paper fray, among a people so avid of news as ours, to drown public opinion in an ocean of print. The printing regulations were inadequate to fit the case; for every pamphlet read aloud in a parliamentary assembly and protected by the constitutional provision of immunity, was thus automatically secure from prosecution. Even in this first stage, giving way would have meant surrender. Thus there followed, step by step, at first hesitatingly and always a little behind the time, measures in the direction of press regulation and discipline, the purpose of which was to protect the vital interests of the State. Parliament thought less than ever of wise self-restraint and obedience to the command of a truly crucial hour. So of course conflicts were inevitable. An incident unimportant in itself led at the beginning of March 1933 to an irreconcilable difference of opinion between the government and the opposition, in the matter of a standing order. As a protest the presiding officer declared that such a conception of the conduct of business could not be carried out, and announced his resignation.

But this was not the time for a parliamentary crisis. It was not Parliament, but the State, that was in danger. Dollfuss intervened. The Nationalrat itself afforded the proper legal handle; and thus had the Parliament, in its old form, showed itself obsolete. From that moment it was clear that there would have to be a fundamental change in the constitution.

The extra-parliamentary forces now bestirred themselves the more, with ever ampler resources and with more and more insistence on all possible sides. Now began the preliminary skirmishes: brawls, more or less harmless surprise attacks—one of the earliest was on the Country Club at Lainz—the beginning campaign leading up to the decisive action of the coming year. Then came attacks with tear gas in several large shops in Vienna, at Christmas time of 1932. The signal was thus given for war and the introduction of tactics for wearing down morale. It was to be assumed that they intended in this way to force Dollfuss to yield.

We inevitably replied with sterner precautions and more extended police measures. On this the visible signs of propaganda multiplied; as usual, the party symbols first appeared in the public lavatories; then came the turn of the walls of houses, doors, shop windows, house fronts; billboards, benches, pavements; the milestones, the asphalt of the highroads, and the trees along them—a shrieking political propaganda took advantage of any and every foot of space to challenge the Viennese and the stranger in the gates, by day and by night. The immediate intention of all this was not the achievement of power in order to govern the country better or more justly. Rather, as the slogans and inscriptions and the political tendencies of the propaganda made quite clear, its aim was to decry Austria and make her an object of scorn. And so, after long and patient waiting and warning, our only possible answer was a rigid attitude of defence. *Putzscharen* (cleaning squads) were organized, whose business it was to see that people found guilty of political demonstrations by means of posting or painting signs were made, under police supervision, to clean them up, to make good injuries and pay for damages. Very often it was found that the immediate perpetrators were unemployed youths, who worked for a fixed rate and were paid by the hour. In such cases it was of course only just that the originators and ringleaders should be called upon to repair the damage.

Noisy demonstrations at meetings and concerts and in moving-picture theatres, for the purpose of provoking disturbances—these marked the next stage. Their inevitable consequence was increasing radicalism from the Left—who always have seen their mortal foe in their opposite on the Right. And when the two opposites came to an armed clash somewhere, then the same game was repeated over and over: each side blamed the other for starting the fray, while both blamed the police for siding with the other party; and the organs of both united in accusing the Chancellor of weakness in not being able to control the witches' Sabbath of unleashed political passion.

But there was nothing weak about Dollfuss. He had no idea of letting his manner and tempo of dealing be dictated to him by anyone. Neither by his foes nor yet by his friends. He would not be over-hasty in bringing things to a head; it was his purpose not to neglect any opportunity which seemed to give promise of unravelling the tangle and avoiding greater sacrifice. He could wait, and he knew that it was not a matter of dealing with the problem of the moment, but rather with the whole situation. Thus, however he delayed, he was resolved on decisive action at the right moment.

The struggle continued on every front.

The rule of academic freedom, which according to unwritten law forbade the police to set foot on university ground, gave plenty of opportunity for demonstrations; often enough, elements which had nothing to do with higher education gathered by prearrangement in the corridors and halls of the universities to create tumult and confusion. But even in the time of the old Austria it was no different, though then matters could be settled and quieted down by warnings and admonitions. But now these disorders were made use of in the political struggle. Undignified scenes were the order of the day. The national anthem—in fact, every public profession of national feeling, on academic soil—was regarded as a provocation and incitement to disorder, according to a previously arranged program, and was prevented by every possible means.

We replied by compelling order. The guardians of law and order set foot for the first time on academic soil, whose extra-territorial privilege thus came to its well-deserved end. The student self-government administration was reformed; here, as elsewhere in Austria and in the world, the rule held that he who had done the wrong must bear the blame. However, everyone might think and believe what he chose, so long as the position of the universities as places of learning, education, and culture remained secure. There was a brief, artificially stimulated burst of indignation, with the inevitable protests—and then quiet.

But the more clearly it appeared that such means of intimidation were unavailing, that Austria was resolved to
carry through at all costs, and in case of need not to shrink
from measures which on the other side of the border had
long since been applied for the preservation of law and
order, the more embitteredly did the struggle rage in the
land, and its supporters did not fail to clutch at the most
desperate means. We reached the period of playing politics
with explosives. At first these had been simple paper bags,
which burst with little else than acoustic effect; then came
bombs, infernal machines, and explosives of every sort; they
served to prepare the atmosphere which is essential for civil
war. Bridges, railway lines, telegraph stations, were as suitable targets as buildings and men whom one wanted to put
out of commission. I will refrain from recounting the
frightful details which were part of the tragic history of
Austria at that time. Nor will I speak of the economic boycott, or the continual attempts to work upon already highly
irritable nerves by spreading disturbing reports, as for instance of the impending forced loan, the State confiscation
of savings accounts, and others of the same kind. I will not
enter upon discussion of the absurd methods which recommended themselves to force the government to retreat: for
instance, the smokers' strike [aimed at the revenues of the
Austrian State tobacco monopoly], the refusal to pay taxes,
the boycott of all public arrangements and functions; the
repeated alarm, which filtered through a hundred channels
into all strata of society, to the effect that at latest in six
weeks the armed Austrian Legion, made up of emigrants to
the German Reich, would march in and take possession of
Austria. These six weeks began in the first place in the
winter of 1932, and lengthened themselves out to three

months as time went on! Nor will I speak of the Legion as such; according to old Austrian tradition there existed a regular recruiting-office for it in Austria; nor of the *"Feme"* murders, which occurred every now and then, nor of the attentats whose purpose was to spread alarm and terror. On none of these would I dwell: they were once; let us hope they may never be again. But brief mention was necessary; they may not be entirely buried in the silence and forgetfulness which comes with the lapse of time. And this for two reasons: one must know of them in order to understand the counter-measures which had to be taken; and also the judgment of the coming years can only arrive at a just picture if there is knowledge of the wounds and the depth of them, and therewith a correct estimate of the time they took to heal.

Such being the state of things, it was inevitable that events seemed sometimes to tumble over each other. In June 1933 a group from the Christian German Athletic Association were marching unsuspiciously near Krems, in Lower Austria, when they were fallen upon from ambush, with hand-grenades. One man was killed and several severely wounded. Thereupon every possibility of activities was forbidden the Austrian National-Socialist party. And here it must be said that that party, financially and in personnel, was dependent on certain forces not at home in Austria. Political emigration had in the course of time increased so much as to be a decisive factor; these people were mostly non-citizens. For every individual who had committed offences against Austrian law and saved himself by flight had been divested of his citizenship. Besides that, in certain parts of Austria district leaders and inspectors had been appointed who likewise did not possess Austrian citizenship; so that for some time now National-Socialism in Austria no longer had the character of an internal political movement.

It was clear to Dollfuss and his co-workers that the coming storm could not be met solely by the Executive or with the means and machinery of State legislation and administration. To the four conditions for the maintenance of Austria's independence that I listed above, another and most important one was now added: the pressure of those Austrians who were on the side of the Fatherland must come into plain sight and be strongly and unitedly applied. But it was a long way to such a goal. In the Council of Ministers itself various currents had to be reckoned with; these were united on the fundamental idea that the State must be defended, but opinions as to the best method of doing this frequently disagreed. It was certainly not easy for the Chancellor to mediate between the Landbund and the Heimatschutz and slowly smooth the way from the earlier concept of a coalition to that of holding a strongly unified line in which everybody voluntarily took the place assigned to him without being wooed by preliminary compromises, promises, or agreements. To create this political unity, to overcome the spirit of party, was the one idea of the Fatherland Front.

The first of May brought the concrete formulation of this idea, though as yet the name, symbol, and form of organization were not decided upon. The Heimatschutz had organized a celebration of the anniversary of the liberation of Vienna from the Turks, with a great parade which was to start from the Park in Schönbrunn. All the forces of the government assembled there. Prince Starhemberg made a speech, in which he put the Heimatschutz at the disposition of the Chancellor for the defence of Austrian freedom, and announced an unequivocal all-Austrian program. Engelbert Dollfuss appeared for the first time in the old uniform of a first lieutenant of the Imperial army. His reply, appealing for clear and unequivocal support of the Austrian idea, was received with a burst of exultant and unmistakable enthusiasm. We were all thrilled by this demonstration of unshakable will. For him who had been seeking Austria for years and had his Fatherland deeply at heart, it was an unforgettable experience. Later I came to look upon it as the hour when the new Austria came to birth.

There were some who stood with us at that time who in the course of the next months, on one ground or another, faced another way. I recall a neighbour of mine, a highly meritorious front officer in the old Fatherland, who had later done good service to its memory; he now performed special service on the staff of the Heimatschutz. He considered with a critical eye my activities as Minister of Justice and said to me (these were literally his words): "Believe me, I know the Nazis personally. There is only one way to deal with them: brutal force. You won't get very far with jailing them. Justice and mildness are of no use at all. There is only one way. . . ." I have not forgotten what he recommended, but we did not act upon it, nor is it useful to keep it in mind. It came back to me clearly years later, when I had to decide on a plea for pardon, made by my erstwhile interlocutor—and, in passing, not without success. He had meanwhile been arrested on a charge of complicity in a bombing attack, as a member of the N.S.D.A.P. Thus times change, and coats with them; but happily only here and there and in isolated cases; mostly, too, when political con-

viction has become too close a neighbour to personal ambition.

The Schönbrunn parade of the spring of 1933 had, as I
have said, broken the ice. Not that it had gone off without
friction. The march through the city had looked very ominous at certain points. Here and there large groups had
assembled; they looked ready to break through the police
cordon and meet the advancing columns with violence.
The Red and the Brown made common cause for once; and
the source of certain missiles could not be determined. But
these were in the minority. Most of the population in
Vienna and Austria saw in the parade a liberation.

The nightmare had passed, a new belief and fresh strength
inspired those who were fighting for Austria, and more especially the necessity for unity and holding together became
clearer than ever.

For the first time all the other defence organizations had
taken part in a demonstration of the Home Defence movement, and after that the idea of forming a common front
never died down. The most various efforts were made in
that direction, but again and again, owing to the special
demands of first one group and then another, they ended in
failure. At length, however, the Chancellor did succeed, at
least along the main lines, in helping the idea of the Fatherland Front to break through. The intention, first of all, was
that the Fatherland Front should be merely a roof under
which all might gather who stood for the freedom of Austria. As a sign of their common creed all the members
pledged themselves to display the badge of the Front. As
such the red, white, and red buttonhole ribbon was used
from the outset. To the Chancellor it was clear that, first of

all, the possibility must be found of making some kind of a
start. It was after all a question of taking into consideration
susceptibilities on all sides and securing the co-operation of
as many people as possible. Thus it became necessary to
dissuade the Christian Socialists from too great an insistence
on the party outlook, in itself quite understandable, but one
which had been outstripped by events. On the other hand
the Heimatschutz had to be convinced that their claim to
totality in the State could not be realized. Finally it had to
be made clear to the Agricultural League and to the other
one-time organizations which had a national outlook that
belief in the independence and freedom of Austria by no
means implied the renunciation of national convictions.

All this inevitably resulted in a certain confusion and
gave scope for the tittle-tattle of scandalmongers, and in particular there was the danger that those who were ready in
the common interest to sacrifice many advantages—for example, the Christian Socialists and also the Heimatschutz—
had the feeling that sacrifice in like manner had not been
demanded from others. The differences of opinion within
the Fatherland Front centred primarily on the question
whether the government and the political tendencies in the
country should be based upon absolute unity and concentration of forces or whether a new form of co-operation on
the lines of a coalition was to be preferred. A section of the
Heimatschutz was for the latter solution, although Prince
Starhemberg constantly advocated the course of unity.

The Chancellor discussed this vital question with me
often and at length, and the conclusion was come to, after
exhaustive and conscientious deliberation, that every new
coalition represented a compromise which made energetic
action, as regards person and policy, impossible, and that

the goal to be aimed at must be beyond question the fusion of all groups in the Fatherland Front and this purpose must be proclaimed without equivocation and put into effect step by step.

Thus after the agitated summer months the time arrived for the second German Catholic Congress, and this opened in Vienna in September 1933. This Congress was deliberately intended to be a congress of the whole of German Catholicism and was associated with the celebrations to commemorate the two hundred and fiftieth anniversary of the liberation of Vienna from the Turks. In this connection Dr. Dollfuss delivered at Vienna's big racecourse a great speech in which, as his program, he announced the effacement of the parties, the overcoming of the party State, the erection of the Fatherland Front and the formation of a new corporate constitution of a Christian Austria of German language. This meeting, on September 11, 1933, was the first general roll-call of the Fatherland Front in Austria.

The General German Catholic Congress did not altogether justify its title. For one thing, tension between the Reich and Austria, which found expression in various ways —the thousand-mark fee [1] deserves particular mention in this connection—prevented participation by the Catholics from the German Reich, and thus the original plan to organize a demonstration of general Catholic culture of a really "Great German" character in the classical meaning of the phrase could not be realized. On the other hand, the German-language Catholics from the states that had formerly been part of the Dual Monarchy were abundantly

---

[1] In order to ruin Austrian tourist traffic, the German government decreed that every German who wished to go to Austria must pay, for the permit to do so, a special fee of a thousand marks (400 dollars).—TRANSLATOR.

represented. The program of the Congress and the choice of subjects put particular emphasis upon the German cultural idea, and the delicate issue involved in the conflicting conceptions of constitutional forms was tactfully avoided. Not one of the important addresses which were delivered at this Congress struck the note of controversy, and not even the suspicion that they saw things from a too one-sided, Austrian standpoint could attach to the majority of the speakers.

In all probability I was the most "suspected" among the Austrians who read papers at the Congress. I spoke on the mission of Austria in the Christian Occident and I ended my address as follows:

"Our creed, and the German culture and German system of law which sprang from it, should continue to give our country her distinct stamp. German law had its origin in the venerable wisdom of our forefathers, and this wisdom has penetrated the classical forms of Roman law adopted in a later period. Thus we have achieved a synthesis of freedom and indispensable restraint which is determined by the ends to be obtained in the common interest. Christian reason in association with the heritage of our nation has shaped this synthesis in which the limits of the duties and the rights of the individual in relation to family, rank, and the community of the State are clearly defined. And we still regard breach of faith as a crime against the national spirit, as our ancestors did. German law and German culture combined with the sense of Catholic responsibility should guide our Fatherland along the difficult and laborious path. Again and again the Austrian troubadour of German culture found in hours of despondency an admonisher who aroused the weary and the discouraged with the words whose magic music captured the world from Vienna:

'Friends, not strains like these; let us strike up pleasanter and more joyous ones. . . .' Out of the genius loci of this city and her mission there ascended the intoxicating rhythm to the stars that links for perpetual ages Rhine and Danube, Vienna and Weimar, Beethoven and Schiller:

Why bow ye down, why down, ye millions,
O world, thy Maker's throne to see?
Look upward, search the star pavilions—
There must His mansions be!"

I do not believe that these words, which reproduce the Austrian interpretation of fundamental issues, can justify the reproach so often and so cheaply made, of treason to the nation, a reproach which became one of the most favoured weapons of thoughtless political twaddle in Austria. Whoever does not want to recognize the truth of this, let him range us Austrians among those whom he calls traitors, but in doing so let him not overlook that in the greatest days of our history the protagonists of German culture in the world and the protagonists of the German mind stood almost without exception on this side, too.

The whole Catholic Congress, even in its preparation, stood for the healthy idea of associating a really national way of thinking with the Catholic and Austrian viewpoint, an idea which had always played a particular part in intellectually alert Catholic circles. Dollfuss, who by the conclusion of a concordat had introduced positive order into many problems concerning the confused legal position of State and Church, certainly imparted to the Congress the authority and the glamour of State participation, and that must have been obvious to anyone who remembered the confessional structure of Austria, its overwhelming Catholic majority, and who had in mind our great traditions. In this connection the Eucharistic Congress of 1912, attended by the old Emperor, is worth recalling. Besides, the impressive manifestation of faith which took place three years before in Hungary on the occasion of the jubilee festival of Saint Emmerich, in the presence of the State dignitaries of all creeds, furnished Austria with a model and with an example. But Dollfuss rigidly avoided using the platform of the Catholic Congress for political purposes. The demonstration of the Fatherland Front at the Vienna racecourse took place, it is true, simultaneously with the Catholic Congress and its meetings, but there was no connection between the two.

Afterwards the attempt was made to represent this Catholic Congress in Vienna, held after the conclusion of the Concordat, as the political trial of strength of Austrian clericalism. But in so far as by clericalism is understood the influence of clerical circles on the government, the power of the clergy in the sphere of the State or, put in other words, a more or less concealed rule of the priests, the reproach was unjustified. Indeed, it must be stated that the trend under Dollfuss and his successor was in quite a contrary direction. Without the co-operation of the Chancellor and even without his previous knowledge, all priests had to give up their seats in Parliament. Catholicism and its organizations separated themselves more and more from politics, it was sternly insisted upon that there should be no interference with the Fatherland Front and its specific tasks. The new epoch was to bring about the precise and clear definition of limits between the spheres of influence between State and Church, and not their amalgamation. The two powers had to show mutual consideration so far as common interests were involved, as for example in the sphere of religious education. The State assumed the obligation of protecting the Church from unjustified attacks and it assured that religious ideas could be put forward without molestation and that they were received with due respect. The Church, on the other hand, pledged herself to loyalty to the State and its authorities.

The deep roots of Catholicism in Austria are the outcome of a historical development lasting a whole thousand years, for which State and Church have much to be grateful. This development was decisive in shaping the whole cultural scene as we have it today; our Austrian landscape, the soul of our Austrian art, the fundamental traits of the Austrian character—all these speak of it. Above and beyond that, there was never any question of religious intolerance; both sides, State and Church, were guaranteed complete liberty, each in its own sphere, obviously including the right of freedom of opinion, of organization, and of criticism; and use was made and will be made of this right.

Both Chancellor Dollfuss and I, his successor in office, repeatedly and solemnly acknowledged the Papal Encyclical *Quadragesimo Anno,* of which Dollfuss spoke in his great speech formulating a program, and again from the speakers' tribune at the meeting of the League Committee at Geneva. But the encyclical is not to be looked on as the Catholic interpretation of political science, nor, generally, as a message intended only for Catholics. Rather does this Papal letter contain the principles of a reform of society which is to lead to the overcoming of materialism and the solution of the social question, irrespective of religious creed.

As regards the Concordat, this, as is well known, had already been prepared by Chancellor Schober, and before Austria, Italy, and after Austria, Germany reached a concordat with the Holy See. The Concordat in Austria worked very well and opened the path of beneficent co-operation between State and Church in the interest of the nation.

The Catholic Congress in Vienna therefore was a milestone on the way of Austria's cultural evolution. In addition to this, the general roll-call of the Fatherland Front brought for the first time complete clarity regarding the future political objectives which Dollfuss, with the enthusiastic consent of his followers, was determined to reach. Shortly after those days foreign and domestic cares appeared anew. With the harnessing of all forces and notwithstanding all resistance Dollfuss held to the course he had mapped out. A concentration as rigid as possible of his own forces within the Fatherland Front, extension and support of the voluntary armed organizations of which the task was to reinforce the forces of the State, constant search after new ways with a view to exorcizing the suffocating distress of economic crisis, and, not least, the untiring and unremitting efforts to induce the opponents of the Right and the Left to think things over and co-operate—these were the constantly recurring themes of all our political measures.

CHAPTER FOURTEEN

The Decision

THE next nine months were marked by three striking events: first the bitter happenings of February 1934 and the enforced settlement with the militant Socialists. Then the new corporative constitution on May 1, 1934, the passing of which was the last legislative act of the Nationalrat, after the elimination of the former opposition. It was announced by the federal President and formally promulgated by Dollfuss. And lastly the conclusion of the Rome protocols, in which economic freedom and the requisites for survival were guaranteed to Austria by understandings with Italy and Hungary.

The question has often been raised whether the February revolt might not have been avoided. Events often look different in retrospect from the appearance they presented to those faced with the task of dealing with them. That we were not spared those events is a fact which, in my view, has deeper roots than the course of our history since 1932. That course perhaps hastened the explosion; it could not have caused it. Its first ground was the political alignment of forces which gave to one side, the Socialists, the power in Vienna, while the other held the provinces. In a federated state such a situation is of course decisive. At the crucial moment there can be no question of sharing the power, because each side needs all of it to gain its ends, and each side would be ruined if the other retained any. A favourable settlement became impossible after the failure of Seipel's efforts to form a national government in 1931. That was the last chance.

The second factor was the character of the peace treaties, which had as an inevitable consequence the heightened extremism of the masses on all sides, and which deprived the State of the means of controlling the situation by its own strength and preventing internal disorders. And so the armed volunteer organizations arose, these, too, divided by their political affiliations into radicals of the Right and the Left. The competition between them, and the enflaming of political passions, were of course contributory factors. At first there had been the comparatively harmless drilling; in the course of time came the machine-guns, the field manœuvres, and finally, on the Socialist side, the use of hand-grenades and hand-made bombs. When two private armies stand facing each other in a country, and the State is not in a position to disarm them both, from then on it is at the mercy of any flying spark; the issue is unavoidable and is only a question of time.

The third factor was the failure of the parliamentary form of government.

There could no longer be any delay in dealing with the

DOLLFUSS ADDRESSING A MEETING OF
THE FATHERLAND FRONT

KARL MARX APARTMENT BUILDING

Headquarters of the Socialists in Vienna, after Bombardment, February 1934

political crisis; that was clear from the moment when the preservation of the State became the only order of the day. The price at which he might preserve peace with the Left was no longer the question with Dollfuss. If he had paid it, his work, and in all likelihood the future existence of Austria, would have been destroyed. There is no doubt that a combination with the Socialist leaders at that moment would have inevitably brought about the very success of the National-Socialists which they sought and failed to achieve with the July *Putsch* of the same year. Certainly the Socialist leaders were not all like-minded; there were extremists and moderates among them, leaders bent on a solution by violence, others who were responsible enough to warn their friends against taking a leap in the dark. In justice it must be admitted that these last were faced in 1934 with a hard, possibly by then insoluble problem; for if they prevailed, then there was danger that the masses of their adherents, accustomed for years to the sound of the radical slogans, would go over to the side of those whose thorough-going extremism seemed to promise more satisfaction. Dollfuss's effort to win over the more moderate elements to his side met with failure; it encountered the unspoken fear of others lest the unity of the party be destroyed. I myself, within my own sphere, was making every effort towards pacification. But whenever we got down to fundamentals, the hopelessness of our efforts always became more apparent. What the Socialists wanted was just the opposite of that which the Chancellor regarded as the corner-stone of the new constitution: they wanted the preservation of parties and party power, and therewith the concession of a state within a state, and that state ready to offer at best only a temporary truce. All that could have been realized if the

Chancellor and his co-workers had abandoned their guiding principle and gone back on their firm conviction that in the abolition of parties lay the only possibility of a successful issue of the struggle for the existence of Austria.

And this did not happen. Thus the leaders of the State bear no responsibility for the unhappy events of February 1934. They did not desire, much less provoke them; and they must be regarded in the light of an explosion of forces, touched off by the fanaticism of the few; these, by reason of their party ideology and their uncontrolled determination to hold power in the State, though it was of interest to them, apparently, only in this single case, at last set off the alarm which brought on the revolt.

On February 12 the usual *Te Deum* was sung in Saint Stephen's in commemoration of the accession of the Pope. It was customary for the government to be present on the occasion. Just before I went to the cathedral, as I remember, I received a telephone call announcing that a high-explosive bomb had been thrown into my house in Innsbruck, then closed, and had done considerable damage. The act had been committed in the course of a terrorist program planned and carried out by Innsbruck National-Socialists. The bomb had been specially prepared, and introduced through the letter-box into the vestibule of the flat, which was in the third storey of a new building. This was my last telephone call before the outbreak of the February revolt.

During the services in the cathedral, which ended at about half past eleven, we became conscious—it was as the last lines of the Papal hymn were being sung—that the lights were growing dim, and they presently went out. I returned to the Ministry of Justice on the Minoritenplatz, to discover that the telephone did not function, and I could not find out what was happening to my property in Innsbruck. Shortly after came the news that the first shots had been exchanged in Linz and that the republican Schutzbund was rising in Vienna.

The rest of the story is well known from the various official announcements. Three anxious days followed, in which Vienna was like an armed camp, and the sounds of disorder in the suburbs reached the centre of the city. The Chancellor had at once taken all steps to inform the public fully of events and in particular to urge the adherents of the Social Democratic workers' party to pause and reflect. It was my task on the first day to clarify the position of the government in a broadcast; later Dollfuss himself went to the microphone to ask that all weapons be laid down, promising immunity if this was done. The frightful and bitter results inevitable in all civil war might now be kept within bounds, they could no longer be prevented. An attempt was afterwards made to represent the uprising as a more or less harmless method of exerting political pressure, which was met by the State with senseless brutality. In reply it must be asserted that the State was confronted by the necessity of defending itself, and for the sake of avoiding further sacrifice of life and property on both sides had to employ all its strength and means of resistance to prevent a spread of the disorder. There can be no talk of inoffensiveness; the irresponsible leaders were inspired by the most deadly seriousness—that is clear from plans found later revealing systematic preparation and proving that it was a question not of defence but of an offence prepared to go to the uttermost extreme. In case the revolt succeeded, a reign of terror was to follow; official buildings were to be destroyed by explosives, revolutionary tribunals already chosen were to be set up, with black lists and all the paraphernalia familiar to us from the Béla Kun period in Hungary and the Kurt Eisner *Putsch* in Munich. The military headquarters of the revolt had long since been prepared, in the municipal housing blocks; the resistance there was formidable, and the executive succeeded in reducing it with the greatest difficulty and considerable losses on both sides.

On the side of the government the losses were 128 dead and 409 wounded, of which 52 dead and 103 wounded came from the ranks of the volunteer organizations alone. On the other side, including injuries and fatalities to non-combatants, the figures were 193 dead and 300 known injured. The leaders of the revolt escaped over the near-by Czechoslovakian frontier.

Much malicious propaganda ensued, asserting that the revolt had been an uprising of the workers against the government. Such representations are a contradiction of the historical truth. The great majority of the working class, even among the organized Socialists, were clear-headed and sensible enough not to lend themselves to a violent experiment which in all human probability could only end in shipwreck. The call to a general strike met with no response; the great majority of the working class, with sound native Austrian good sense, declined to make common cause with the republican Schutzbund. And even among the leaders of the Schutzbund there had been, a considerable time before, a split, in which unfortunately the radical and activist elements retained the upper hand.

The government, the army, the police, the gendarmerie, and the volunteer organizations had performed their diffi-

cult task. The Fatherland owes them lasting thanks. Those
who stood on the other side of the barricades fought in part
out of fanaticism, in part they obeyed the call to mobilization with their usual discipline. Sincere sympathy is due for
the tragic fate of those who fought and fell in good faith.
Those who fight honestly and mistakenly are not to be
classed with those who against their better knowledge kindled the flame and made the others suffer for their own guilt.

Dollfuss bent all his strength to convince the adherents
of the former Social Democratic Party that nothing was
further from his mind than to give the worker a worse position in the new State or to value him less highly. Certainly
the worker needed a new Austria prepared to do everything
possible, in the social and economic field, to convince the
worker that if he gave his unreserved allegiance to the
Fatherland idea he had nothing to lose and everything to
gain. Aside from the unavoidable hardships of the post-
revolutionary period the leaders of the State were going
systematically to work to heal all the wounds; they would
lose no opportunity to lend a hand in building the bridge
which was intended to lead from negative theory to practical collaboration and the sharing of responsibility. Especial stress was laid upon the formation and strengthening
of the trade unions—wherein, of course, there could be no
thought of retaining the former political trade-unionism,
any more than of the retention of the party system. The
new political structure of the state, and its embodiment in
the constitution—then on the eve of completion—had the
conquest of all party spirit as its first aim and fundamental
premise.

The fighters on the government side lay in rows in the
Central Cemetery in Vienna. We stood at their graves in

the cutting cold of a February storm that almost took our
breaths away; and in all our minds was the thought that
these to whom the Fatherland was paying last honours had
saved our homes from consequences beyond our own imagination. Today we know what in all human probability
would have been the consequences if that February out-
burst had not been quickly and safely quelled. Events
which since July 1936 have come to pass in Spain would
have been the inevitable consequence for Austria. Dollfuss
often said that those February hours were the bitterest of
his life. And in such times it is no light office to be at the
head of the Ministry of Justice. But Austria performed its
painful duty—and that not only with reference to our own
country. The German people and German culture were
thereby protected from serious, probably irreparable harm.
But for all those who understand what it means to make
ruin in the heart of Europe and to whom the preservation of
peace is no empty phrase, the sacrifices of that time must
be matter for serious reflection.

Dollfuss had now for a long time been fighting a battle
on two fronts, and one which sometimes seemed to be without hope of success. He never neglected any occasion which
could serve the tranquillization of the country and the rein-
forcement of the Austrian platform. He made repeated
speeches in all quarters and sought to bring about negotiations—though never without making clear that the fundamental lines were already laid down and, in the interest of
his program, could never be called into question. As early
as the spring of 1933, when the National-Socialist agitation
grew more and more unchecked and extreme, he endeavoured in the course of his duties to guide his opponents

into the path of quiet and reasonable progress in the interest of the country. With the knowledge of the Chancellor, Rintelen and Buresch undertook to carry on personal negotiations with the leaders of the Austrian National-Socialists. The Chancellor appointed me as a person in his special confidence to share in the exchange of views. On the opposed side stood Theo Habicht and Proksch. We met in the blue room of the Ministry of Education. I remember the conversation quite precisely, as my first and last encounter with the well-known Theo Habicht, who was a member of the German Reichstag and leader of the Austrian National-Socialists. Herr Proksch was a railway official, of Sudeten-German origin.

The sense of Herr Habicht's remarks was that he thought there was a possibility of a political coalition between the Austrian N.S.D.A.P. and the Christian Socialists. On the other hand, the Heimatschutz presented a definite obstacle, and he must insist on their elimination from the government. He proposed that in their place National-Socialists should be admitted into the cabinet, to a number which he stated, but which I have forgotten. It was a question of three or at most four posts. The cabinet should proceed at once to an election, and the National-Socialists would guarantee that whatever their result, Dollfuss should remain at the head of the cabinet. This was a concession which they were ready to make, on grounds of foreign policy. The Austrian reply, which I took pains to emphasize, was that sentiments of loyalty would make it impossible for us to consider the elimination or overlooking of the Heimatschutz. Herr Habicht answered that, to his knowledge, the other party was not so finical in matters of loyalty. With regard to the elections, we went very carefully into the well-

known Austrian attitude, as it had been repeatedly and publicly set forth by the Chancellor. Thus the interview, which
was intended to clear the ground, was without any result;
and another meeting was arranged for, after a report had
been made to the Chancellor. There was no resumption
of the discussion. It was already clear, as the succeeding
year was to bring us repeated proof, that when there was a
possibility, through the exchange of ideas, of bringing about
a relief of tension and reaching a compromise on disputed
points, there were always, in the last and decisive hour,
radical forces at work on both sides, which so charged the
atmosphere with electricity that every possibility of further
dealing was excluded. This was shown particularly at the
turn of the year, in 1933, when Dollfuss declared his readiness to meet a representative from the Berlin Foreign Office
and discuss the possibilities of concluding a peace. This
was no sooner known than on the whole distance from
Mariazell to Vienna the bombs began to explode more than
ever, and thus, on psychological grounds if no others, all
conversation was out of the question—even if the other
spokesman had not been Herr Habicht, who, after all that
had happened, was inevitably regarded in Austria as a hard
burden to carry.

These repeated efforts to get together were certainly based
on a sound and correct idea and perhaps only suffered from
the fact that there were too many independent attempts in
different directions. During the progress of them the Chancellor asked me—late in the evening of October 30, 1933
—whether I could be ready within an hour to travel to
Munich to take part in a political discussion. A personal
acquaintance had told him that with the knowledge of the
German Chancellor and at the instance of influential circles

of the N.S.D.A.P. in Germany, a discussion had been arranged for with an accredited representative of the Austrian Chancellor. Its purpose was to clarify the point of view of both sides and to prepare the ground for a further exchange of views between Dollfuss and Hitler. I accepted the commission and said that I was ready for the trip, without having told anyone in Vienna of my intention, not even my wife. The train left within the hour, and I could no longer get it at the West Station, but it was held for me at one farther on. When I entered it, I had the clearest feeling that despite all the careful efforts at secrecy this somewhat suddenly undertaken political mission would not remain unknown.

I reached Munich on the morning of the 31st. I was received with correctness and cordiality and taken, with every sign of care to avoid notice, to a private house. From there, after a little while, I was conducted by the S.S. leader Himmler to the villa of the Führer's representative, Minister Hess, in the suburbs. My reception and the ensuing conversation observed all the proper forms. But, to my surprise, I was soon convinced that the suppositions on which I had made the journey were not correct. The German Chancellor had obviously no knowledge of the meeting, and his representative was clearly surprised at the time of my arrival. He first asked me whether I was empowered to carry on negotiations. Contrary to our understanding and view, it also transpired that Herr Theo Habicht knew of the appointment and that no result could be expected without his contributing to it. I explained that I came with the knowledge of the Chancellor, in a purely personal and entirely confidential capacity, and that I had no commission to deal with concrete problems. But the view which I represented

was after all that of the Chancellor, who laid great stress
upon getting the situation cleared up and perhaps obviating
certain misunderstandings. Austria was in no way to be
regarded as a suppliant. The fundamental condition for
success was the recognition that we were dealing as two
equal partners; Austria was entirely ready, she would come
half-way and was anxious to remove misunderstandings; but
there could be no negotiations save on the ground that her
honour, freedom, and independence were respected. If
these premises were clear, she saw no reason not to bend
every effort to live with the German Reich in the light of
old tradition and on the best of understandings, Austria
had never given reason for doubt that with respect to the
conditions of the peace treaties she had the same attitude as
the Reich and would always be prepared to support German
racial interests.

Reichsminister Hess in reply developed the point of view
of the Reich, and in particular referred to events in Austria
which, in his opinion, were injurious to the honour of the
Reich. In the first instance, there was the matter of the
national insignia, which had been forbidden in Austria;
further, there was the violent language of the Austrian
press; lastly, the ban against the N.S.D.A.P.

As for the insignia, it might be pointed out that the display of the Reich colours, the red, white, and black, was
under no interdict in Austria. At that time the swastika
flag was not the sole and only banner of the Reich; the black,
white, red and the swastika were both displayed—in other
words, two political symbols. As for the press, I was able to
refer to activity on the other side, in which radio propaganda played a particular role. Moreover, we had already
in Austria a law in force which imposed severe punishment

upon attacks and insults against members of foreign governments and heads of states. As for the desire for readmission of the N.S.D.A.P., I pointed out that Austria was faced with a sheer impossibility, because neither the new constitution soon to come into effect nor the structure of the State as a whole could tolerate any parties. This, then, was a demand which even in principle admitted of no discussion. As for the other points, the problem of the press and the display of insignia, I thought a friendly solution was possible, and I was at all times ready to represent such to my Chancellor. I could easily conceive of collaboration with the Austrian National-Socialists, at the moment when they were ready to become members of the united Austrian front. But it must be made clear that this was a purely domestic matter.

The conversation lasted about an hour. It was agreed to preserve the strictest secrecy. And this agreement was observed on both sides. In the meantime the substance of the talk has long since been overtaken by events; likewise there were clear references to the meeting in other publications.

The conversation had no immediate influence or success. By the agreements of July 11, 1936, which were given to the public, and the arrangements which were likewise published, it was made clear that there was an abiding will to overcome the obstacles, and that natural, friendly relations between the two states were being striven for; while at the same time the fundamentals were laid down, outside of which no agreement was possible.

In the early afternoon of the same day I returned by plane to Vienna. Chance would have it that the première of Grillparzer's *König Ottokar's Glück und Ende* was being given at the Burgtheater that same evening. And nothing stood in the way of my gratifying a long-cherished desire and

enjoying that noble epic of our Austrian Fatherland, composed by one of the greatest masters of the German tongue.

It was an ill fortune that for the time no success attended
our efforts to put an end to the strife. That Dollfuss was
always prepared to deal, in any way which would not compromise the fundamental Austrian tenets, of that I am the
living witness.

In the spring of 1934 came the solemn promulgation of
the new Austrian constitution, which took place on the 1st
of May in the Stadium at Vienna, accompanied by a mighty
youth demonstration and a symbolic procession of the newly
formed corporations. A part of the constitution went into
effect at once; the remainder was subject to some delay, and
provisional measures were taken for the transition period.
The labour of editing was chiefly the work of Dr. Ender; it
received the unanimous assent of the ministerial council, as
also that of public opinion in Austria, so far as it was united
on the platform of the Fatherland Front. The transition
period was unavoidable, because considerable time was
needed for the formation of the occupational corporations,
and some definition was necessary before it was put into
practice in daily life.

And thus the foundation was laid for the structure of the
new State; our next pressing duty was to look after its economic progress. The Chancellor took repeated journeys
to Rome and Budapest; the Rome protocols, sponsored by
the decisive influence of the Italian Duce, Benito Mussolini, were successful in establishing the economy of Austria
upon a firm basis, and therewith confirming and strengthening her international position. Mussolini not only had

full understanding of our country's needs; he also met our Chancellor upon a human basis of personal sympathy and understanding. The time was close at hand for a visit to Italy by the Chancellor when everything was brought to an abrupt stop by the events of July 25, 1934. I would not re-open old wounds; likewise those events are still too fresh in the memory of contemporaries to need further description. Those whom fate made immediate partakers—and there are many of them—will not forget that day. When the first news of the coup at the Chancellery reached me at the near-by Ministry of Education on the Minoritenplatz, the im-pression it made was unforgettable; as for the events which followed, they will remain with me all the days of my life. We were paralysed with horror when, long after five o'clock, the first authentic news came to the Ministry of Defense on the Stubenring, where the members of the cabinet had gathered, and we were told that Chancellor Dollfuss was no longer among the living. The effect of the news can only be measured by those who knew well the aims and achieve-ments of Engelbert Dollfuss, who perceived the bearing of the tragedy, and before whom now for the second time the abyss yawned, in which Austria seemed to be sinking. 1918 —1934! It seemed to us, indeed, that we Austrians were destined a second time to lose our Fatherland. Not by our choice—we were all clear as to that.

The course of events was given in the official account is-sued by the government press service in the ensuing months. Later many legends became attached to the shocking story. Engelbert Dollfuss fell on the field of his labours, as a model German, a faithful Catholic, the hero and martyr of his Austrian Fatherland. Even in the hour of his death, when in all human probability he must have been weighed down with anguish over the fate of his life-work, he had no thought of yielding to violence. Evidence for the fact lies in the depositions of the two police officials whose testimony was taken on July 31 and August 4; they took care of the dying Chancellor in his last hours.

Police Sergeant Johann Greifeneder on July 31 deposed as follows: "I was on guard duty in the Chancellor's office in the fourth storey of the Ballhausplatz, near the accountants' office. My hours were from ten to one.

"Just before one I heard a noise on the stairs and went out and opened the door to the staircase. Opposite me were five or six men in uniform; they shouted at me: 'Hands up!' I looked down to the third storey and saw two more men in uniform point a pistol at my colleague, Messinger, and disarm him. It went through my head that I must be one of the last to be disarmed. I could not offer any opposition. They took me down to the third storey, where I had to wait on the landing; there were eight or nine more men in uniform there with drawn pistols. Meanwhile others were bringing down the officials out of the Chancellery in the fourth storey, shouting at them: 'Hands up!' They waited till everybody was there. I remarked that it was not a good idea to keep so many people there, it was too heavy a load for the staircase. One of them yelled at me: 'We're doing the commanding here, you have nothing to say about it.' Then a non-commissioned officer came and gave the order to go down into the courtyard. Here the civilians were separated from us; they left us in the first courtyard near the main gate. The whole thing may have taken ten to twelve minutes.

"Between half past one and a quarter to two, one of the rebels came up to us in the courtyard and asked my colleague, District Inspector Jellinek, if we knew that the Chancellor had been wounded. When we said no, he asked if we would like to see him, and of course we told him yes. He led us up at once, Jellinek and me, and we found the Chancellor in the so-called corner salon, by the window near the Congress Hall. He was lying on his back with his hands spread out. We demanded that a doctor be summoned. They directed us to the 'major,' who was standing in the courtyard. We went and pleaded that a doctor be sent for; he refused, saying that nobody was allowed to leave. Jellinek then went into the rear courtyard and asked if there was a doctor among those held there. The answer was no; so then he asked if anybody had a bandaging kit. While he was still there, a rebel came into the front courtyard with a bandaging kit and asked if anybody knew how to put on a bandage. My colleague Messinger and I volunteered and were taken upstairs under guard.

"We found the Chancellor still in the same position. He was unconscious. One rebel slit his clothes with the scissors, cut away the shirt, gave us the bandages, and went away. There were some other putschists in the room; one of them sat at the writing-desk smoking a cigarette. I held the Chancellor's head and Messinger applied the bandage. I said to Messinger that we must get him to bed somewhere, so we pulled up the red sofa and laid him on it. Some of the putschists helped us. Then we washed the Chancellor and moistened his forehead with cologne. One putschist by mistake put lysoform on the Chancellor's lips; we wiped it away with cotton.

"Then the Chancellor came to himself. His first question was whether the other ministers were all right. I told him so far as I knew they were. Then the Chancellor told us:

'A major came, a captain, and several soldiers and shot at me.' He asked if he could speak with a minister, and mentioned first Minister Schuschnigg. We asked one of the putschists and he directed us to go to the major. But one of them went and fetched him; I think it was the captain. The major said: 'Herr Chancellor, you called me, what is it you want? If you had not defended yourself you would be all right too.' The Chancellor said: 'But I was a soldier.' He repeated his wish to speak with Dr. Schuschnigg, but the major said: 'Schuschnigg is not here.' Then the Chancellor asked for Karwinsky [then State Secretary of Police], but the major did not answer. He got up and brought Minister Fey, after we had waited a long time, during which the Chancellor asked if he could not have a doctor or be taken to a hospital; he also asked for a priest. We begged them to send for one, but in vain; and I tried to console the Chancellor, telling him it was only a flesh wound and he did not need a doctor. But he seemed to realize that he was badly hurt; he asked us to raise his arms and legs; we did, and he said: 'I can't feel anything, I am paralysed.' He said: 'Children, you are so good to me; why weren't the others good? I only wanted peace. We are the ones who have always been attacked, we had to defend ourselves—may God forgive the others.'

"Then Minister Fey came, under guard; I sat on the arm of the sofa and could hear everything that was said. I put a fresh bandage round the heart. The Chancellor spoke very friendly to Fey and asked how he was. Fey said: 'As you see, I am all right.' Then the Chancellor asked him about the other members of the government, and Fey told him they were all all right. The Chancellor begged Fey to ask the Premier of Italy, Mussolini, to look after his wife and children. Fey agreed. Then the Chancellor said he wanted to have Schuschnigg form a government; if Schuschnigg was no longer living, then the Police President, Skubl, should undertake it. Then a putschist came and leaned over the major and said: 'Herr Chancellor, come to the point. All that is of no interest to us; give the order that the executive shall not take action against the Chancellery until Rintelen has taken over the government.' The Chancellor expressed the wish that all unnecessary bloodshed be avoided. Finally the Chancellor said to Fey: 'Look after my wife and children.' Then the putschists pushed Major Fey away, and led him out on the balcony. What happened there I don't know. The Chancellor complained again about not having a doctor, he was afraid he would choke with the mucus that came up. But it was not mucus that gave him the choking feeling, it was blood coming up and we kept wiping it away from his mouth. Then he rattled more and more in his throat and gradually he lost consciousness.

"The Chancellor's last words were: 'I send my love to my wife and children.' Then there was more rattling and twitching and then he died. That was about a quarter to four in the afternoon; the death agony lasted at most five minutes."

Continuing on August 4, Police Sergeant Johann Greifeneder spoke as follows:

"In completion of my statement of July 31, in answer to questions I have only the following to say: the Herr Chancellor certainly did not give his assent to the proposal that Rintelen be entrusted with the government.

"When the putschist major spoke first alone with the Chancellor, I heard nothing of a proposal concerning Rintelen. With reference to the conversation which was after-wards carried on in Minister Fey's presence, as I have already stated, it was not the putschist major but another putschist who came in and proposed that the Herr Chancellor entrust Rintelen with forming a government and give the order that the executive should not take action against the Chancellery. The Chancellor made no direct answer to that; he only thought a few seconds and then said that bloodshed must be avoided. He said nothing about Rintelen. On the contrary, I remember quite definitely, as I said in my first deposition, that the Chancellor told Minister Fey he wanted Schuschnigg to take over the government, and in case he was dead, Police President Skubl.

"Summing up, I depose that I never left the room during the critical period and therefore must have heard everything essential that was said. The Herr Chancellor spoke low, but his voice was clear, and I never moved farther from the couch than to the writing-desk to put on fresh bandages. The distance might be about three feet."

Police Sergeant Rudolf Messinger made the following statement, taken on July 31, 1934:

"About a quarter to two some putschists came and asked if anybody knew how to put on a bandage. We (Greifeneder and I) offered and were taken up to the first floor by a guard of putschists. I did not then know who was wounded, until we came up and I saw the Herr Chancellor lying unconscious in the corner salon, by the first window next the entrance to the Congress Hall. He was lying on his back with his arms stretched out. His right coat-sleeve was slit. We asked if there were any bandages. One of the putschists brought a black bag with a first-aid outfit; another cut the Chancellor's clothes away, and his shirt. . . . The Chancellor opened his eyes and said: 'Could I speak with one of my ministers?' There were ten or fifteen putschists in the room, including a captain; he must have had the major sent for. The major came and said: 'Herr Chancellor, you have called for me, what is it you want?' The Chancellor: 'Could I speak with one of my ministers? How are they?' Putsch major: 'They are all quite all right.' Chancellor: 'Tell Mussolini he should care for my wife and children.' Putsch major: 'Herr Chancellor, give the order that Rintelen shall be entrusted with the government, and that the executive are not to undertake hostilities against the Chancellery.' Then the putsch major went away and Major Fey came, guarded by several rebels with revolvers. The Chancellor was then fully conscious; he said: 'How are you, Fey, and how are the others?' Fey: 'Thank you, I am all right, as you see, and so are the others.' Chancellor: 'Tell Mussolini he must look after my wife and children.' Their conversation could not have pleased the putschists; one of them came up with his revolver drawn, and another with his watch in his hand. The latter said: 'Come to the point; we are not interested in your arrangements. Give Major Fey the order that Rintelen is to form the new government, and that the executive must not undertake any hostilities against the Chancellery.' The Chancellor answered to that: 'Minister Schuschnigg is to be entrusted with the government, or in case he is dead, Police President Skubl.' Then one of the putschists said that the fifteen minutes were up, and Minister Fey was pushed away. I do not know where they took him. As he left, the Chancellor said: 'Please look after my wife and children.'

"The putschists tried to get into connection with Ravag, the broadcasting station, by means of a radio set on the desk in the room where the Chancellor was. Also they tried to get the telephone to function. After Fey was taken away, the Chancellor said he was very thirsty. We moistened his lips with cotton soaked in water. He said: 'Children, you are so good to me. Why aren't the others? I have only wanted peace. We have never attacked, we have always had to defend ourselves. May God forgive them.'

"The putschists brought Minister Fey back a little later. He was to speak on the telephone, which they had got fixed up. I don't know to whom, nor what he said. He seemed to be reading something into the phone from a paper he had in his hand. Then they took him out on the balcony to make a speech. We did not pay much attention, being taken up with attending to the Chancellor, who was gravely wounded. . . ."

Police Sergeant Messinger, resuming his deposition on August 4, spoke as follows:

"In completion of my statement of July 31, in answer to questions I can only add as follows: When the putsch major spoke with the Chancellor in Minister Fey's absence and told him to give orders that Rintelen should form a government and the executive should not take hostile measures against the Chancellery, the Chancellor, so far as I can recall, said something about Minister Schuschnigg, and also that the shedding of blood must be avoided. I cannot remember that he said anything about Dr. Rintelen. I must emphasize the fact that I was busy with the Chancellor and could not give my entire attention to what was said. When Minister Fey was brought in, the conversation went as I deposed on July 31. I clearly recall that Minister Schuschnigg and alternatively Police President Skubl were named by the Chancellor as those to whom the new government

WORKMEN CELEBRATING THE NEW CONSTITUTION, MAY 1, 1934

MANIFESTATION OF MOURNING FOR DOLLFUSS ON
THE HELDENPLATZ, VIENNA, AUGUST 8, 1934

should be entrusted. The Herr Chancellor said nothing about Rintelen in my presence. I was present in the room during the entire conversation and did not leave the Chancellor while he was alive. I must add that from time to time I went over to the writing-desk, a few steps away, to dip the bandages in water. But I can definitely say that the Herr Chancellor did not speak to the putsch major or Minister Fey anything about Rintelen being entrusted with the formation of a government.

"I might add that during the first conversation between the Herr Chancellor and the putsch major the former asked what sort of proposal he was making, and the putsch major answered with the proposal I mentioned, about Rintelen, after which the Herr Chancellor said something about Minister Schuschnigg. . . ."

Shortly thereafter the great funeral ceremonies of the Fatherland Front were held in Vienna. Hundreds of thousands of people stood packed together in the Heldenplatz and filled all the streets leading into it.

I cite the following from a speech which I made in Mariazell on the 2nd of August:

"It has been established that the Austrian Chancellor, Dr. Engelbert Dollfuss, was shot down at a distance of four to six inches, and that there was no reason for the assassination, because the leaders of the revolt could see as they burst in that the door through which Dr. Dollfuss would have fled at the last minute was bolted and that they could have arrested him without trouble. It was intentional, deliberate, and arranged.

"I have no doubt that this was so. Further, it has been established that the dying Chancellor was denied the services of a doctor and a priest, for which he repeatedly asked; and that there was no ground for the refusal, because it would have been quite possible to bring both the doctor and the priest.

"There were isolated local outbreaks in various places, which the executive put down. The situation so developed in the next three days that various local revolts were attempted, particularly in Styria and Carinthia, sporadically in the border districts, and were put down only with the forcible intervention of the executive. The conclusion is to be drawn that the rebels had been kept entirely in the dark by their leaders as to the actual events and may for some time have believed that the coup in Vienna had been successful. But the overwhelming majority of the Austrian people stood with Chancellor Dollfuss.

"In this connection I adduce the fact that this extraordinarily clever and well-organized *Putsch* was able to move only a very small percentage of the Austrian population to assemble behind its instigators, while the overwhelming majority stood in mourning at the bier of the Chancellor and leader, Dr. Dollfuss."

To that there is no more to add, even today.

The excitement among the people was indescribable. On the evening of July 25 the news spread that the putschists in the Chancellery were, according to their original wish, to be taken under military convoy, in lorries, and set across the German border. I was told at the time that in case this plan was attempted there could be no guarantee that it would succeed. The peasants were up, on the whole road through Lower Austria; it was out of the question, in face of the violent embitterment which animated particularly the population of the Chancellor's own home district, that a single one of them would get through alive. This was equally true for the convoy as for the putschists.

Such a convoy to the German border, as was well known, had been assured in writing, only provided there had been no loss of life in the Chancellery.

The general mourning for Dollfuss was very movingly displayed as his funeral procession passed through the streets of Vienna to his grave. The vast throngs were shaken with excitement easy to understand. "Revenge for the murdered Chancellor!" was a cry heard more than once as the procession passed through the Ringstrasse. Prince Starhemberg made a most affecting farewell address on the square before the Rathaus; it closed with the declaration of loyalty which united us all at this hour. I took leave of the dead leader at the tomb at Hietzinger. And on this occasion was coined the later oft-repeated political rallying-cry, which then as now, and now most of all, expresses our purpose and aim: "Straight ahead—for Austria!"

CHAPTER FIFTEEN

Redemption—the Will and the Way

ON THE heaviest day in the history of the new Austria, July 25th, 1934, I was asked by the President of the Federation to take over the government provisionally. In the succeeding days I was faced with difficult and crucial decisions. The confidence in me displayed by the head of the State, but also pressing and vital factors in the fields of politics and economics finally caused me to take over the chancellorship— unwillingly and with great hesitation. Engelbert Dollfuss, at the beginning of his term of office, had once said to me that he regarded me as his successor; not long before his death he mentioned the subject again, and said he had no idea of remaining in office in perpetuity. When his task was done and the constitution was in operation, he meant to resign the chancellorship and serve his Fatherland in another field. More than once I was seized with alarm at the thought that destiny might summon me to fill Dollfuss's place; I had had plenty of opportunity to view at close range his achievements in office and the demands they made upon him. And it was clear to me that whoever held it must renounce much, perhaps everything. And our views, even in this more personal aspect, were very much alike. Dollfuss regarded the limelight and the elevated position as at best a necessary evil, they did not suit his native character, which was easy and unforced. He would always avoid them wherever possible. I have never understood those restless spirits who think of the world as a place where one must always be hatching plots and pulling wires, who like to see everything stirred up, who cannot conceive of complete agreement among responsible men, or of voluntary subordination by one man to another; to whom the making and breaking of ministers, the solving of cross-word puzzles in the field of politics, has become a fantastic acrobatic sport. I recall many a conversation touching on this theme. Scarcely had Dollfuss taken office when I learned to my astonishment that people were whispering of my schemes to unsaddle him. At first I was indignant at such gossip; but one gets used to everything and quickly learns that scarcely anybody possessing definite political views is spared the cross-fire of idle rumour. When such tattle as this concerned us both, I always told Dollfuss of it, and we laughed together. That long before July 25 there were gamblers in the political game who were playing for serious stakes is only too clear from the sequel. For instance, I had a singular conversation with a well-known Austrian politician employed abroad. That was two months before the catastrophe of July, on the occasion of the opening of the Austrian pavilion in the biennial international art exhibition in Venice. My interlocutor expressed the opinion that the economic situation in Austria was headed for inevitable collapse. Among other things, he based his view on the market crisis in Styrian apples, at which we were just then holding our breaths. It would be useful, he thought, if I would try to secure a permanent position outside of the political field; there were various precedents, and it was time to think of such things.

At about the same time, and from the same source, the question was put to me whether, in case I had to form a government, I would be ready to work with my interlocutor. He was quite prepared to put himself at the service of such a cabinet, under my leadership. At the time I did not take such conversations very seriously; I was convinced that my interlocutor was simply cautiously sounding me, and obviously playing an assumed role, in order to see if he could count upon me in case of need. I never entertained a doubt that for me there was but one chancellor, whose name was Engelbert Dollfuss, and my friends and I had an unchanging determination to go with him through thick and thin. Naturally I found it rather offensive to be credited with such remarkable naïveté when there was, so far as I knew, no ground for it.

But now the hour of decision was at hand; in the midst of tragedy, on the afternoon of July 25, I received the summons of the President of the Federation to form a government. I begged him to delay. The old government should remain in office at least long enough to bury its deceased leader. Vice-Chancellor Prince Starhemberg was abroad for a short time at the outbreak of the revolt. When he heard the news he hastened back by plane. It was also in deference to him, since he was Dollfuss's proxy in the government and the Fatherland Front, that I considered a postponement advisable and communicated this proposal to the head of the State.

I had a most friendly talk with Starhemberg. He was being constantly urged by his friends to canvass for the chancellorship. And on account of the turbulence in his movement he was naturally in a difficult position. But with extraordinary tact and selflessness he declared himself ready to take cognizance of the political exigencies as represented by various leading personages and in consonance with the views of the head of the State. We quickly agreed on the selection of our co-workers and agreed that our task was to carry on the work of Dollfuss in his spirit and on the lines he had laid down.

To ensure the unity and allegiance of all those who stood for such a course, to avoid wounding sensibilities, and to obviate from the start any appearance of divergent views among the heirs of Dollfuss, we agreed that Starhemberg should take over the leadership of the Fatherland Front, with me acting as his second in command; on the other hand, as Vice-Chancellor, he would be mine in the conduct of the administration.

It was I myself who proposed this arrangement. Accordingly, the division of the political power, and the concept which grew out of it, were not to be taken as the issue of a demand made upon me. The solution was quite natural; within the Fatherland Front it was perfectly understood and welcomed. Dollfuss himself had designated Starhemberg as his proxy in the leadership of the Fatherland Front. And the reasons for the choice remained in force after the death of the first leader and founder of the Front. It was imperative to prevent the red-white-red Front from being confronted with a green-white one; for this would have meant in the end nothing less than a revival of the painfully laid party spirit, and a coalition instead of a concentration. The Heimatschutz, in the hour of greatest trial, had gathered beneath its green-white banners and at the decisive moment had paid for its allegiance to Austria with a split in its own ranks. It considered itself the pioneer of the new order; for a long time its declared goal had been the achievement of complete power in the State; it had made considerable sacrifices in the struggles of 1934 and was now afraid of being put out of action. New matter for bitterness and agitation must result from such feelings, and the taxing the Fatherland with forgetfulness and ingratitude; and all that could easily become fresh fuel for radicalism, which added to all other difficulties by political dissensions in its own camp.

I agreed with Prince Starhemberg that the pressing need of the hour was to combat such tendencies. We were both clear that we could achieve the downfall of party spirit only by sternly assembling our utmost powers and eliminating all unnecessary friction. Further, we saw that awkwardnesses were unavoidable and that the process of assimilation of diverse political elements would take considerable time. We realized that our first and most important political task was the cautious but thorough absorption into the organized Fatherland Front of all those political elements which found themselves united in the spirit of Austria; we agreed, in memory of Dollfuss, to devote all our powers to this great enterprise.

At the same time, we would embark on the unification of all the voluntary defence organizations. The plan was for Prince Starhemberg to take over the direction of a common and united defensive front, into which all such groups should be assimilated while at the same time the organic unity of each should be preserved.

Thus, then, we held before our eyes as the unchanging goal of our policy the straight and consistent pursuit of Dollfuss's course: the preservation and the independence of a free Austrian Fatherland; the achievement of the corporative structure; and the establishment of the constitution. To arrive at this end we had to set up certain premises, which often presupposed a provisional procedure. In the first place, the political forces concerned, notably the voluntary organizations, had to make heavy sacrifices, which might not be forgotten or disregarded. Questions of personal prestige must give way before practical necessities; many a person must abandon conceptions founded on political tendencies of the past. We had to fix our goal and lay down our route in a variety of fields, in order to ensure progress:

We had to make clear once and for all Austria's attitude towards its neighbours and the world at large. This task lay in the field of foreign politics.

Then we must attack the problem of consolidating and building up the domestic political front, for most important matters were pending when Dollfuss was snatched away at the height of his powers. There could be no question of their remaining in the *status quo*—that would have endangered the whole of our labour. One was the conquest of the last remnants of coalition politics, with all its deficiencies, personal and factual. The last flickerings of rivalry between the various organizations and groups had to be quenched— they had, even in Dollfuss's time, given lively concern. We had carefully to harmonize the various political passwords; to make systematic war on subversive propaganda; bring about a recession of the abnormal conditions which followed the revolt of July 1934; and make an honest and sincere effort to relieve the tension of the overcharged atmosphere and bring about a gradual peace. We had to get hold of the youth, within the schools and without, and teach them to understand the Fatherland and the Austrian idea, to fill them with enthusiasm for it and rouse in them a consciousness of the fact that faith in Austria is reconcilable with a national point of view; that German boys and girls in Austria will best serve their Fatherland by freely and proudly acknowledging themselves Austrians. We had to make good what had been lost in the first fifteen years in consequence of the existing line-up of political forces and the goals the leaders had set themselves.

Such was the combination of tasks set the leaders of the State and the Front in the field of domestic politics. And they had to find a satisfying solution if the main lines of Dollfuss's life-work were to be preserved.

But if we were to pursue a safe and successful course in both the foreign and the domestic field, something else was needful: an entire reorganization of the policy of defence. Austria's defence forces must be built up, and the armed voluntary organizations must be unitedly withdrawn from the political field and made serviceable to the controlling function of all bearers of arms, the defence of the country, in the most literal sense.

For all this, the successful overcoming of the economic crisis remained of the first importance. We had to make it possible for the country to survive; to that end the fight against unemployment and the awakening and strengthening of confidence in the Fatherland and its powers stood in the forefront of the political program. Connected with it was a problem of greater importance than the national question, which in the new Austria is no question at all, but is always being shoved into the limelight of the political conflict, although nobody attacks it, nobody denies it, nobody doubts, and therefore there is no danger and no reason for defence. But whoever honestly means well by the Austrian people, and finds no gratification in the clamour of the rusty trumpets which were sounding the same alarm in 1848, 1870, 1900, and 1914—such a man must rather concern himself with the hope of finding a solution to that other and as yet unsolved problem: the social question in Austria.

Whereas the collapse of the old Austria solved the national problem in summary fashion, the crumbling of the Monarchy and the developments of the first fifteen years of the new State flung up the social problem in sharper and sharper form. Here much constructive work is to be done; it lay to the hand of everybody who felt sincerely responsible for shaping the destinies of our German stock in Austria and improving its daily lot. All ranks depend upon the success of our program of economic reconstruction: the impoverished and proletarianized middle classes, the hosts of the small bourgeoisie in the cities, the professional and academic as well as the commercial groups; the peasant in the mountains of western Austria, struggling to wring his daily bread from the soil; lastly the army of workers in industry and trade—in short, every section and stratum of our population. And they all suffer from its frustration or delay. Let the captains of the out-of-work, in their political camps, whatever labels they wear, realize that. The man who subscribes to the thesis that Austria is incapable of living may abide the issue for himself. But he must not overlook the fact that it is an irresponsible attitude to look forward to new destruction as the goal of all possible effort, only for the sake of proving himself in the right. And even so, he could not prove it, if there were an end to the deliberate attempts at obstruction, either by acts of sabotage or by the senseless and idle propagation of alarms and rumours. The social problem in general and the problem of the working classes in particular is not a political problem today in Austria; rather it is pre-eminently an economic one.

And therefore economic stability is the real guarantee of a permanently and firmly established new Austria.

The political attitude of Austria vis-à-vis the rest of the world is conditioned in general by the possibilities of a small State, and in particular by the cultural and geo-political conditions of the country, which mark out the path that history has decreed we shall tread. The small State as such has three ways in which it can maintain itself:

One, strict neutrality on lines laid down by international law, good for all future possibilities of international complications. The maintenance of such a neutrality is entirely dependent on the market value of international alliances and contractual obligations. It will be the more secure the more strongly it displays a disposition to defend itself; and the less alluring by reason of that disposition is the risk of a breach of contract on the plea of necessity.

The second possibility is combination with a bloc of powers and inclusion in a more or less close alliance, which can mean anything, from a mutual hands-off pact to an agreement for mutual assistance.

The third method rejects any unilateral bond, concludes no alliances but rather makes compacts of friendliness, takes every occasion to co-operate with other states on a broad basis, is always prepared to act as intermediary—in short, represents that political attitude which we in Austria call the open window.

If we decide on this third way, it is pre-eminently because it gives us the best guarantee of the peaceful accomplishment of those tasks which are laid upon Austria as her meaning and mission.

Now, as always, we feel ourselves called to be the bridge and the mediator between the peoples and states which once belonged to the Empire of the old Austria and which now lead their own independent lives. This mediating office is laid on us in the cultural and the economic field of politics. It differs from our former one in that it remains remote from the field of power politics. It is further our destiny, co-ordinated with the one just mentioned, to uphold our connection with the larger German cultural group, and by being a free, independent German state, while also playing the modest role which our historical development has prescribed to us, to serve the whole race to which we belong and which we acknowledge, in its intellectual and economic development, and therewith likewise its importance in the world. To make hard or impossible the fulfilment of this task would be a piece of short-sightedness, advantaging no one and in the long run preventing the peoples of middle Europe from living in peaceful neighbourliness. And that could never redound to the prosperity of our own people. I do not believe in the permanent triumph of revolution and forced settlements in the field of international relations. The stronger state, of course, can, if it is lucky, succeed in changing the map. But history teaches that such changes may put off the solution of problems but never bring it about. But I believe in the evolutionary power of historical

forces to build up and give shape to the new and the expedient without destroying the old values. Thus I have
never envisaged our political destiny as lying in a choice
between the ostensible opposites Germany and Mittel-
europa—that is, between the Danube Pact and the *Anschluss*—but rather in the resolution of these opposites;
and that is possible if none of the middle-European states
feel themselves threatened by Germany, nor Germany by a
confederation of these states—that is to say, if a middle-
European combination can be found which should include
Germany. This peaceful path to a reconstruction of middle-European ideas is unthinkable without our free and
independent Austria; and an Austrian policy supported by
this conviction and conscious of its responsibility, can pursue its German course, to which she has always kept, and
never leave it, even in circumstances of the utmost difficulty.
Just as little will Austria be able to relinquish friendly relations with the neighbours with whom she shares memories
of a common Austrian past; even though she encounter
mistrust and cross-purposes; while, on the other hand, she
will never cease to emphasize her German mission and the
bond of her German blood.

Austria has acknowledged herself in her constitution to
be a German State.

That State would be without meaning if it did not lay
stress on being taken literally in its will to freedom and independence. But that being secure, then despite all the
reverses of her history, a straight line leads from the first to
the third Austria, and it would be for us to show that under
entirely altered conditions and on a quite different political
plane a little State achieved what the great power once
failed to achieve by war. All which, in view of the world

situation and the actual state of the political weather in central Europe today, may sound utopian. I cannot deny that forcible solutions are more in the foreground and seem to have more prospect of realization than patient planning and give-and-take.

But strength and tolerance are not really opposites. Just as little may patience and a spirit of compromise be confused with yielding and retreating.

How much would we not have regarded as utopian a generation ago which yet has come to pass! Though it is not always with unmitigated joy that we recognize the fact. The fact remains that our Austria's own history was a hard schooling to her, on the path from the improbable to the possible event. We have well learned the lesson that everything changes in time, nothing is final—even when it is most convinced of the finality and the immortality of its own thesis.

In the first weeks after I took over the chancellorship I embarked upon the official visits to friendly neighbouring powers. Our friendly relations with Hungary may be taken for granted without further comment, by those who are mindful of our centuries-long historical bond. Historical events have obviated many former occasions for conflict; both sides look back upon the road they took in common, not without remembering the common errors and mistakes of yesterday. Engelbert Dollfuss, in collaboration with the Hungarian government, guided the economic relations of the two states into new and hopeful paths, and overcame that diffidence which in the first years after the revolution, the setting up of the new boundaries, and the manifold occasions for mistrust, threatened to hamper the close and friendly relations of the two states. It is certainly not too much to say that Austrians and Hungarians today understand each other much better than they did in the old days when they were one.

Minister-President Julius Gömbös, since deceased, stood at that time at the head of the Hungarian government. He was on terms of friendship with Dollfuss; I too have learned to see and prize in him a tireless and upright patriot, a friend to Austria and a responsible colleague, with whom repeated conferences brought me together in Budapest, Vienna, and Rome. Julius von Gömbös did not conceal his original profession; he liked to think in military terms; and especially in the military field common memories and destinies are a permanent and storm-proof bridge whereon Austrians and Hungarians can always find each other. Likewise the cultural treaties, in the cause of which the Hungarian Minister Bálint Homan performed such worthy service, now began to bear more and more fruit.

In the August days of 1934 I was reminded in Budapest of another visit which I had been privileged to pay some years before, not far away from the Presidency, on the Nestor of Hungarian statesmen, now deceased, Count Albert Apponyi, in his palace in Ofen. Count Apponyi is to us in Austria the perfect type of Magyar magnate. The world saw, in the keen face of this man, even up to his advanced age, the best representative of the Hungarian nation. He was a man of most varied experience and ripe political judgment, with an amazing fund of knowledge, an incredible mastery of languages, a culture of compelling power. More than once in the various capitals of Europe, not least in Geneva, seat of the League, he mounted the platform to discuss the problems which agitated the world.

PARADE OF THE HEIMATWEHR ON THE HELDENPLATZ, VIENNA,
OCTOBER 28, 1935

ABOVE: *Secretary of State Guido Schmidt in Berlin, with German Foreign Minister Baron Neurath and Minister of War General Blomberg, November 1936.* BELOW: *Schuschnigg in Paris with French Premier Flandin and Foreign Minister Laval, February 1935.*

The organization of peace was to him a burning issue. Count Apponyi was a Catholic, a legitimist, and a Democrat. The talk I had with him in 1930 he began by a reference to the need for co-operation between our two countries. He put all his trust in the League of Nations, in this point representing the same views as Seipel; as a Hungarian, aware of his cultural traditions, he held the parliamentary system in high honour. He had no use for talk about the crisis in democracy, which at that time in Austria occupied all our minds. He was for the preservation of all the traditional forms of democracy, entirely, of course, from the Hungarian point of view; and all his past opposition from the time of the old Empire seemed to rise up when he said: "Believe me, one must keep all the valves open; otherwise there will certainly be an explosion. . . . And there must be in existence an inviolable authority, which stands above the age: that is the symbol of the sacred crown of Saint Stephen." A large portrait of the hereditary King stood on his writing-table. "If I am legitimist," he went on, in the same sense, "it is not by taking counsel of my feelings, or because my people had anything for which to thank the dynasty, but because the historical symbol is for us a necessity of life."

I had the impression that the revolution and the subsequent developments had in many fields raised the same problems in Hungary as in Austria—among them the problem of the generations, the disparity of thought between the old and the young, who seem unable to come together.

August 1934 brought me my first personal encounter with the head of the Italian government, Benito Mussolini. Upon that first meeting, in Florence, followed others, in Rome, Forlì, and Venice. What Mussolini is, and what the

Duce means for his country, can only be measured by him
who comes to Italy with open mind, having known pre-
Fascist Italy. Italian Fascism makes its appeal not, in the
first instance, to the "haves," the rich, the capitalists, the
successful men. It seeks rather to get hold of the masses,
the small people, the workers, the peasants, the youth. And
to all appearance it has succeeded in very great measure.
Concentrated energy, strength of resolution, clear political
concepts, consistent thought, glowing national patriotism,
statesmanlike understanding—not even with all this does
one get a complete picture of the man. Seeing him only on
the rostrum, borne up and inspired by the loud plaudits all
about him, or on some gala occasion, in full dress, with the
chain of his order, you cannot, I think, take the measure of
his personality. Only personal contact and objective conversation can give the right impression. Not that his eyes
would be different, but their language would be; they can
then convey the knowledge that not only hardness but also
kindness, much humanity, much culture, reside together in
that characteristic, typically Latin head. Two phrases from
the Duce's speeches seem characteristic to me: "The hardest
and the most important thing is: to be so strong that one
can remain good." And: "Force? Yes. But force is not a
school which we keep, nor a system which we are introducing—nor, which would be worst of all, an æsthetic which we
are teaching. The use of force is magnanimous, it is chival-
rous, it is, in a surgical sense, healing." For us Austrians the
utterances of Mussolini, which appeared in the *Popolo
d'Italia* on February 13, 1935 under the title *"La Missione
storica dell' Austria"* are of especial interest (*Scritti e Dis-
corsi di Benito Mussolini*, Volume IX). The article concludes with the words: "I believe that by the end of the year,

with the renewed strengthening of the State and the recovery of the economic situation, everybody will be convinced that Austria can live; and thus that a second German State can exist in Europe, German, but master of its own destiny (*può cioè esistere un secondo Stato tedesco in Europa, tedesco, ma padrone del suo destino*)."

The Rome protocols, signed by Austria, Italy, and Hungary, were extended in the course of time. The needs of our country met everywhere full understanding, no less in the cultural than in the economic field. I was always especially struck by the importance attached to an extensive intelligence service and everything else of a similar nature. And in Fascist Italy special emphasis has been laid from the first on that important problem of national education and the training and control of youth.

In all the councils and pronouncements dealing with the Rome protocols, one idea constantly recurred: the desire for co-operation without any effort to form a coalition or any aim directed at outside parties. It was a fact, established and repeatedly emphasized, that other states might have the right to participate. The Rome protocols also expressly conveyed "full agreement with regard to the guiding principles and methods for preserving the integrity and independence of Austria"; these words were contained in the communiqué issued on August 22, 1934 at the close of the conversations in Florence. "This integrity and independence," the statement went on to say, "in which, of course, complete autonomy is included, are of interest and importance to Europe, and form an indispensable basis for the preservation of peace in the region of the Danube." Herein lies the political importance of the protocols for Austria. And up to the present day the situation has not altered.

Mussolini took occasion, in 1922, to say that treaties are like chapters in the book of history; but they are not the final word. To this very just observation it remains to add that certain conclusions follow from a logical arrangement of the chapters, which for him who knows how to read the book of history will aid in the avoidance of misinterpretations and surprises. The possibility of friendly relations and close co-operation, especially with Germany, always lay open—even as early as in Dollfuss's time—upon the just-mentioned basis; all of the participants have always felt them to be highly desirable.

I would take this occasion to give especial mention to one other matter: Italy has never, either in 1934 or later, made even an attempt to interfere in the domestic politics of Austria. There has never been a doubt that she has paid scrupulous respect to Austria's independence and her right to choose the political forms best suited to her. Reproaches and surmises to this effect have been entirely unfounded.

And in referring to this attitude of Rome towards Austria's internal affairs, I would also include the spiritual Rome, which we always paid a separate visit on each of our visits to the Italian capital. The signing of the Concordat of 1934 brought me into personal touch with Vatican circles. I shall never forget my negotiations with the Cardinal Secretary of State, Eugenio Pacelli, whose lofty spirituality and priestly dignity were most impressive; nor the great celebrations in Saint Peter's. But most of all will remain in my memory the repeated audiences with His Holiness the Pope. The Holy Father and Cardinal Pacelli both spoke excellent German and used it in all our conversations. And in particular the Pope showed the liveliest sympathy for our concerns and was amazingly well informed about Austrian affairs. But aside from that, the assertions that the Vatican intermeddled in Austrian internal affairs belong in the realm of maliciously invented legend. Neither the Vatican nor the Church at large ever attempted to exert influence in either the foreign or the domestic policies of Austria. Our conversations had to do exclusively with the relations between State and Church; they were, accordingly, on purely religious and churchly matters, which have nothing to do with politics in the large sense. The idea that the government was getting orders from the Vatican, or that the Vatican sought to exercise influence upon the administration, has been spread by the invention of fantastic stories, the purpose of which was to becloud public opinion and prepare the ground for a feud against religion, which might then be directed to political ends.

In the first year of my office I went to Paris, accompanied by the then Foreign Minister Egon Berger-Waldenegg. Our purpose was to establish contact with responsible circles and inform them of Austria's political and economic progress and the possibility of developing the relations between the two states. In Paris I had conversations with the then Premier Flandin and Foreign Minister Laval; in London with Prime Minister MacDonald and Sir John Simon, the Secretary for Foreign Affairs—these last of especial importance, as I could explain and clarify the events of July 1934. We received a warm and friendly welcome in both London and Paris, which was highly gratifying. I was profoundly impressed by my London visit.

The following year I made a brief visit to Prague, on the invitation of the Industrial Association, before which I delivered an address on the subject of economic co-operation between our two countries. These economic interests were closely interwoven, as anyone can realize who grasped the economic structure of the old Austria. It is natural that many bonds still existed between the two states in the way of economic and commercial interests important to both. My visit to Prague gave me a much-desired opportunity for conversation with the President, Eduard Beneš, and the Premier, Milan Hodza, whom I later met many times in Vienna.

The September session of the League of Nations in Geneva had brought me in touch with the leading men of western Europe, among them Mr. Anthony Eden, afterwards English Minister for Foreign Affairs. The Geneva sittings made a striking impression on me. The principal business of the session was the admission of Soviet Russia into the League. All the great powers, including Italy, who were members of the League, voted for her admission, including ourselves. I recall a courageous speech of the Swiss delegate Motta, defending the negative attitude of his country. The session also brought me into touch with Barthou, then the French Foreign Minister. This witty Frenchman, an enthusiastic admirer of Wagner and Beethoven, took leave of me with the half-jesting, half-serious words: *"Ne restaurez pas les Habsbourgs."* A short time after, he was assassinated in Marseille.

The question of the Monarchy in Austria was just then agitating the European mind. Some people could not understand why legitimist propaganda was tolerated in Austria, others wished for the abolition of all restrictions. The Austrian point of view was clear and unequivocal. Any propaganda which affirmed the Austrian State as such and was in harmony with the constitution, which, accordingly, did not abandon the platform of the Fatherland Front, was regarded as unobjectionable. Wherever those inviolable limits were passed, it was necessary to recall them to the memory. One thing it was necessary to remember: The form of a state cannot be of supreme importance when its very existence is debatable. Therefore the new Austria did not demand from any of its representatives a definite acknowledgment concerning its outward constitutional form. But it did demand respect for its great tradition and its historical importance, without which Austria itself would be unthinkable. He who agrees that Austria should be preserved must also find proper and expedient the unhindered cultivation of her great traditions. Aside from which, it remains the inviolable Austrian viewpoint that the question of the form which the State shall assume is entirely a domestic matter, in which no other state can intervene. Of course, it goes without saying that only the Austria of today is meant. A monarchism based on the Pragmatic Sanction, for instance, had no possibility of realization—of this I was convinced. Nor can the question of the origins of the Republic play any role today in judging the constitutionality of the form of the State. Thus a discussion of the possible difference between a legitimist and a legal authority must be regarded as purely academic. The decisive fact is that the decision as to the form of government a state shall have must be made simply and solely to depend on the weal or woe of the State and its people. In the long view, a historical development is not furthered by impatient pressure, nor can it be prevented by delays and hesitations. The inevitable follows its own steadfast laws; this is also true when the time-span by which we measure, limited as it is to probable events and too prone to lose sight of future possibilities, is not long enough to be of any use. Yet regard to such possibilities must be the task of those who are charged with the duty of preserving undiminished the existence and the tranquil, peaceful prosperity of Austria.

In the meantime the excitement of the years 1934 and 1935 has long since died down, and the world has come to understand that it is not to the purpose to keep bringing up problems which, if they were left alone, would not be imperative. Finally, it is the clear duty of the leaders of Austria to show that, aside from any personal attitude, they possess enough sense of responsibility to judge what will best serve the peace of the country. It is a mistake to envisage Austria as placed before alternatives. He who believes in our country knows her vital power. The form of federation may seem sometimes good, sometimes bad. But the Fatherland would be in an ill case if this were the all-important factor. On the other hand, every German Austrian must remember that, despite all detraction, our Imperial house deserved endlessly well of land and people; their services meet us on every hand, and they deserve our gratitude.

CHAPTER SIXTEEN

Fragments from a Diary

December 1, 1934:

The hard struggle of 1934 is over. It has cost great sacrifices and many losses. "We have never attacked, we have always been driven to the defensive." Dollfuss uttered those words just before he died. They were the truth. Austria was saved, and—so far as human eye could see—peace was saved too. There must be an amazing strength indwelling in our Austria; its historical mission cannot be ended, otherwise it must have collapsed altogether in face of the general attack of the year 1934. The world economic crisis laid a paralysing hand on trade; there was the desperate struggle of domestic politics: every economic program was to be rendered impossible, every attempt at rescue prevented as though by force. Railway lines and bridges were the subject of attempted bombing; notices were posted in all the great centres of tourist traffic warning strangers against visiting the scene of political unrest; there was a strong concerted effort to bring about the failure of the Salzburg Festival, an enterprise as important economically as it was artistically and culturally. There were explosions in the Residenz, the Festspielhaus, and the Bristol Hotel. Dollfuss had just returned from an inspection in the Grossglocknerstrasse; he had talked with the workmen, and read in their eyes their pride and confidence in their own achievement; he had seen Rehrl, the Governor-General, who had set up an imperishable monument, as truly Austrian as it was German, by his epoch-making operations in the Grossglocknerstrasse and the Salzburg Festival administration. He had pressed Rehrl's hand and rejoiced with him in the priceless and unique charms of the city on the Salzach. Then Dollfuss lay on his bier, a cry rose up from the whole country; and at Salzburg they opened with *Fidelio*!

Es sucht der Bruder seine Brüder
Und kann er helfen, hilft er gern. . . .

Yes. There is something about loyalties. He who understands, and knows the powers indwelling in them, cannot yield—at any price at all. He stands upright and goes his way. For either the work to which one has set one's hand is good, right, and necessary, in which case one must go on with it to the end; or else it is ephemeral, wrong, bad, in which case it should not have been begun. Either way, it is out of the question to yield to intimidation, however harsh.

Time must inevitably show whether, despite the unfavourable circumstances, it will be possible to finish the Grossglocknerstrasse and make the rest of the world as strongly aware of the Salzburg Festivals as they undoubtedly deserve.

A peculiar tragedy lies in the slow civil war of the past year, which, months before the events of July, was shaking the country to its foundations. Both sides have regarded it as a struggle for freedom. But the ideal of freedom, that priceless possession of the modern, advanced human being, may not be made a mockery. A struggle for freedom always presupposes preservation, never destruction; it demands strong and striking evidence that there is a possibility for the development of its own powers; it is not summoning armed and organized strength to the end of crushing them. It is concerned with building up, not with operations to clear the ground. It employs arguments comprehensible to the simplest mind. Madness and crime alone would seek the destruction of their own country, simply that thereafter they must be grateful for the help of the greater and stronger power. All that, under other conditions and with different labels, we have gone through once already: Austrians have undergone it once—under pressure from the stronger. That was in 1918.

Shall we go through it all again?

So it came about that our losses in life and property, which certainly, put to constructive ends, would have been used to better purposes, and all the moneys of the State, which it needed for its defence and which thus were lost to its economy, have after all had their good side:

Something has suddenly become a reality which the whole world long held for impossible: Austria has found herself; a passionate resolve has blazed up everywhere throughout the land: the faith and consciousness of being standard-bearers in a struggle for freedom.

It took the incredible pressure and the concentrated attacks of its enemies, the frightful sacrifices of a lamentable civil war, to create anew, out of the second, sickly Austria, the third, the Dollfuss Austria.

The task now at hand is the healing of wounds, the summons to deliberation; for the unhappy issue of these events was of course unlimited extremism and embitterment. As usual in such cases, the spiritual instigators had escaped responsibility by a timely flight across the borders. In all the countries of Austria the great masses of the population passionately demanded stern punishment for those who lent themselves to the *Putsch*. Much calm and deliberate reflection was needed.

Of course, stern action was inevitable too; if necessary, harshness. So then, those who paid the penalty were naturally made martyrs of by their friends. The "persecution of nationalist sentiment" became a slogan. As though nationalist sentiment could excuse from punishment even though it led to crime! Opinions and motives are nowhere in the world grounds for escaping punishment. They must not be confused with the problem of responsibility; and that was never in doubt, either in February or in July. Moreover, what reasonable excuse could there be for any nationalist sentiment which had as its premise the destruction or even the injury of an Austria German to its core?

And so the appeasement is no easy matter. I have wished for and striven for it in all sincerity, and shall continue to seek it with all the means in my power. Many who stood on the other side are likewise honourably resolved and ready for that end. And if even so we proceed but slowly, it is because the ultra-radicals do not want to realize that they are losing ground. At some moment or other they launch a torpedo and tear all the threads. What they want is clearly impossible: the recognition of the party and a coalition with it for legislation and government. Those times are over for ever; quite aside from the fact that the assumption of totality automatically does away with any other view. It is impossible for opposition to sit down at the table with us; only those can do so who are prepared to surrender their own views. The representatives of the Austrian idea were not to be dislodged; to bring them to confusion would be even more impossible. For all Austrians alike the same is true. The former Socialists have not a jot less right to appeasement and a share in the work; but the premises remain the same for all: confession of faith to Austria, recognition of her constitution, cognizance of the Fatherland Front, and co-operation with it when the way to active political work is open; abandonment of parties, of whatever kind or however named, for which there is no room in the new State.

On these fundamental points there can be no debate. No one who agrees with them will be asked about his earlier party affiliations or the tendency of his general views. His co-operation will be welcomed.

I visited Styria in pursuance of my official duties. There, as in Carinthia, conflicts are habitually more acute than in the other parts of Austria. The administrative and military branches there paid heavy toll both in February and in July. In a city in the heart of Styria, where the political atmosphere was heavily charged, I inquired after the prospects for a relaxing of the tension. For answer I was led to a city gate on the edge of the town, where a pensioned lieutenant-colonel had been shot down by a young man at five paces, as he was peacefully going his way as a defender of his home. An officer of long and honourable service, with a wife and minor children, who had committed no crime save that of being openly an Austrian. And the bearers of his name—as is the fact in so many cases—speak better German and have spoken it longer than the youth who fired the fatal shot. Here, too, we have a typical instance of the German-Austrian destiny.

All that is still remembered. The widow and children are still on the spot; the doer of the deed is known; I could hear the tension of it quivering in the voice of the local leader of the Fatherland Front, personally known to me as a peace-seeking and conciliatory man.

These are the reasons why the process of appeasement is so slow. Only time can heal some wounds!

December 1, 1935:

The constitution is being completed step by step. It is no use to worry over the hundreds of small local irritations and difficulties. Individual wishes, whether of persons or of groups, must take second place. The great thing is not to falsify the great fundamental idea.

It is too true that conscientious heirs have no light task when they try faithfully to carry out the behests laid upon them. There is no hope or claim, in any conceivable field, that has not been represented by its sponsors as a legacy from the Dollfuss regime. Engelbert Dollfuss and Seipel had the same experience. After Dollfuss's death all and sundry invoked his wishes, unmindful of the fact that they had made up an interpretation of them to suit themselves. And many, too, who in his lifetime wanted to go their own way and often enough made his work very hard for him, now found their feet on Dollfuss's path, with the assumption, of course, that it led to the goal of their own desires. There were those who felt that there was too much talk of Pan-Germanism, walking with those who deplored the frequent allusions to Austria as a member of the German cultural family. There were those who found there was too much talk about Austrian, others about German affairs; those who thought that the monarchical tradition was too much in the background, alongside others who felt that legitimist development was unduly held in check. Some found that too Catholic a line was being taken, others regretted the realization of the Christian State. Some thought we spoke too much, others too little, of the ideal of the State. To some, parties were an abomination; to others, the only hope of salvation. There were the partisans of the armed volunteer organizations and their opponents. All these assembled together, and all of them finally acknowledged the Fatherland idea—by no means in such small numbers as our opponents would like to make people think. And despite all conflicting opinions, it was surely good that it was so! And it was all after the mind of Engelbert Dollfuss—though in the single case he would probably have objected to having his name invoked. That is the way, in Austria: we abuse everything and everybody; and those who do not know us often get a wrong impression. But whoever is beguiled into joining in the chorus may find to his chagrin that the Austrian prefers not to have other folk mix in.

Above and beyond all conflicts of opinion, it was the business of the government to hold a clear and direct course. And this most of all in the matter of putting through the constitution. The task was the easier in that we had a solid and determined nucleus which had made up its mind to achieve an effective and unswerving following; and on such a nucleus everything depends in the moment of decision—in the political field as well. This nucleus is the actual marrow of the Fatherland Front; it is more important than

all those masses with their membership cards running up
into the millions.

The Dollfuss constitution undertook to strike out in new
ways. Thus we cannot rely on the old models. There are
three large possibilities: we might altogether give up the
idea of a written constitution, which is possible when a tradition hundreds of years old is effective in the population
and has become a matter of course; when it has got into the
bones and grown to be the fundamental unwritten law of
the whole major and collateral structure of the State. England is in this happy state. Again, there is the possibility of
taking over, in some form or other, the principle of *"L'État,
c'est moi."* The I does not need to be a single person. It
may comprise a number of persons, or even a party. That
is the totalitarian state, with its own life-rhythm and peculiar philosophy. I find it fundamentally false and erroneous
to reject or accept it, absolutely. Where it exists—in Italy
and Germany—it may be, in its basic forms, entirely right
and in consonance with its own aims; which does not mean
that, taken as a pattern for imitation, it would be equally
successful always and everywhere. We must not forget that
at the beginning of those epochs which led up to the totalitarian states, there came the collapse of the old European
order, the peace treaties, and Russia; the Soviet Union inscribed on its banner the ideological conquest of the world.
Her revolution has been, to a considerable extent, successful; but in another form than that envisaged by the com-
munistic idealists. So, then, we faced at last a completely
novel political phenomenon: the wide-spread, victorious
national counter-revolution.

What we had to do was to replace a written constitution
with a new written constitutional law. To it fell the task

of superseding the democratic-parliamentary form, which
for us, in our particular situation, had shown itself in time
of need incapable of serving the country as a sustaining and
conservative foundation. Thus in Austria arose the State
composed of states, with authoritarian leadership, assuming
to itself as a state no totalitarian rights. It expressly con-
fesses itself in the constitution to be a Christian state. This
acknowledgment, to be sure, does not exclude the separation of effective departments of state and of Christian community; but it is ready to respect the mutual co-operation of
both parties in those definite fields which according to our
constitution they must deal with in common. I mean the
schools, the education of youth, the care of souls, and extended jurisdiction of personal rights. It was in order to
conduct this co-operation without friction that as early as
1933 the Concordat was signed with the Catholic Church.
There is no inherent difficulty in the way of similar compo-
sitions with other confessions. The new constitution was
often described as the constitution of the *Encyclica Quadragesimo Anno.* The description is unclear and misleading,
for the encyclicals of the Holy Father were never intended
as the record of a state constitution; they only furnished
fundamental standards for the reform and regeneration of
a socially well-organized society. The main lines of this
Papal encyclical were acknowledged in Austria as being
fundamental and correct in direction; this attitude has its
result in the attempted corporative organization of society.
The corporations are introduced into the constitution in
such a way that they choose their delegates by a free vote
and send them to the economic council of the union;
further, they have a share in the appointment of the provincial and municipal diets, and, more than that, possess

their own chambers, in which they can regulate professional affairs in their own field of activity. The plan is that by progressive development the State shall be relieved from dealing with those affairs which the corporations are in a position to deal with themselves in their own sphere of influence. This fundamentally new arrangement concerns a host of unsolved problems. Its realization can only progress by stages. The principal thing is, not only to get the great mass of the dependent, workers and employees, into the corporate bodies, but also to assure them proper co-operation and responsibility. This in no way controverts the healthy continuation of the trade-union idea, which is certainly developing in Austria in a most promising way. What must be avoided is the revival of the political trade-union idea, in order not to endanger the unity of our structure.

The new Austrian constitution, accordingly, does not in any way deny or seek to root out the healthy democratic ideal. Rather its effort has been to lift it to a new level and make it effective in other than a merely formal way. I consider it an indispensable premise in Austria that the people shall have a voice. We must only have a guarantee that this right shall not be abused or taken, under any pretext, as opportunity for making a platform against the State and the Fatherland. To prevent this, the building up of the Fatherland Front must be, as before, our most pressing political task. The co-operation of the Fatherland Front and the corporative bodies must result in shaping a fixed organization between the states, such as will put beyond question the tranquil and steady development of the Fatherland; that will ensure a division of labour in legislation, made from a practical point of view, and leave proper room for the adjustment of conflicts, which will always be unavoidable, but which must never be allowed to endanger the community. Within this large frame there is enough room and freedom of movement for all, even for those who in 1934 rose against Austria. And therewith a plain and impassable limit is also drawn to the continuing efforts after appeasement.

People have sought to represent the new State as purely authoritarian; this because the authoritarian idea is firmly fixed in the constitution. But this authoritarian idea means nothing more than an unequivocal statement of responsibilities and duties. And in the constitution itself the limits to arbitrary misuse are fixed. The headship of the State is once for all set above the authoritarian, responsible direction of the business of the government, and to the State appertains the right of appointing and recalling, secured in a genuinely democratic way. Moreover, there are numerous safeguards provided in the constitution itself, which guarantee that the clear dividing line between authoritarian government and forcible dictatorship shall not be overstepped. During the transitional period, which will come to an end with the completion of the corporative structure, the precaution is taken that temporary appointments take the place of the occupational franchise which will follow. Thus inside the year the temporary advisory bodies were set up in the departments of legislation, Privy Council, Economic Council, and Cultural Council of the federation. But even these appointments, in every case, followed the suggestion of those groups to which later will fall the right of free vote. Only for the Council of State does the principle of appointment continue to remain in force. Finally it must not be overlooked that the Provincial Council is among the advisory bodies of national legislation and that it consists of the financial sections of the various provinces.

Likewise the federalistic organization of our State of itself affords sufficient warrant that the authoritarian idea in Austria will not be exaggerated.

The flawless execution of the constitution and the completion of the corporative structure will require years of work. We shall have to employ the interim in achieving progress on our chosen path of building up our economic structure and that of our domestic politics, and firmly establishing our gains in the popular consciousness. To that end we must emphasize more than heretofore the integrality of the Fatherland line in Austria. There can be no rivalries; every Austrian must learn to think first of the Fatherland and the community of the people and only afterwards of its separate parts, its societies, corporations, and unions. Above all, one must not get the impression that in the camp of the Fatherland Front many aims struggle for the power; this in order that uncertainties may not arise, that our progress may not be slowed down, and that those fundamental solutions which must inevitably come shall be realized with the least possible delay. To this end there must be a clear, consistent course in our foreign policy, a more decisive attitude towards the upbuilding of Austria's defensive power, integration of the course of domestic policies, and the achievement and termination of what I have called the process of internal appeasement. We must become clear about who is willing to work with us and who has remained definitely and permanently in the negative. This year was certainly not one of the easiest.

Personally, too, I have found it hard enough. But the lot of the individual counts for little when what we are all concerned with is the whole.

October 10, 1936:

Today the military service bill became law. The recruits
are marching into the barracks, and a sorry chapter of the
servitude of the Fatherland is closed. How quickly times
change, how fast things develop! Fifteen years ago uniforms
and military service were proscribed; ten years ago no one
would have thought it possible to reintroduce an army
raised from the people; five years ago we should have met
with the stormy opposition of a considerable number of the
European states; three years ago there still persisted in Austria itself in regard to conscription much irresolution, mistrust, and obstruction.

Today there could be hardly a measure so certain of
unanimous approval as that for the reintroduction of compulsory service. The soldier's uniform and profession stand
once more in high honour, loyal to the ancient tradition;
there may have been unfriendly utterances here and there
abroad, but in general the stronger feeling has been that one
cannot deny the right of self-defence to a state with the will
to live. In our own country the law was hailed as a liberation from humiliating chains.

The law was by no means a sudden thing, but the issue of
a long and consistent development. It was Carl Vaugoin,
for long years Minister for War, who by patient, persistent
labour incontestably laid the foundations for the future
reconstruction of the Austrian army. At that time there was
much complaint that the soldiery were being made political-
minded. That was partly right and partly wrong. It was
right because a political-minded soldier-in-arms is never in
the long run a welcome spectacle, and a whole political-
minded army would be, according to our conceptions, anything but ideal; though most of the phenomena of the period

after the revolution were certainly equally unideal. But the reproach was wrong because the entrance of partisan politics into our professional army was a phenomenon of the time, bound up with the fact that no sphere of our life at that time escaped them. Nevertheless, a large measure of our Austrian tradition did survive throughout the parliamentary period, otherwise so barren from the point of view of traditional Austrian thought; and that this was true remains the inestimable service of the army administration, the war-proved officers and under-officers. It cannot be wondered at that the transition to entirely altered conditions, under Dollfuss's leadership and that of the veteran commander Major-General Prince Schönburg, did not take place without difficulties and dislocations. That it did succeed was proof of the exemplary professional loyalty and enthusiasm which had under the most exacting conditions remained alive and saw to it that the instrument of defence, the highest test of a state, was preserved to the Fatherland. The Austrian people helped too, by their sound understanding of genuine soldiership and the profession of arms, to develop from modest beginnings and with the most modest means, to raise our army to a respectable level.

At the end of the unhappy year of 1934 we had an army of only some thirty thousand in round numbers, including officers. Our flying arm, then only at its beginnings, numbered 65 planes, of which 40 were only fit for training-purposes.

It was plain that we must bend all our efforts to reach in the shortest possible time the necessary complement of trained arms and ranks. Not because Austria was suddenly attacked by the ambition to subscribe to an offensive militarism; that was remote, even to the monarchy. Years be-

fore the outbreak of the war the Imperial War Minister
Schönaich sounded the alarm, impressing upon us the decay
of the army; it was never wholly heeded, yet never wholly
forgotten among us. Our tiny little State of today surely
needs to make no large gestures. But it must show that it is
ready to strain all its powers to protect the borders of the
Fatherland; it must stand on its own feet when it is necessary to preserve the homeland from entanglements of every
sort; it must be able to put beyond doubt that even today
Austria, despite her very unfavourable situation, is by no
means prepared to serve in any event, against her will, as a
basis for operations. Accordingly the army is for our friends
a fixed quantity, to be relied upon; and for everybody a
factor with which everybody must reckon when he makes
his plans. For our own economy and the peaceful activity
of our country the defence force is and remains the condition of tranquillity and the fortress guarding our steady
reconstruction. For the power of defence signifies strength,
and strength means the assurance of space to live in; without
it the will to peaceful constructiveness cannot serve.

The times have fundamentally changed since 1920. The
anti-militaristic attitude of the early revolutionary period
was not to be interpreted as merely a reaction to the experiences of the war. It was, besides being that, the issue
and upshot of socialistic propaganda, which dominated our
city streets with the slogan: "No More War!" Certainly
there could be no objection to the sentiment, if it were
really practical politics; if it would not mean the paralysis
of the will to defence and therewith the weakening of the
strength of the people; above all, if it were uncontestable
that the words were sincerely meant, which was unfortunately not the case. Otherwise the ban against civil war

must have been fulminated first of all. More than that, it has been shown that anti-militarism becomes a socialistic dogma in any state, only when, on one or another ground, the armed force of one's own country is regarded with suspicion. The red armies and therewith the great state of Soviet Russia afford the most striking evidence of this: it likes, and with much justice, to describe itself as the first military power in the world.

This socialistic mistrust of the military, however, was present in Austria in quite extraordinary degree; it grew stronger the more the various voluntary organizations sought to fill in the gaps which were made by the peace treaties in the defence force of the State.

From the political point of view, of course, armed and organized groups can have no permanent mission or end in themselves; they can have a possibility of development only so far and so long as the State is not able to claim for itself the monopoly of bearing arms. The reintroduction of universal compulsory service put the voluntary groups perforce in face of an entirely altered situation. To leave them permanently by themselves, as they were, would have meant harmful confusion and friction in many directions and in many respects.

The aim therefore had to be all possible closing up and unification of leadership while preserving the old, well-tried comradeship; absorption into the general aims of the defence of the State, and thus the linking up with the military power, became indispensable. This was the origin of the front militia.

Careful and cautious progress towards the goal clearly indicated by the whole situation was the most urgent requirement; for we must not only take care not to wound natural sensibilities, but also take care not to create the impression that the services and sacrifices of the voluntary groups had been forgotten, or that there was planned a political repression of those forces which had given them their significance. It was to be expected, and did in fact happen, that this reproach was here and there levelled, however unjustly. For him who stood in the line it was in the last analysis unimportant whether he did his military service in the old group or in the new front militia, which, though led by professionals, was yet built up in the same way on a voluntary basis, and had as its task the preservation of the old group traditions. The military command actually facilitated his absorption into the frame of the group that had been voluntarily taken over, since it avoided on principle every sort and kind of personal and essential rivalry in leadership. Whoever had occupied a position as leader or commander, to him was open entrance into the militia in the same capacity, in so far as it turned on military employment. If he were a political leader—and there was not always a clear demarcation—then the new development indicated to him his place in the Fatherland Front, which could only gain in centralization and striking-power thereby.

Despite which, it was unavoidable that here and there regrettable wounds remained open. That was true of all of them, the home defence as well as the members of the other armies. Because I myself was intimately associated with the Storm Troops and had my most faithful colleagues among them—my closest collaborator, the Minister of Education, Pernter, belongs to them—I can very well appreciate the inward depression which was bound up with the new development, and precisely for the activist elements in the Fatherland. That the transition proceeded without important difficulties must be ascribed to the insight and the understanding attitude of the responsible leaders. And not least was the service of the general secretary of the Fatherland Front, Guido Zernatto, who though himself of the Heimatschutz, yet recognized the demands of the time and served them single-mindedly.

As early as in May there came a break in the domestic political situation. Vice-Chancellor Prince Starhemberg left the government, the conduct of which was united with that of the Fatherland Front. Thus there was the same situation as in Dollfuss' time: in order to put beyond question the existing unity in the political direction and to secure it for the future, there followed its legal consolidation by means of supplementing the law pertaining to the Fatherland Front.

This new orientation of things was, so far as I was concerned, neither prepared beforehand nor was it decided on and striven for. Reproaches to that effect, heard on and off at the beginning, were entirely in error. That it so fell out, and perhaps had to be, was rather due to compelling practical reasons lying outside the sphere of personal influence. From the time of the old Austria we had carried over the word "dualism" into our vocabulary. Formerly it had legalistic reference; the Austrian quite rightly had never liked the sound of it. But of late one had got the habit of understanding by the word "dualism" that kind of division of power in domestic politics which after the death of Dollfuss had happened because of the separation of government and Fatherland Front.

At that time everything had to be done which could prevent a disruptive policy in the government camp and strengthen the unified front. With reference to the given situation and the entire historical development, I still consider that the solution of July 1934 was right. Also in the long view, despite repeated doubts which come up increasingly from time to time from outside, I have held to the dualistic solution to the uttermost. At last I tried, in March 1936, on the occasion of a speech before the cultural section of the Storm Troops, to give an ideological basis to our dualism in the conduct of domestic politics. According to my notion, the division into two of the political power might be good sense in that it led to the possibility of a control which was calculated to meet the danger of an exaggeration of the authoritarian system. Here the precondition was the relation of the two leaders, sustained in full mutual confidence and defined with the greatest care. Up till February of 1936 the division of labour had been held to in essentials, despite all difficulties. Mutual confidence, cooperation, loyalty, we had. All attempts, from one or the other side, to play off one of us against the other and take a hand in the game were repulsed by us both with equal firmness and consistency. We were bent on upright and honest community of aims and showed ourselves on every possible occasion to be so. The last great demonstration of this resolute solidarity in the spirit of Dollfuss was given in the speeches, on the occasion of the first appeal of the leadership of the Fatherland Front after the death of its founder, on January 19, 1936. The line taken by the leader of the Fatherland Front was the genuine Dollfuss line, in all its purity and entirety, and moved—certainly without throwing out any previous feelers—in that train of thought which I myself also represented. But from then on, the domestic crisis emerged, at first slowly, then at a steadily mounting and in time headlong pace. It ended by seriously shaking our co-operation. But I do not at all see the explanation of the division in any deep-seated divergence of opinion as to the final goal or the general direction of our policy.

The difficulties were not in the least those of personal relations; neither of us could foresee them or determine their development; thus we were powerless to overcome them. My profound conviction is that they could be traced back, essentially, to certain circles, certain persons who stood between us and sought to influence first one and then the other. They were never to be got hold of; and their goal was the radicalization of individual tendencies in the Fatherland camp. The national leader, Prince Starhemberg, was reproached with too great yieldingness towards the Chancellor. This reproach, which was expressed in various private meetings and was vigorously employed by obviously interested parties to create opinion, produced from the other side in answer the complaint of the former Christian Socialist party circles that I had displayed too little resistance to the Heimatschutz and its leadership. Prince Starhemberg was consequently put in a difficult position, since every emphasis upon the unity idea of the Fatherland Front roused the suspicion in various quarters that he was abandoning the plain and unadulterated creed of the Fatherland Front. I in my turn encountered much misunderstanding, on the ground that I had turned the Storm Troops into a cultural organization. For those of all parties who objected to this imperative measure, the time seemed to have come to sound the alarm. Thus the tension between the various groups, but especially inside the Fatherland Front as such, became constantly greater. The division of labour in the political administration naturally laid it open to be courted by all those—and they are always present in such situations

SCHUSCHNIGG ADDRESSING A MEETING,
OCTOBER 18, 1936

GÖMBÖS (LEFT) AND SCHUSCHNIGG (RIGHT) IN ROME
For a Conference between Mussolini and Austrian and Hungarian Diplomats,
March 31, 1936

ACME

—who felt themselves slighted because they could not reach the goal of their political aspirations, and thought their services had been underestimated, or perhaps had other grounds for dissatisfaction with the way things were going. In addition to all this, it was quite understandable that even well-disposed friends sometimes interpreted as weakness something which I had done or left undone, which, however, indicated nothing more than the constant effort to hold together an always difficult and delicate situation. Then there were certain incidents, each in itself of no great importance, but taken together giving a false impression both inside Austria and abroad. Add the propaganda of our opponents, who had continued to hope for the collapse of the domestic front and saw in every supposed breach in the closed line of the Fatherland Front a fresh incentive to attack. And lastly there were tale-bearings and intrigue; it is hard to say whether these were due more to malice, or tactlessness, or over-active business sense. Anyhow, the moment was given me for clarifying the situation when private groups, lying quite outside any political responsibility, sought to give the impression that the organization of the government and of politics in Austria was their affair, and the acting parties nothing but puppets who preserved their political existence by favour of these circles. But it was not possible, either for Prince Starhemberg or for me, in the long run, to sustain a purely formal responsibility without being able to have our own way. Each of us had his own quite clear conceptions, which as a matter of fact came to much the same thing in the end, but with divergencies, quite naturally, of method and temperament. We fully agreed that there was danger in delay, if we could not achieve a close concentration of the Fatherland forces

which should be visible even from the outside. My idea
was that, according to the sense and wording of the constitution, the politics of the Fatherland Front were to be directed jointly by the national leader and the federal Chancellor. I concede at once that this idea, under the given
conditions, was a half-measure and gave no assurance that
friction would be avoided in the future. Prince Starhemberg in the end could not assent to this view, nor to certain
other changes of a practical and personal nature which I
considered advisable. Thus came the change in the government, because there seemed no ground to be certain of
further fruitful co-operation.

I held that in the long run the strictest concentration of
all forces and the clear political aim of a unified leadership
were indispensable to success. Without them, in the given
conditions, there could be, as experience showed us, no
possibility of effectual action. Confidence was paralysed in
the great mass of our followers; a feeling of insecurity took
the upper hand; the door was opened for a host of legends
and rumours—all this, in the last analysis, not because there
was any justifiable ground for personal reproach, nor can
anyone speak of personal blame; but simply because the
necessary decisions were either not made or else were greatly
delayed; and at critical moments a divided government is
unthinkable, since the unavoidable loss of time of itself out-
strips and nullifies the execution of necessary measures.
There are, in politics too, moments to which Napoleon's
saying applies: that a mediocre general, acting by himself,
has more chance than five superior ones who must consult
each other.

I was from the beginning clear in my own mind that the
decision taken in May of this year would neither be under-

stood nor welcomed by anyone at first sight. It would certainly have been more convenient to avoid it and leave matters with the division of responsibility. But it was my conviction that a further putting off of the solution was no longer to be reconciled with the interests of Austria. Prince Starhemberg might certainly be of a different opinion in details; but he loyally and correctly subordinated his own view to the practical exigencies. The way to unification was open; we must now enter upon and tread it, without hesitation, in stern consistency.

The effort to strengthen the Fatherland Front from within had to go hand in hand with endeavours to stabilize the State from without. For a long time there had been attempts to smooth the troubled waters between Austria and the German Reich and bring them into a normal course; to restore the situation which only a few years before, in the old and in the new Austria, had existed as a matter of course, in the country's relationship to the whole of the German people. For some time now there had been impediments of a political nature, sometimes foreign, sometimes domestic. But now the time was ripe, and the treaty of July 11 came into force, in which both partners bound themselves to undertake certain duties: The government of the German Reich declared that it "recognized the full sovereignty of the Austrian union, and promised to regard the Austrian form of government and its domestic policy, including the question of Austrian National-Socialism, as a purely Austrian affair, upon which it promised to exert no influence, either direct or indirect."

The Austrian government on its side gave a similar assurance to respect the form of government within the Reich;

further, it stated that it would "in general and in particular,
in its relations with the German Reich, hold to those fundamental principles which correspond to the fact that Austria
acknowledges herself to be a German state." Express reference was made to the maintenance of the Rome protocols
as well as the position of Austria vis-à-vis Italy and Hungary,
as participants in the protocols.

In this declaration the Austrian government expressly
reiterated what Dollfuss had at various times emphasized in
his program speeches. The treaty did not contain a word
which could not have been subscribed to without a thought
on some earlier occasion by Dollfuss or his successor in office. Its content, indeed, corresponded entirely to the principles which had again and again been set up in the treaty
preambles of past years, when every time there had been
some upset which prevented the conclusion of the negotiations, so that all the previous attempts had come to nothing.
At the same time with the publication of the treaty the main
lines of the content of oral understandings became known
in Germany and Austria, the aim of which was to create a
favourable atmosphere for the agreement and to liquidate
once and for all the unnatural situation of the last years.
These understandings dealt with the regulation of the
treatment of Austrian subjects in the Reich and German
subjects in Austria; the formation of mutual cultural relations; the treatment of press regulations; the emigration
question; national insignia and anthems; economic relations, with special reference to tourist traffic; agreed treatment of foreign politics in matters touching both sides,
wherein Austria expressed her readiness "to pursue her
aims with reference to the peaceful aspirations of the foreign policy of the government of the Reich" and to enter

from time to time upon an exchange of opinions concerning matters of common interest. There was attached to the agreements a declaration of the Austrian Chancellor according to which he was prepared to carry through a far-reaching political amnesty, from which only those should be excluded who had been guilty of serious ordinary crime. In Point B of the aide-mémoire the following statement is laid down, which I cite for the sake of clarity: "The Chancellor declares that he is prepared, to the end of achieving genuine peace, at a proper time, which is envisaged as being in the near future, to admit to collaboration and political responsibility representatives of the former so-called national opposition; in which case it would be a question of personalities and the Chancellor would reserve to himself the right of choice. The agreement consists herein: that these persons in the confidence of the Chancellor shall be entrusted with the task of providing for the inner appeasement of the national opposition, according to a plan previously arranged with the Chancellor, and for their participation in the upbuilding of a united political will in Austria."

Further on I will speak of the illegal propaganda concerning alleged secret agreements in which the Austrian government had undertaken binding obligations above and beyond those mentioned. I have encountered more than one of these legends. In particular, of course, there was never a word of a reorganization of the government, because that would be a typical case of a question of purely domestic politics. On the other hand, the principles are clearly laid down which should guide a possible development greatly desired by us, to open to everybody the way of political co-operation. That we honourably struggled for the appeasement of the country I have often enough and clearly enough publicly emphasized, particularly on the occasion of the promulgation of the treaty of July 11. Again, I more than once repeated the conditions under which political co-operation is possible in Austria. The basic conditions remain the same: the renunciation of party, membership in the Fatherland Front, recognition of the constitution. Concerning these premises there was no doubt whatever, on July 11 and afterwards, between the partners to the treaty. I was ready and resolved to spare no effort to reach the desired goal; to smooth the path of conciliation within and without and re-establish the situation corresponding to the natural relation between two German states who have so much in common, not only in language and culture but also in history and destiny.

October 1, 1937:

The year has not so far kept to the promise of 1936. Yet it would be wrong to overlook the progress which has been made. Not all the problems which occupy us have found complete solution. But we have come nearer to solution, or at least certainly to clarity as to the possibility of a solution.

Beyond the borders of Austria many gloomy and threatening shadows darken the world: in Spain and the Far East cannon are thundering; the effort to preserve peace is more present and more anxious than ever before. It is no longer merely the munitions factories that are interested in war; it sometimes seems as though the great state-shaping ideologies of the time can no longer live together in peace. But it is not a question of converting others so much as of forcing them to respect their neighbour's view. Each one by itself desires peace. But no one of them, of course, wants to let another play the missionary; so that beyond a doubt, if the general sense of the contract of July 11 between Germany and Austria could be made operative throughout the world, the universal recognition of the fundamental principle that no influence, direct or indirect, must be exerted upon the chosen form of government of another state, it might be an effective means of keeping the peace, in the small and the great. So long, however, as only a part of the world demands that the other part shall not mix in, but at the same time finds ways and means to penetrate with its ideas and its own arms deliveries, so long the danger will be present. We Austrians are not directly affected, but we anxiously follow the course of events, because the memory of 1914 warns us how easy it is for a spark to set off an explosion when great heaps of explosives lie all over the place. Perhaps we should not have so extensively altered the boundaries of the states of central Europe, but instead have drawn the border of Europe much farther to the West and away from Russia. We should have concerned ourselves less with thinking in continents and more with thinking as Europeans; less with organizing the world and more with the reasonable organization of Europe. Then perhaps today there would not be certain problems which have now become burning and which seem insoluble precisely because the boundaries have been drawn wrong.

The deepest source of error has always been mistrust. Mistrust begets short-sightedness. And the two were sponsors at the peace treaties of 1919. And therefore things turned out as they should not have done, when one remembers the eight million dead of the last war.

The Austria of the old days would have had an important voice in the shaping of things. Its successors singly and together have been pretty powerless, without much to say. It must be and remain our effort to serve with all our powers the cause of peace, order, and reason and sympathetically follow every endeavour to oppose authority to anarchy, culture to barbarism, the mind of the West to the automatism of the East. From the Austrian point of view, the dichotomy is not that of fascism and democracy, but that of East and West. In the West, for one country the necessary and suitable form may be fascism, for another democracy. For us the prescribed way is the corporative state, which, God willing, will be realized as a whole in the coming year.

The situation of Austria in foreign politics has not changed during the past year. It can scarcely do so in the future. To build up our strength, to stand as much as possible on our own feet while excluding the idea of autarchy, which is an impossible one for a small state—these remain the imperative order of the day. The cultivation of relations with our neighbours, in an economic as well as a political sense, is naturally of especial importance. Our attitude towards the German Reich demands on more than one ground especial consideration. Not that the small state may flatter itself that it can essentially influence the great one in its views, aims, or plans; but there must be no doubt that in the new Austria exists the same readiness to neighbourly friendliness, the same desire for smooth co-operation, that always existed in the old. What Austria can do to this end it has done and will be ready to go on doing, to the widest extent. Our boundaries have long been drawn for us with unequivocal clearness. Austria has embarked upon her own constitutional development; she regards the adherence to the fundamentals of the Dollfuss constitution not only as her bounden duty, which she is ready to fulfil to the uttermost, but also as the realization of the historical task and cultural mission which our present epoch has prescribed to her. Thus Austria can never, despite all her recognition of that long stretch of common road, marked by common stock, speech, and wide tracts of common culture, never move far from the great, decisive cultural and political line which has no longer much to do with policies but much with her conception of the world. More than that, there would be no ground for taking up an opposed position and persisting in an attitude of mistrust. In word and meaning the treaty of July 11 is entirely sufficient to assure a peaceful and friendly association. But it is to be taken literally. Illegal groups in Austria level the reproach against the administration that they have not held strictly to the compact. The reproach is wrong. We have done everything to keep the compact, even when it was in more than one way made hard for us. The hardship lay in the fact that certain circles took it upon themselves to carry through their own plans with the help of the treaty, when they were themselves not in harmony with it. Those to whom Austro-German amity was dear, and not the triumph of National-Socialistic totalitarianism in Austria, had no ground to force the State to intervene, by constant stirring up of factitious conflicts, and then to accuse us of a breach of contract. We bound ourselves, so far as we are responsible, to respect the political constitution of the Reich; and we have defined the conditions for the achievement of peace and also the co-operative function of the former "national opposition" in smoothing the way for the upbuilding of a united political will in Austria. We have not and could not have bound ourselves to give immunity to those who transgress against the laws of the State and thus to give them a privileged position above all other citizens of Austria. The conditions for co-operation in all the fields of political responsibility have been stated by us more than once. There is nothing to add to them. All possible measures which could be taken to smooth the way have been taken without exception, without regard for the reception they would receive. That they would on the one hand evoke much unrest and distrust, because after all that had happened they were considered much too far-reaching, was as clear as it was predictable from experience that the tactics of the other side would represent every complaisance as insufficient and every concession as a triumph for the illegal warfare, by which the achievements of the government were ostensibly set at defiance!

All this is unessential if the path we have entered on can, so far as human beings can judge, lead to the goal. The idea that increased pressure and illegal activity can lead to success is as erroneous as the attempts to provoke Austria to deviate from the treaty of July 11. Moreover, all the things which happen in our own country and refer to arrangements of domestic policy are in the end without important meaning. It remains much more important to arrive again at the point where Austrian recognition of its essential Germanness shall not be misused and made the pretext for demonstrations against our own country, and where honest and natural pleasure in German progress and German success may have undisturbed expression, as has always been the case. It was the case, because a pro-German anti-Austrian equation did not exist. What was formerly possible it must in our time be possible to bring to pass in actuality. But that it was formerly possible shows clearly enough that the Austrian government bears no blame for the change.

The truth is that the political conflict of the last years has displayed phenomena of a particularly unpleasant kind. Political conflicts there have always been. Distorted phenomena could not always be avoided. But the propaganda of hatred, which of late has set at variance not only members of the same profession but very often the closest relationships and even families, which invades the realms of art and sport, science and society, does not stop at the door of the schoolroom, but seeks to engage the very children in the broil—that phenomenon is very new and has in general as little in common with the Austrian character as it has with the cultivation of the healthy national spirit which has always been at home in our country. The consequence of this convulsion has naturally been that the words "German" and "Austrian" have gradually come to represent opposed ideas. When again we have come so far that, as in former times, the most conservative Austrian does not shun the implications of the conception of Pan-Germanism, and likewise the other, in the foreground of whose interests is the national idea, shall find it reconcilable with his folk-conceptions that the military word of command should be the same in Austria as in Germany; when he arrives at the point of letting Austria and Austrian performance count for what they are instead of seeing in them a national derogation; when he reminds himself of the old Bismarck and his warning to the hotheads of our country that they should show themselves good Austrians at home because then they would be the best Germans—when we are again so far, then we can seriously speak of peace and reconciliation. In such case Germans of the Reich could wear their national insignia in Austria without our having the feeling that they are a sort of Gessler hat and not the insignia of a friendly power; in such case there would be, not only on one side, the surrender of every sort of exaggerated propaganda, the aim of which stands clearly written on its forehead, but also on the other side the will to respect the new Austria, whether in the form of the cross of the Fatherland Front or its insignia, as the symbol of a free German state, which has nothing in common with partisanship or separatism, but is regarded as the coequal and justified insignia and profession of a German stock.

Indeed, despite all assertions to the contrary on both sides, we have since July 11 made progress, in the broad field of a return to normal conditions in general, as well as in a relief of tension in the domestic field. Anyone who fundamentally overlooks and denies the fact thereby betrays the fact that he would actually be more in favour of setting the treaty aside.

The treaty has beyond doubt been productive of good to the broad masses of the interested parties. It has proved itself a thoroughly effective means of combating that unhappy civil war which broke out in our country in 1934. Pursued in sincerity, in letter and spirit, it will show itself capable of even better results. Certainly for those in Austria who felt themselves called to be the mouthpiece of the conflict, it does not mean the attainment of their aims; hence their dissatisfaction and their attempt to hamper and oppose every favourable further development. But their goal was never the meaning or purpose of the treaty; rather it was designed to put a period to the struggle, not to exchange weapons and begin a new one!

It remains resolved to serve the whole German people, and in particular the people of Austria, who long for quiet, undisturbed constructive upbuilding and the possibility of peaceful work; not to open up a new arena of conflict in the field of domestic politics. Of that all reasonable and thoughtful people who call Austria their Fatherland have had enough and more than enough; largely because they have a clear warning in their memories of the second Austria and have not forgotten that the first Austria broke, in great part, upon the violence of its interior political strife.

The progress of pacification and the observance of her word by Austria can be seen most clearly in the statistics of detentions and arrests:

From July 11, 1936 up to the end of the year 18,648 persons were amnestied who had come into conflict with the law on account of illegal National-Socialist activity. This includes remissions of sentence as well as the suspension of court and police actions.

As political prisoners there were also in detention (in Camp Wöllersdorf, and to the end of April 1934 also Kaisersteinbruch):

>   on November   1, 1934, 4,990 persons
>   on November   1, 1935,   326   "
>   on November   1, 1936,   133   "
>   on October   1, 1937,   45   "

Concentration camps have existed in Austria since February 1, 1934.

In judicial arrest for political crimes:

>   on December 15, 1934, 2,499 persons
>   on November   1, 1935, 2,193   "
>   on November   1, 1936,   817   "
>   on October   1, 1937, 1,207   "

This includes prisoners accused and also those already sentenced.

The number of those condemned by the Austrian courts for political activity is as follows:

1934	5,467 persons
1935	2,844 "
1936	2,186 "
1937 (first half)	806 "

The official summary of the number of persons under arrest on political counts follows:

November 1, 1935	1,934
November 1, 1936	1,086
Average for 1937	900

These figures comprise all the political arrests and accordingly include all those persons, of whatever political bias, who broke the law forbidding political activity to the proscribed parties. The so-called peace policy can of course never extend to single groups only; the radicalism of both Left and Right twice during 1934 attempted to advance by violence. Both times the result cost a lamentable loss of life; the July insurrection began with the murder of our leader on the Ballplatz. The new Austria sincerely sought to overcome, on both sides, the consequences of these unhappy revolts. For both sides, accordingly, must be enforced the same conditions for peace. He who is so minded can partake of it; he who sticks to his own program of impeding the result cannot prevent those responsible in the State from carrying out their peaceful purposes towards the others. The just and equal basis for all is and remains our corporative constitution.

The scope of the amnesty was considerably greater than, in pursuance of the treaty of July 1936, had been the intention. The number of those affected by it shows clearly the progress in domestic appeasement which we had made, despite all assertions to the contrary made for purposes of propaganda. The scope and the lessons of the amnesty were such that the line we took could not receive universal agreement and understanding. But universal understanding and valuation of the policy of the responsible heads of a state are not the decisive factor; rather, whether and in how far it is capable of serving the common weal. It does not matter whether he who bears the right and the burden of the decisions is judged as weak or strong, yielding or stubborn, harsh or compliant; the question is: has his action been in the end good or bad, wrong or justified? Neither the impression of the moment nor the failure or success at a given stage is the decisive fact. The ultimate balance alone can show; and that is above all true in the sphere of politics; for single systems as well as universal ones.

The year 1937 was to be devoted especially not only to interior pacification but also to the work of economic reconstruction. The fight against unemployment remained our greatest concern; the assertions of many to the contrary, we have, thank God, made considerable progress in this field. The new Austria has honourably stood the test of that burden of recent years. The figures show it.

The number of unemployed on relief averaged: in 1932, 310,000 persons; in 1933, the year of the severest crisis, 330,000; in 1934, 281,000; in 1935, 263,000; in 1936, 259,-000. The average for 1937, in all probability, will be some 233,000 persons.

The monthly average of unemployment was 176,000 persons in September 1937, whereas in the previous September it was 216,974.

In considering these figures we must not leave out of account the fact that economic consolidation in many undertakings made possible a transition from short-time to full-time work, and also that considerable numbers in those groups which do not come into consideration in unemployment relief because they did not satisfy certain legal conditions could be absorbed into employment. In the year 1937, for the first time in a long period, certain industries reported that unemployment had entirely disappeared.

Likewise in other fields economic statistics reveal an undeniable improvement.

Austrian exports have increased in quantity and value since 1933. The value relation of imports to exports, which in 1932 was as 181 to 100, had in 1936 become 131 to 100, and in the first eight months of 1937, 121 to 100. The unfavourable trade balance, which in 1929 stood far above one billion schillings, had gone down by 1936 to below 300,000,000. The current year (1937) will in all likelihood show a further considerable improvement.

The capacity of Austrian economy to develop is especially clear from the mounting figures of production. The following statistics are taken from a lecture on "The Foundations of Austrian Economy," delivered by Dr. Victor Kienböck, president of the Austrian National Bank, in September 1937, in the Viennese Association for Business Interests. The production figures for 1923 and 1936 are compared and give the following picture (I cite only a few essential products):

		Domestic		Imported
Wheat	1923	33%	of the requirements	67%
	1936	63%		37%
Rye	1923	76%		24%
	1936	81%		19%
Potatoes	1923	95%		5%
	1936	100%		no imports

The potato production increased in this time from about 1,500,000 tons to about 2,750,000 tons.

		Domestic		Imported
Sugar	1923	31%		69%
	1936	99%		1%

Expressed in quantity, the production of sugar rose from about 52,000 tons in 1923 to an average of 211,000 between 1934 and 1936.

The year 1923 showed an excess of imports as follows:

milk and cream	22,000	tons
butter	1,700	"
cheese	c. 3,800	"

But in 1936 the excess of imports was turned into an excess of exports, as follows:

milk and cream	c. 12,500	tons
butter	c. 3,800	"
cheese	c. 3,400	"

The production of electrical energy in 1923 ran to 1,900,-000,000 kilowatt hours; in 1936, to 2,550,000,000 kilowatt hours.

Exports were:

1923	20,000,000	kilowatt hours
1936	341,000,000	" "

Wood exports were about 915,000 tons in 1923; they rose in 1936 to 1,350,000 tons.

The rising line of production statistics is especially clear in iron ore, pig iron, steel, cellulose, and paper.

Tourist traffic in Austria also, as is well known, shows a very gratifying upward turn; and the figures for the current year (1937) are still mounting.

A comparison of Austria's foreign debt also reveals a favourable development. It shows that the foreign debt of the Fatherland fell from 4,251,000,000 schillings (about 1,012,000,000 dollars at par) in 1923 to 2,063,000,000 schillings (about 491,000,000 dollars) in 1936; in other words, nearly 51 per cent. The amount needed in 1932 for the service of the debt ran to some 282,000,000 schillings (67,-100,000 dollars), while for 1937 only 110,000,000 schillings (26,180,000 dollars) had to be set aside for the purpose. Precisely this statement is by no means uninteresting, because it is well known that the reproach of increasing financial enslavement to foreign countries was one of the favourite weapons in the fight against the creators and steadfast defenders of the new Austria.

Austria's domestic debt (consolidated debts and other credits for the State, the provinces, and municipalities) amounted at the end of 1932 to a round 1,731,000,000 schillings (412,000,000 dollars); the figure at the end of 1936 was 2,082,000,000 schillings (495,500,000 dollars). Thus in this respect, too, Austria does not need to fear a comparison with her neighbours.

Despite all these figures, which cannot be done away with by denying them, there are again and again political agents who make their living by painting the coming catastrophe and the spectre of financial collapse in dark colours on the Austrian wall. A glance at the currency situation is enough to stamp all this transparent propaganda as lies. In this connection I may point out that the bank rate even at the beginning of 1932—that is, some half-year before Dollfuss took office—was 8 per cent, and that it has stood steadily at 3.5 per cent since July 1935.

These figures, which might be supplemented by others from the most varied fields, speak in no uncertain terms for the likelihood that Austrian economics can survive and expand. Certainly they offer no ground for arrogance; but they afford a distinct hope of tranquillity and security, and controvert, more strongly than any argument, all maliciously or recklessly displayed defeatism.

Finally, the year 1937 affords a welcome opportunity to test the progress which we have made in the social consolidation of the country. It is evident and undeniable that the events of February 1934 were a shattering blow for the great mass of the members of the Socialist workers' movement. And here, too, we can only count on the passage of time for the healing of wounds and the giving up of all forcible measures. The gradual progress of reconciliation in this field is especially valuable and significant.

We have ground for justified optimism on two counts:

The membership of the Austrian trade-union federation, which came into existence at the instigation of Chancellor Dollfuss after the dissolution of the free trade unions and the prohibition of all activity on the part of the Social Democratic Party in February 1934, was 148,000 persons at the end of 1934. At the end of 1936 it already had a membership of 400,000, a considerable increase over the whole membership of the free trade unions when they were in existence.

The period from October 1 to December 31, 1936 saw

the election of the workers' representatives in the factories. The setting up of the lists of candidates was to follow, by arrangement with the administration and the respective unions and after consultation with the Fatherland Front. In 3,515 industries with 213,570 voters, there were 9,358 representatives to be elected. There was a voting average of 91.9 per cent. Of the 9,358 persons chosen, 5,719 had already been appointed as mandatories and were only having their appointments confirmed. In addition were the 3,639 newly elected representatives, of whom, indeed, only 10 to 15 per cent of the mandatories to be chosen by alterations in the lists of candidates since the election won their mandates. The elections were carried out with complete freedom, opportunity being afforded to the whole body of employees to select men whom they trusted to represent their interests. The gratifying result of the elections shows the sound relations and the agreement existing between the body of Austrian workers and employees; also the frictionless co-operation of the political and economic bodies concerned, and accordingly between the trade-union federation and the Fatherland Front. Here too, then, is factual evidence that the efforts of illegal propagandists have been unsuccessful.

There is certainly no ground for complete satisfaction with what we have so far accomplished; but there is still less for considering that we have achieved nothing at all; for denying every step in advance and painting everything in the gloomiest colours, to the end of convincing Austria and the world that all effort in Austria is in vain.

The truth is, that nowhere in the world are things all shadow or all sunshine. When the one convincing proof can only be given by a process of long, slow trial; when, accordingly, one cannot perform the radical cure which would consist, for all the dissatisfied, in their being able to live on Austrian soil without Austria or its government—when all this is unfortunately not within the realm of possibility, one must have the sense to stop making untenable comparisons; one must not contrast the light from abroad with one's own dark side, nor speak in the same breath of what has been done in foreign countries and what here remains still remote; one must not envy the man with bigger boots because he can take longer strides, and want to reach the height with him no matter what the cost. It remains a question whether everybody is adapted to the same greatness; whether one does not come in the end to the same goal by taking shorter steps and perhaps with less strain. One cannot enjoy at the same time the resounding effects of a dictatorship and the easier rhythm of democratic music; one must not strive at once for the blessings of autarchy and the opening of the frontier. One may not decide to give up certain comforts without realizing that that means to forget one's own spoilt and fastidious habits; one may not continue to ask: What has the other man done? and never: Where do we ourselves stand? One must never lose the ground from under one's feet and move on in dreams and forgetfulness. Those years do not lie so far back that we cannot remember them, when we learned to understand what we lost in the old Fatherland; many Austrians and many others in the world became aware of its advantages and blessings—when it was too late!

CONCLUSION

HANS HAMMERSTEIN delivered a lecture, in the year 1935, which he called "The Face of Austrian Culture." In it he emphasized the fact that it is not very easy to understand Austrian history, but harder still to make comprehensible the Austrian idea. "Ask a number of good average Austrians," said the speaker, "what Austria is, and you would get various eloquent, for the most part even witty answers; but scarcely one exhaustive and satisfying; several doubtful; none, I am afraid, which gave out the true radiance of a genuine faith. But take Austria away from the Austrians, and they would all at once know what they have lost."

"Austria," says Hammerstein in another place, "is, in the best sense of the word, climatically and humanly well-tempered."

That has ever been so, even when we ourselves would not have it so. There are times when it requires much self-command to preserve the right moderation; excess of all kinds is only too infectious. In the first Austria it always belonged to the art of government to avoid all extremes. The Empire went well when it pursued this policy; that is true above all for those whom it is the final aim and goal of all governmental regulation to serve and advantage. Only when its equilibrium was attacked from all sides and destroyed, only when the waves of political passion mounted higher and higher and broke far outside those narrow circles where political conflict is regarded as the business of life, only then did the old Austria begin to tremble in all its joints.

For it was not a state like other states; it had its own notions, its own laws, its own way of life, and, above all, its own problems to solve. At the moment when it was made to conform to all other states and had to realize, in its own borders, ideas and methods essentially foreign to it and enter into rivalry with unequal weapons, in that moment its doom was sealed.

But whatever might be mistaken and faulty in detail, as a whole the old Austria deserves beyond a doubt to be held in honourable memory, to be justly estimated and granted a good repute, even though she did not succeed in solving all the problems with which new developments brought her face to face—among which, of course, one cannot fail to think especially of the manifold and various national problems and conflicts. After all, it is easy to criticize, hard to be moderate—and until now nobody has succeeded in doing any better.

Everywhere, where once the first Austria stood, there now stand, almost twenty years after her overthrow, a considerable host of the same unsolved problems; we shall not contribute to their solution by silence or disregard, or by seeking to get rid of them by more radical means than those natural to the former tolerant, moderate old Austria. The first Austria is today no longer a danger to anyone; it will never come back in its old guise. But it would be good, in many respects, to go to school to it. Legislation and administration would certainly not suffer thereby.

If one were to undertake a journey round the whole great space which once lay inside the Austrian boundary-posts, one would still find frequent traces of the old Austria. And what is still alive there does not bear such bad witness. Much has been painstakingly wiped out, because it seemed dangerous to the new time and its ideas; yet memories break through, softly but clearly, and their voice is strange. Its accents are not physical, not national, not political, nor may one give them political interpretation. For it is not in longing for the forms of the past, but in reverence for undying spirit and for a special way of thought which eases the social life of us human beings, that we acknowledge our perpetual debt to our good old Austrian heritage.

When we speak, in this connection, of the Austrian character, we take no thought of politics. We must, at last and finally, be clear, at least in our own country, as to the essence of our peculiar characteristics. That we use different words —that, for instance, we mostly say *"Grüss Gott"* instead of *"Sieg Heil"*—therein, certainly, does not lie our special individuality. For we might easily say something else. Nor does it lie in the laxer conventions, the smaller gift for organization and propaganda, wherein we sometimes display our inferiority complexes and sundry other of our lamentable bad habits. No, it lies rather in our gift of avoiding hard corners, of reconciling opposites, of purveying German spirit and culture to the world in such a wise as to win from the world not only positive and respectful admiration, but also love and personal sympathy. That is and remains the mission of the Austrian, who now as much as ever, as standard-bearer of his race, stands on the bridge which con-

nects differing cultures. And so we must not break our
heads over the question whether this Austrian actually
exists or perhaps was only built up because he was a necessary conception. In any case, what we have to do, without
shrinking or reservation, is to confess ourselves Austrians.
In the second Austria, many of us believed that such a confession was the beginning of our twilight as a nation. But
those were the people who always and by conviction see
everything in this country in shades of grey. We shall not
convert them. To look into the depths, to see rightly where
the spiritual values lie—that is a gift from God; no effort or
persuasion can give it—nothing save experience.

The hard compulsion of the time brought it about that
we owed the Fatherland much, in the years of the second
Austria, and could not pay; hence, perhaps, we make the
impression that we are ashamed of ourselves.

Anton Wildgans sounds the call in his speech on Austria:
"We workers on the structure of this new Austria do not
need to deny the old. On the contrary, we clearly understand that we still have it to thank for almost everything,
even though the heritage which was bequeathed us is laden
with affliction and cursing. But the property is valuable:
it has the values of an honourable culture and a special type
of human being; and of these two only shall we speak."

Out of conflict and need the third Austria was born. At
the bier of Engelbert Dollfuss might have been spoken the
words with which Hugo von Hofmannsthal concluded a
speech in memory of Prince Eugene, in the year 1914:
"This Austria is a creation of the spirit, and again and again
some envious power seeks to rend it. But a man who is a
man can do the unbelievable; and over and over, at given
intervals, providence summons up the man from whom

great things are demanded and he answers the call."

But do not some of us have dark hours when we still doubt Austria? Doubt whether she still has significance, whether she can still stand on her feet. Whether it is still worth while for us to acknowledge ourselves Austrians, of an Austrian Fatherland.

The answer can only be a thousandfold yes. The form, the body, can perish; the spirit remains, it is imperishable; only we must hearken to the teaching of history and the voice of our greatest men.

Doubters there have been in this country, almost as long as its name has endured. And yet it has survived the Thirty Years' War, the disorders of the eighteenth century and the Napoleonic period, the destructive decades before the World war; lastly, and despite all, wounded to death yet still alive, it survived even that.

And then again, for the third time, it awaked to new life, when already in our country the standard-bearers were fewer and fewer who openly avowed their allegiance to the mission and meaning of the Austrian Fatherland. All that cannot be meaningless.

The dispute over Austria and Austrian values was in Schiller's time just as present as in our day. Otherwise the well-known protest in *Wallenstein's Death* would be unexplainable: "The Austrian has a fatherland and loves it and has reason, too, to love it."

One of our greatest, Franz Grillparzer, who himself had all the marks of the typical Austrian, in character and destiny, uttered many an acid and embittered word against his country, levelled many a scathing condemnation, yet always returned to his Austrian profession of faith. Again and again, in many forms, he sang the "song of songs," the song of the Fatherland:

O thou good land! O Fatherland, between
Italy the child and Germany the man
Thou liest there, a youth with rosy cheeks.
May God preserve to thee thy youthful feeling
And make that good which others have corrupted!

And in modern times, though still in years when no one
foresaw what was to come, it was Hermann Bahr, who, coming from quite another camp, had even in 1908 a prophetic
eye, and inscribed in the album of Austrian youth: "One
thing only can I wish you: have faith in Austria! For years
I have been crying: have faith in Austria! And my last word
shall be: have faith in Austria! Austria is nowhere else but
in our longing and our self-reliance. Deep in the heart of
the working man Austria is hiding. A new youth must come
and lift it up. Then, when it appears, a light, the light from
our joyous natures, will shine over all the peoples" (*Buch
der Jugend*).

After him followed Hugo von Hofmannsthal, who likewise, long before the dawn of the third Austria, concluded
a speech on "Austria as Mirrored in Her Poesy" with the
words: "Without a breath of spiritual universalism a future
Austria can neither be wished for nor believed in."

And Anton Wildgans wrote in 1929:

Austria is clept our land.
When He with gracious hand
Shaped and so richly dowed,
God hath our Austria loved.

His contemporary, Hofmannsthal, said: "Austria first became spirit in its music; and in this form it conquered the
world."

Many people have become Austrians, who were born in

other German countries: one of the greatest, who did his
life-work among us, who, living in Vienna, conquered the
world, and whose legacy and grave we cherish: Ludwig van
Beethoven.

And in a time when, as but now, it seemed as though
Austria's hour of destiny had struck, the hour of the War of
Liberation, the greatest of the masters set to music the words
of the composer of the soldier songs, Heinrich von Collin:

> If she but will,
> Our Austria is always above all;
> She wills, she wills!

Chance has willed that this phrase of Beethoven came to
light among the buried treasures of our archives, in the year
1934. So be it, then: she wills it!

INDEX

Abram, 106

Adler, Friedrich, 36

Adler, Victor, 43

Agrarian League, *see* Agricultural League

Agricultural League, 78, 102, 114, 134, 156, 168, 173, 175, 176, 182, 205, 208

Alexander III, Emperor, 6

Alpenland, 63

Alpine Montan-Gesellschaft, 129

Andrassy, 6

Anschluss with Germany, Austrian, 47, 48, 76, 78, 192, 250

Apponyi, Albert, 252–3

Arbeiter-Zeitung, Vienna, 47, 49–52, 119, 120

Austria: area, 3, 11; population, 3, 11, 16–19; constitution, 3–4; nationalities, 15–18, 19, 22, 31–3; German culture, 18–19, 70, 115, 140, 161, 193, 209–11, 222, 249, 290, 304–5; parliamentary system, 19, 84, 92–105, 112, 153–5, 216; flags, 30–1; revolution, 39–54; Republic established, 44, 48, 50; social legislation, 53, 84; post-war, 55–63, 83, 86–91; inflation, 59–60, 83, 86; foreign politics, 60–1, 248, 255–6, 286–92; relations with Germany, 61, 69, 182–4, 226–7, 283–6, 287, 288–92, *and see Anschluss,* Pan-Germanism; plebiscites on union with Germany, 62–3; obtains financial credit from League of Nations, 71–2, 73; economic crisis, 85, 86, 88, 151–5, 156, 161, 246–8, 261; postwar youth, 86–91, 105; constitutional reform, 121–4; defence movement, 127–44, 207, 273–83, *and see* Fatherland Front; transport strike, 132–3; unemployment, 151, 156, 158, 159, 295–6; tourist trade, 158, 298; reform of legal code, 163–4, 187–8; struggle for independence, 195–214; revolts of 1934,

i

A NOTE ON THE TYPE

THIS BOOK is set on the Linotype in Baskerville. The punches for this face were cut under the supervision of George W. Jones, the eminent English printer and the designer of Granjon and Estienne. Linotype Baskerville is a facsimile cutting from type cast from the original matrices of a face designed by John Baskerville, a writing-master of Birmingham, for his own private press. The original face was the forerunner of the "modern" group of type faces, known today as Scotch, Bodoni, etc. After his death in 1775, Baskerville's punches and matrices were sold in France and were used to produce the sumptuous Kehl edition of Voltaire's works.

This book was composed, printed, and bound by H. Wolff, New York. The paper was made by S. D. Warren Co., Boston. The binding was designed by Georg Salter.